# MARYLAND CRUISING GUIDE

2008-2009

Editor: Mickey Courtney

**COVER PHOTO**

"Sunset on the West River"

A stunning winter sunset scene on the West River looking toward the historic town of Galesville, MD, as seen from the Shady Side peninsula. Galesville has a colorful history of agriculture, boat building, crabbing, fishing, oystering, steamboat transportation, fine dining, yachting, and as a summer vacation spot.

Photographer, Don Wagner, is an avid sailor in both cruising and racing. Don is a retired engineer and a resident of Shady Side, MD. His photographic interests focus on Chesapeake Bay scenes; birds, boats, lighthouses, and bay-wide activities.

## PREFACE

This chart book was first designed and printed in 1961 by Williams & Heintz Map Corporation for the Tidewater Fisheries Commission. It was revised every two years for the Department of Natural Resources. In 1997 Williams & Heintz took over publication and continues to update and reprint every other year.

Since the publication of the 2006-2007 edition of the Maryland Cruising Guide, more than 300 corrections were made to produce the 2008-2009 edition. These corrections include aids to navigation in the upper bay ship channels and other ranges such as Craighill, Tolchester, and Elk River channel. There are also many changes in the Potomac River, and the back bays of Ocean City. In addition to the actual corrections made, hundreds more positions were checked for accuracy.

We have used the latest NOAA charts and Local Notices to Mariners to give you the most up-to-date charts. This book covers all of Maryland's Chesapeake Bay waters from the mouth of the Potomac up to Washington, D.C, Ocean City, and to the C & D Canal. Marine facilities, ramps, and other helpful lists are incorporated in this book. The same standards of accuracy and quality are continued in its successor, the VIRGINIA CRUISING GUIDE, which also is published and printed by Williams & Heintz Map Corporation.

Publisher:

**Williams & Heintz Map Corporation**
**8119 Central Avenue**
**Capitol Heights, MD 20743**

Contact us:
(301) 336-1144
(800) 338-6228
www.whmap.com

Charts based on NAD-83

## USING THIS GUIDE

The charts in this guide are reproductions of selected National Oceanic and Atmospheric Administration (NOAA) charts. Charts 1 through 20 are at a scale of 1:80,000. The insets are in various scales from 1:40,000 to 1:20,000. The charts were corrected utilizing the information published in the U.S. Coast Guard Local Notice to Mariners through February 26, 2008.

**Every effort was made to ensure the accuracy of this publication. However, due to the constant changes occurring on the waterways, the mariner is cautioned not to use this publication for navigation. Use the current NOAA charts corrected through the use of the U.S. Coast Guard Local Notice to Mariners.**

You may obtain the Local Notice to Mariners from the Coast Guard website at www.navcen.uscg.gov.

The courses shown on the charts are magnetic and the distances are in nautical miles. There are approximately 6076.1 feet ( 1852 meters ) in a nautical mile. One nautical mile is equal to approximately 1.15 statute miles. The unit of speed is the knot, which is one nautical mile per hour.

## BOATING SAFETY INSTRUCTION

Any person born on or after **July 1, 1972** may not operate a numbered or documented pleasure vessel without first obtaining a **certificate of boating safety education**. A minimum of eight hours of instruction is required. The Maryland Natural Resources Police offer a state boating course and also offer an equivalency exam. For details, contact:

Maryland Natural Resources Police
Safety Education Division
1804 West Street, Suite 300
Annapolis, Maryland 21401
Telephone 410-260-3280
FAX 410-260-3292
Website www.dnr.md.gov

Two great national boating organizations, the **United States Power Squadrons** and the **U.S. Coast Guard Auxiliary** offer excellent basic boating courses which meet the requirement for the Certificate of Boating Safety Education. Both organizations offer high quality advanced courses.

For further information, contact your local Power Squadron or local Coast Guard Auxiliary Flotilla or write:

District Education Officer
District 5
c/o U.S. Power Squadrons
P.O. Box 30423
Raleigh, NC 27622

or:

U.S. Coast Guard Auxiliary
5th District Director
431 Crawford Street
Portsmouth, VA 23704

Phone Toll Free 1-800-336-2628 for boating course information.

## MARINAS

Marina locations are shown on the charts by way of encircled numbers. Pages iv-vi contain a list of marinas and the services offered. Marinas with marine sewage pumpout facilities are shown with red numbers encircled in red. (161)

The locations of public boat ramps are shown by the symbol  on the charts at the locations of the ramps.

**If you own or operate a marina and wish to have your marina listed, please contact the editor of this publication for details. If your marina is currently listed and the name has been changed and/or there are changes to the services offered, please notify the editor.**

## GOOD CRUISING PRACTICES

- First, check the weather. Your VHF radio or a commercially available "weather radio" will give you the latest marine weather information. Know your boat's limitations and your limitations before you consider getting underway when the weather is less than favorable.
- File a Float Plan with a friend with your itinerary. This will aid authorities should you be in need of assistance.
- Make sure all U.S. Coast Guard required safety equipment is on board, is in serviceable condition, and is readily available. Brief your guests on the locations of safety equipment, safety procedures, and emergency procedures. A throwable personal flotation device (PFD) must be immediately available. It is preferable that all persons on board wear a PFD. If pets are on board, it is good practice to have them wear a safety harness to help recover them should they fall overboard. PFDs for pets are available.
- Have a first aid kit, a tool box, and spare parts on board.
- Have an anchor with rode, lines, fenders, and a boat hook on board.
- Check your sound producing device (horn or whistle) and your navigation lights if you plan to be underway at night.
- Check your fuel tanks. Have enough fuel for the intended trip with a 1/3 reserve.
- Check all thru-hull fittings/seacocks, belts, hoses, and engine fluid levels.
- Check batteries and disconnect shore power if so equipped.
- Stow all gear properly.
- Do not overload. Distribute weight evenly and maintain adequate freeboard at all times.
- Obey the Navigation Rules. Not doing so is the greatest cause of collision.
- Keep a sharp lookout, not only to avoid collisions with other boats, but also with objects that could damage your hull or propeller.
- Be especially careful when operating in any area where there are swimmers. They are difficult to see.
- Watch your wake. It may capsize a small boat or cause damage to boats or property along the shore. You are responsible.
- If you capsize, remain with the boat if it continues to float. You are more easily located by a search plane or boat, and attempts to swim to a distant shore are often unsuccessful.
- Always instruct at least one other person on board in the rudiments of boat handling in case you become disabled or fall overboard.
- Many of the smaller tributaries have speed limits, usually six knots. Watch for orange and white buoys marking such areas.
- When taking on fuel, make sure the boat is secured properly. Shut down engine(s), set main electrical switch(es) to off, close hatches, doors, and portholes. Have fire extinguishers readily available. Make sure any source of flame is extinguished. Make sure that the fuel nozzle is in contact with the fill opening to prevent static sparks. Have a cloth or fuel absorbent material to clean up any spilled fuel on deck. Carry extra fuel only in approved containers.
- After fueling, open all doors, hatches, and portholes to ventilate the boat. Wipe up any spills, check bilges and fuel connections for leaks, and sniff for fuel fumes. Run the bilge blower. Start engine.

**The prudent mariner will not rely on any single aid to navigation, particularly on floating aids, nor on any single method of navigation. Floating aids may be off station, lights may be extinguished and electronic navigation aids (GPS, Loran) may give erroneous information or fail. Learn the basic navigation methods - piloting and dead reckoning.**

## SPEED / TIME / DISTANCE

Speed ( knots ) = Distance ( nautical miles ) /Time ( hours )

Time ( hours ) = Distance ( nautical miles ) / Speed ( knots )

Distance ( nautical miles ) = Speed (knots ) x Time ( hours )

## COMPASS CONVERSIONS

Add West
Subtract East

True
Variation
Magnetic
Deviation
Compass

Subtract West
Add East

When following a magnetic course, make sure that your compass has been adjusted to minimize deviation or that you have a deviation table. When plotting a course, make sure you apply the variation shown on the chart inside the nearest compass rose and apply deviation if necessary.

**NOT TO BE USED FOR NAVIGATION. USE THE CURRENT NOAA CHARTS CORRECTED BY LOCAL NOTICES TO MARINERS**

# LIST OF ASSISTANCE FIRMS

## Fast Response towboats to Your Assistance

The professional marine assistance firms listed below have met the rigorous inspection standards of CMTAA. The monitor VHF channel 16 and normally respond to locations within about 25 miles of the port indicated.

Chesapeake Marine Towing & Assistance Association
A Regional Chapter of C-PORT

| No. | Firm | Boats / Phone |
|---|---|---|
| 1 | **TowBoatU.S.®** Upper Chesapeake<br>Capt. James McCarthy<br>Upper Chesapeake Bay | *Enterprise & Sassafras*<br>*North East & Patriot*<br>410/885-5988 |
| 2 | **TowBoatU.S.®** Middle River<br>Capt. Dennis Warwick<br>Middle River | *Desperado & Mahican*<br>410/335-3760 |
| 3 | **Deckelman's Bay Assist**<br>Capt. Jack Deckelman<br>*Hornet, Capt'n Jeff, Thomas Point & Captain Brian* | 410/391-6482 |
| 4 | **SEA TOW®** Upper Chesapeake<br>Capt. T. J. Buhite, Jr.<br>Upper Chesapeake | *Middle River & Baltimore*<br>410/335-6818 |
| 5 | **SEA TOW®** Northern Chesapeake<br>Capt. Gary O'Reilly<br>Sassafras, Bohemia, Elk, Northeast, Susquehanna Rivers | *Eagle, Glory & James J.*<br>410/885-5044 |
| 6 | **TowBoatU.S.®** Baltimore<br>Capt. Frank Dolan<br>Patapsco River | *Ten & Ten II*<br>410/255-8700 |
| 7 | **Deckelman's Bay Assist**<br>Capt. Mort Deckelman<br>*Popeye, Towboat Hammer & Towboat Rock* | 410/778-6777 |
| 8 | **SEA TOW®** Annapolis<br>Capt. Dave DuVall<br>Annapolis, Kent Narrows & Cambridge | *Obvious Solution I & II*<br>*Distress Reliever & Sea Cure*<br>410/267-7650 |
| 9 | **TowBOAT/US®** Annapolis<br>Capt. Hamilton Gale<br>Annapolis | *Recovery, Retriever II*<br>*Reliant & Rescue*<br>410/263-1260 |
| 10 | **Undertow Marine Services**<br>Capt. Don Dunbar<br>Rhode River | *Undertow*<br>410/798-0458 |
| 11 | **TowBoatU.S.®** Tow Jamm<br>Mary Gilmer<br>Knapps Narrows, Kent Narrows & Cambridge | *Tow Jamm 1, 2 & 3*<br>410/745-3000 |
| 12 | **TowBoatU.S.®** Herring Bay<br>Capt. Bill Conlyn<br>Herring Bay | *Herring Bay I & II*<br>301/466-5151 |
| 13 | **TowBoatU.S.®** Potomac<br>Capt. Terry Hill<br>Upper Potomac River | *Salvor, Capt Wise, Alexandria*<br>*Woodbridge, Marlborough Point*<br>703/670-0080 |
| 14 | **TowBoatU.S.®** Ocean City<br>Capt. Greg Hall<br>Offshore & Back Bay | *Wester Diver, Titan America*<br>*& MD Salvor*<br>410/289-7894 |
| | **Non-Member Towers** | |
| | **TowBoatU.S.®** Solomons<br>Michael Shaw<br>Solomons | 410/326-6801 |
| | **TowBoatU.S.®** Cobb Island<br>Charles Chapman III<br>Lower Potomac River | 301/259-4066 |
| | **SEA TOW®** Southern Maryland<br>Capt. Bill Merritt<br>Solomons | 301/737-1611 |

**Features:**
- Inspected fast response towboats
- 24-hour service daily
- USCG licensed captains
- Major credit cards accepted

**Services:**
- Towing
- Jump starts
- Degrounding
- Salvage
- Dewatering
- Diving
- Fuel drops
- Prop disentanglement
- Float plan service

**Contact the firm of your choice by:**
- VHF Radio Channel 16
- Telephone or cellular phone
- Through the USCG

**National Dispatch Centers:**
**SEA TOW®:** 1-800-4SEATOW
**TowBOAT/US®:** 1-800-391-4869

Getting Help On the Water Brochure with information on marine assistance is available from CMTAA. Contact any listed towing firm.

# FOR ASSISTANCE

If you are in need of immediate assistance, which means that there is **immediate danger to life or property**, use the following procedure:

- 1. Select channel 16 on your VHF radio.
- 2. Key the mike and say: **"MAYDAY...MAYDAY...MAYDAY,"** speak clearly and distinctly.
- 3. State the vessel name: **"THIS IS (BOAT NAME)...(BOAT NAME)... (BOAT NAME)...."**
- 4. State your position in as much detail and as accurately as possible: **"MAYDAY (BOAT NAME) POSITION IS** (vessel position in latitude and longitude or the bearing and distance from a well-known landmark)."
- 5. State the nature of distress: **"WE ARE** (taking on water, on fire, etc.)."
- 6. If no answer is received, repeat the distress call.

The above procedure is used **only if life and/or property are in immediate danger.**

If you need assistance and there is no immediate threat to life or property, follow the below procedure:

- Contact the U.S. Coast Guard on channel 16 VHF.
- When contact is made, the Coast Guard will request that you switch and answer on a working channel (usually ch. 22A or sometimes ch. 12 ).
- After requesting some specific information such as the nature of your distress, the description of your boat, type of assistance needed and other information, they will ask if you have a friend or a commercial tower you would like them to contact to assist you. If you do not request anyone specific to be contacted, the Coast Guard will broadcast a Marine Assistance Request Broadcast (MARB). Should no one respond to the MARB, the Coast Guard will respond to assist you.
- To save time, you may call a towing firm directly on channel 16 or by cellular phone. A list of commercial assistance towing firms is provided.

NRP

The Maryland Natural Resources Police has units stationed throughout the Bay. Contact them on channel 16. In case of emergency or to report violations you may also telephone 410-260-8888 and NON-emergency, telephone 410-260-8940.

# MARINA INDEX

| Name | Chart No. | Marina No. |
|---|---|---|
| 54th Street Marina | 19 | 1 |
| A & B Yachtsmen, Inc. | 3, 5, Inset-20 | 2 |
| A & M Marine Service Inc. | 6 | 3 |
| Absolute Marine Services | 3 | 4 |
| Advanced Marina | 19 | 5 |
| Alexandria City Marina | 18 | 6 |
| All Star Marine | 2, 3 | 7 |
| Anacostia Marina, Inc. | 18 | 8 |
| Anchor Bay East Marina | 3 | 9 |
| Anchor Bay Marina & Ship Store | 3 | 10 |
| Anchor Inn | 3 | 11 |
| Anchor Marina | 1 | 12 |
| Anchor Yacht Basin | 5 | 13 |
| Anchorage Marina | 3, Inset-10 | 14 |
| Anderson's Marine Service | 3 | 15 |
| Angler Marina | 19 | 16 |
| Angler's Restaurant & Marina | 4, 6 | 17 |
| Annapolis City Dock | 3, 5, Inset-20 | 18 |
| Annapolis City Marina, Ltd. | 3, 5, Inset-20 | 19 |
| Annapolis Landing Marina | 3, 5, Inset-20 | 20 |
| Annapolis Maryland Capital Yacht Club | 3, 5, Inset-20 | 21 |
| Annapolis Waterfront Marriott/Pusser's Landing | 3, 5, Inset-20 | 22 |
| Annapolis Yacht Club | 3, 5, Inset-20 | 23 |
| Annapolis Yacht Sales & Services, Inc. | 3, 5, Inset-20 | 24 |
| Aqua-Land Marina | 16 | 25 |
| Aquia Creek Marina & Boatyard | 17 | 26 |
| Atlantic Marina on the Magothy | 3 | 27 |
| Avalon Yacht Basin | 1 | 28 |
| Back Creek Inn Bed & Breakfast | 8, 9 | 29 |
| Back Creek Marina | 3, 5, Inset-20 | 30 |
| Backyard Boats | 5 | 31 |
| Bahia Marina | 19 | 32 |
| Baltimore Inner Harbor Marine Center | 3, 5, Inset-20 | 33 |
| Baltimore Marine Center at Lighthouse Point | 3, 5, Inset-20 | 34 |
| Baltimore Marine Center-Pier 7 | 3, 5, Inset-20 | 35 |
| Baltimore Yacht Basin | 3, 5, Inset-20 | 36 |
| Baltimore Yacht Club | 2, 3 | 37 |
| Bar Harbor RV Park & Marina | 2, 3 | 38 |
| Barnacle Bill's Marine | 19 | 39 |
| Bay Boat Works, Inc. | 1 | 40 |
| Bay Boats Supply & Marina | 2, 3 | 41 |
| Bay Bridge Marina | 3, 5, 6 | 42 |
| Bay Harbour Boatyard | 5 | 43 |
| Bay Hundred Restaurant | 5, 6 | 44 |
| Bay View Marina | 5 | 45 |
| Bayside Landing Park | 2, 4 | 46 |
| Beacon Light Marina | 2, 3 | 47 |
| Belle Haven Marina, Inc. | 18 | 48 |
| Belmont Bay Harbor (Coastal Properties) | 17, 18 | 49 |
| Benedict Marina | 9 | 50 |
| Bert Jabin's Yacht Yard | 3, 5, Inset-20 | 51 |
| Bill's Boats | 2, 3 | 52 |
| Black Dog Boat Works | 7 | 53 |
| Blackstone Marina | 8, 9 | 54 |
| Blue Water Marina | 5 | 55 |
| Boatel California | 8, 9 | 56 |
| Boating Center of Baltimore | 2, 3 | 57 |
| Bohemia Anchorage, Inc. | 1 | 58 |
| Bohemia Bay Yacht Harbour | 1 | 59 |
| Bohemia Vista Yacht Basin | 1 | 60 |
| Bowleys Marina (Coastal Properties) | 2, 3 | 61 |
| Branson Cove Marina | 15 | 62 |
| Breezy Point Marina | 8, 9 | 63 |
| Broomes Island Marina | 8, 9 | 64 |
| Buedal's Marina & Boatyard | 3 | 65 |
| Bunky's Charter Boats | 8, 9 | 66 |
| Burr Yacht Sales | 5 | 67 |
| Bush River Boat Works, Inc. | 2 | 68 |
| Buzzard Point Marina | 18 | 69 |
| Buzz's Marina | 10, 14 | 70 |
| Cadle Creek Marina | 5 | 71 |
| Calvert Marina | 8, 9 | 72 |
| Cambridge Municipal Yacht Basin | 7 | 73 |
| Campbell's Bachelor Point Yacht Co. | 6, 7 | 74 |
| Campbell's Boatyard at Jack's Point | 6, 7 | 75 |
| Campbell's Town Creek Boatyard | 6, 7 | 76 |
| Cape St. Mary's Marina | 9 | 77 |
| Capital Yacht Club | 18 | 78 |
| Captain Bill Bunting | 19 | 79 |
| Captain Billy's Crabhouse | 16 | 80 |
| Captain John Beach Marina | 17, 18 | 81 |
| Captain John's Crabhouse & Marina | 16 | 82 |
| Captain's Galley | 19 | 83 |
| Casa Rio Marina, Inc. | 5 | 84 |
| Castle Harbor Marina | 4, 5, 6 | 85 |
| Catamarans | 8, 9 | 86 |
| Cather Marine, Inc. | 15, 16 | 87 |
| Cedar Cove Marina | 15 | 88 |
| Centerville Public Landing | 4 | 89 |
| Chandlery Dock (at Fawcett) | 3, 5, Inset-20 | 90 |
| Charlestown Marina | 1 | 91 |
| Chesapeake Harbour Marina | 3, 5, Inset-20 | 92 |
| Chesapeake Inn Restaurant & Marina | 1 | 93 |
| Chesapeake Maritime Museum | 6, 7 | 94 |
| Chesapeake Yachting Center | 2, 3 | 95 |
| Chestertown Marina | 4 | 96 |
| Choptank-Towne Yacht Basin | 7 | 97 |
| City of Baltimore Public Docks - Inner Harbor | 3, Inset-10 | 98 |
| Clark's Landing Shadyside | 5 | 99 |
| Clarke's Landing (Hollywood) | 8, 9 | 100 |
| Coan River Marina | 14, 15 | 101 |
| Cobb Island Marina | 16 | 102 |
| Cockrell Marine Railway | 14 | 103 |
| Cole's Point Plantation | 15 | 104 |
| Colonial Beach Yacht Center | 16 | 105 |
| Colton's Point Marina | 15, 16 | 106 |
| Columbia Island Marina | 18 | 107 |
| Comb's Creek Marina | 15 | 108 |
| Comfort Inn/Beacon Marina | 8, 9 | 109 |
| Courtney Boat Yard | 10, 14 | 110 |
| Courtney's Restaurant & Seafood | 14 | 111 |
| Cove | 1 | 112 |
| Cox's Point Park Ramp | 3 | 113 |
| Crab Claw Restaurant | 6, 7 | 114 |
| Crisfield Fishing Center | 12, 13 | 115 |
| Crisfield Propeller & Seamark Marine | 12, 13 | 116 |
| Crockett's Marina & Boatyard | 12, 13 | 117 |
| Cuts & Case Inc. | 6, 7 | 118 |
| Cutter Marine, Inc. | 2, 3 | 119 |
| Cypress Marine | 3 | 120 |
| Dahlgren Marine Works | 16, 17 | 121 |
| Deckelman's Boat Yard | 2, 3 | 122 |
| Deep Creek Marina | 3 | 123 |
| Dennis Point Marina, Inc. | 14, 15 | 124 |
| Dickerson Harbor | 6, 7 | 125 |
| DiGiovanni's Dock of the Bay | 8, 9 | 126 |
| Dock O' The Bay | 15 | 127 |
| Dockside, LLC | 8, 9 | 128 |
| Dorchester Street Dock | 19 | 129 |
| Driftwood Inn, Inc. | 3 | 130 |
| Drury's Marina | 10, 14 | 131 |
| Duffy Creek Marina | 1 | 132 |
| Dundee Creek Marina | 2 | 133 |
| Eastern Bay Marina, Inc./Crab Alley Marina | 4, 5, 6 | 134 |
| Easton Point Marina | 6, 7 | 135 |
| Eastport Yacht Club | 3, 5, Inset-20 | 136 |
| Eastport Yacht Yard | 3, 5, Inset-20 | 137 |
| Edwards Boat Yard | 2, 3 | 138 |
| Elk Neck State Park Rogues Harbor | 1 | 139 |
| Elk Point Marina | 1 | 140 |
| Essex Marina & Boat Sales | 2, 3 | 141 |
| E-Z Cruz Marina | 17, 18 | 142 |
| Fairview Beach Tim's II | 17 | 143 |
| Fairview Beach Yacht Club, Inc. | 17 | 144 |
| Fairview Marina | 3 | 145 |
| Fairwinds Marina | 3 | 146 |
| Fawcett Boat Supplies, Inc. | 3, 5, Inset-20 | 147 |
| Ferry Point Marina Yacht Yard | 3 | 148 |
| Fisherman's Marina | 19 | 149 |
| Fisherman's Inn & Crabdeck Restaurants | 4, 6 | 150 |
| Fishing Creek Landings | 5 | 151 |
| Flag Harbor Condo Marina | 8, 9 | 152 |

| Name | Chart No. | Marina No. |
|---|---|---|
| Florida Marina & Boat Sales, Inc. | 3 | 153 |
| Flying Point Marina | 2, 3 | 154 |
| Fort Belvoir Marina | 18 | 155 |
| Fort Washington Marina | 18 | 156 |
| Galesville Yacht Yard, Inc. | 5 | 157 |
| Galloway Creek Marina | 2, 3 | 158 |
| Gangplank Marina (Coastal Properties) | 18 | 159 |
| Gates Marine | 5 | 160 |
| Gateway Marina & Ship's Store | 7 | 161 |
| Generation III Marina | 7 | 162 |
| George L. Quade's Store & Boat Rentals | 16 | 163 |
| Georgetown Yacht Basin | 1 | 164 |
| Gibson Island Yacht Squadron | 3 | 165 |
| Gilligan's Pier | 16 | 166 |
| Goldsborough's Marine | 12, 13 | 167 |
| Goose Bay Marina, Inc. | 16, 17 | 168 |
| Goose Harbor Marina | 2, 3 | 169 |
| Granary Marina | 1 | 170 |
| Gratitude Marina | 2, 4 | 171 |
| Gratitude Yachting Center | 2, 4 | 172 |
| Great Oak Landing | 2 | 173 |
| Green Point Landing | 2 | 174 |
| Gregg Neck Boat Yard | 1 | 175 |
| Gunpowder Cove Marina | 2 | 176 |
| H. C. Parker Marina | 16 | 177 |
| Hall's Landing | 1 | 178 |
| Hamilton Harbour Marina | 3 | 179 |
| Hammock Island Marina | 3 | 180 |
| Hampton's Landing Marina | 17 | 181 |
| Hance's Point Yacht Club | 1 | 182 |
| Happy Clam | 16 | 183 |
| Harbor Hills Yacht Club | 5 | 184 |
| Harbor Island Marina, Inc. | 8, 9 | 185 |
| Harbor View Marina (Coastal Properties) | 3, Inset-10 | 186 |
| Harbour Cove Marina | 5 | 187 |
| Harbour Island Marina | 19 | 188 |
| Harbour North Marina | 1 | 189 |
| Hargis Marina | 19 | 190 |
| Harris Crab House | 4, 6 | 191 |
| Harrison Yacht Sales | 4, 6 | 192 |
| Harrison's Country Inn | 5, 6 | 193 |
| Harry Hogan Machine Shop | 15 | 194 |
| Hartge Yacht Yard | 5 | 195 |
| Haven Harbour Marina | 2, 4 | 196 |
| Havre de Grace City Yacht Basin | 1 | 197 |
| Havre de Grace Marina - Log Pond | 1 | 198 |
| Havre de Grace Marina (Water Street) | 1 | 199 |
| Henderson Wharf Marina | 3, Inset-10 | 200 |
| Herrington Harbour North | 5 | 201 |
| Herrington Harbour South | 5 | 202 |
| Higgins Yacht Yard | 6, 7 | 203 |
| Hinckley Yacht Services | 6, 7 | 204 |
| Hoffmaster's Marina | 17, 18 | 205 |
| Holiday Hill Marina | 5 | 206 |
| Holiday Inn Select Solomons | 8, 9 | 207 |
| Holiday Point Marina | 5 | 208 |
| Holly Neck Marina | 2, 3 | 209 |
| Hope Springs Marina | 17 | 210 |
| Hop's Marina | 16 | 211 |
| Horn Point Harbor Marina (CPM) | 3, 5, Inset-20 | 212 |
| Hyatt Regency Ches. Bay Golf Resort Spa & Marina | 7 | 213 |
| Iman's Boat Yard | 3 | 214 |
| Inn at Perry Cabin | 6, 7 | 215 |
| Inner Harbor East Marina | 3, Inset-10 | 216 |
| Island View Marina | 4, 5, 6 | 217 |
| Jack's Boat House | 18 | 218 |
| Jackson Marine Sales/Shelter Cove Marina | 1 | 219 |
| James Creek Marina | 18 | 220 |
| Jane's Island State Park | 12, 13 | 221 |
| K.B. Derr and Son | 8, 9 | 222 |
| Kennersley Point Marina | 4 | 223 |
| Kent Island Yacht Club | 4, 6 | 224 |
| Kent Narrows Yacht Yard | 4, 6 | 225 |
| Kentmorr Harbour Marina | 5, 6 | 226 |
| Kinsale Harbor Yacht Club | 15 | 227 |
| Knapps Narrows Marina and Inn | 5, 6 | 228 |
| Krentz Marine Railway | 15 | 229 |
| Lankford Bay Marina | 2, 4 | 230 |
| Leatherbury Point Marina | 5 | 231 |
| Lee's Marina | 1 | 232 |
| Leesylvania State Park | 17, 18 | 233 |
| Leonardtown Wharf | 15 | 234 |
| Leroy's Marina | 14 | 235 |
| Lewisetta Marina | 14, 15 | 236 |
| Liberty Yacht Club & Marina | 5 | 237 |
| Lippincott Marine | 4, 6 | 238 |
| Little Island Marina | 5 | 239 |
| Locust Point Marina | 1 | 240 |
| Londontowne Marina | 5 | 241 |
| Long Beach Marina | 2, 3 | 242 |
| Long Cove Marina | 4 | 243 |
| Long Point Marina, Inc. | 1 | 244 |
| Losten Marina | 1 | 245 |
| Lower Machodoc Marine, Inc. | 15 | 246 |
| Lowes Wharf Marina Inn | 5, 6 | 247 |
| M.R. Props (at McDaniel Yacht Basin) | 1 | 248 |
| Madison Bay Marina & Campground | 7, 8 | 249 |
| Magothy Marina | 3 | 250 |
| Markel's Boatyard | 3 | 251 |
| Markley's Marina, Inc. | 2, 3 | 252 |
| Maryland Marina | 2, 3 | 253 |
| Maryland Yacht Club | 3 | 254 |
| Masthead Restaurant at Pier Street Marina | 6, 7 | 255 |
| Maurgale Inn & Marina | 3 | 256 |
| McDaniel Yacht Basin, Inc. | 1 | 257 |
| Mears Marina | 3, 5, Inset-20 | 258 |
| Mears Point Marina | 4, 6 | 259 |
| Mears Yacht Haven (Coastal Properties) | 6, 7 | 260 |
| Middle Branch Moorings | 3 | 261 |
| Mid-Shore Electronics | 7 | 262 |
| Mike's Restaurant & Crab House | 5 | 263 |
| Milburn Landing | 12 | 264 |
| Miles River Yacht Club | 6, 7 | 265 |
| Monroe Bay Landing | 16 | 266 |
| Moonlight Bay Inn and Marina | 2, 4 | 267 |
| National Harbor Marina (CPM) | 18 | 268 |
| Nightingale Motel & Marina | 16 | 269 |
| Norman Creek Marina, Inc. | 3 | 270 |
| North East River Marina | 1 | 271 |
| North East Yacht Sales | 1 | 272 |
| North Point Marina | 2, 4 | 273 |
| Northeast River Yacht Club | 1 | 274 |
| Oak Grove Marine Center | 5 | 275 |
| Oak Harbor Marina | 3 | 276 |
| Occoquan Harbor Marina, Inc. | 17, 18 | 277 |
| Ocean City Fisherman's Marina | 19 | 278 |
| Ocean City Fishing Center | 19 | 279 |
| Ocean City Fishing Center Bayside | 19 | 280 |
| Ocean City Yacht Club | 19 | 281 |
| Ocean Pines Marina | 19 | 282 |
| Old Bay Marina | 3 | 283 |
| Old Town Marina | 19 | 284 |
| Olde Towne Marina, Ltd. | 3, 5, Inset-20 | 285 |
| Olverson's Lodge Creek Marina | 15 | 286 |
| Osprey Point Marina | 2, 4 | 287 |
| Outdoor World Harbor View | 16 | 288 |
| Owens Marina | 1 | 289 |
| Oxford Boat Yard (Coastal Properties) | 6, 7 | 290 |
| Oxford Yacht Agency | 6, 7 | 291 |
| Parrish Creek Marina & Boatyard | 5 | 292 |
| Pasadena Boatel & Beach Club | 3 | 293 |
| Pasadena Yacht Yard, Inc. | 3 | 294 |
| Patuxent Beach Marina | 8, 9 | 295 |
| Penn's Beach Marina | 1 | 296 |
| Perryville Yacht Club | 1 | 297 |
| Pete's Marina | 2, 3 | 298 |
| Petrini Shipyard, Inc. | 3, 5, Inset-20 | 299 |
| Phil's Marina | 10, 14 | 300 |
| Phipps Marine Railway | 5 | 301 |
| Pier 7 Marina | 5 | 302 |
| Pilot House Marina & Boat Sales | 17, 18 | 303 |
| Pine Cove Marina | 8, 9 | 304 |

| Name | Chart No. | Marina No |
|---|---|---|
| Piney Narrows Yacht Haven | 4, 6 | 305 |
| Pirates Cove Restaurant | 5 | 306 |
| Pirate's Den Marina | 16 | 307 |
| Pleasure Cove Marina | 3 | 308 |
| Pocomoke City Municipal Marina | 12 | 309 |
| Podickory Point | 3 | 310 |
| Pohick Bay Regional Park | 17, 18 | 311 |
| Point Lookout Boating Facility | 10, 14 | 312 |
| Point Lookout Marina | 10, 14 | 313 |
| Point Lookout State Park | 10, 14 | 314 |
| Port Annapolis Marina | 3, 5, Inset-20 | 315 |
| Port Covington Maritime Center | 3, Inset-10 | 316 |
| Port Kinsale Marina & Resort | 15 | 317 |
| Port of Salisbury Marina (CPM) | 11 | 318 |
| Port Tobacco Marina & Restaurant | 16 | 319 |
| Port Tobacco Marina, Inc. | 16 | 320 |
| Porter's Seneca Marina | 2, 3 | 321 |
| Potomac Marine & Canvas Co. | 17, 18 | 322 |
| Powley Marina | 10, 11 | 323 |
| Prince William Marine Sales | 17, 18 | 324 |
| Queen Anne Marina | 5, 6 | 325 |
| Ragged Point Marina | 15 | 326 |
| Ray's Pier Restaurant | 9 | 327 |
| Rhode River Marina | 5 | 328 |
| Richmond's Marina | 1 | 329 |
| Riley's Marina Sales & Service, Inc. | 2, 3 | 330 |
| Rippons Harbor | 10 | 331 |
| River Watch Restaurant & Marina | 2, 3 | 332 |
| Riverside Marine, Inc. | 3 | 333 |
| Robertson's Crab House | 16 | 334 |
| Rock Hall Landing Marina | 2 | 335 |
| Rock Hall Marine Railway | 2, 4 | 336 |
| Rockhold Creek Marina & Yacht Repair | 5 | 337 |
| Rocky Point Park | 2, 3 | 338 |
| Rod & Reel | 5 | 339 |
| Rolph's Wharf Marina | 4 | 340 |
| Rudy's Marina | 3 | 341 |
| Sailing Associates, Inc. | 1 | 342 |
| Sailing Emporium, Inc. | 2, 4 | 343 |
| Sandy Point State Park | 3 | 344 |
| Sarles Boat & Engine Shop, Inc. | 3, 5, Inset-20 | 345 |
| Sassafras Harbor Marina | 1 | 346 |
| Schaefer's Canal House | 1 | 347 |
| Scheible's Fishing Center. Inc. | 14 | 348 |
| Schooners Landing Restaurant | 6, 7 | 349 |
| Scotchman's Creek Marina | 1 | 350 |
| Scott Marine Sales & Service | 3, 4, 6 | 351 |
| Scott's Point Marina | 4 | 352 |
| Sea Mark Marine | 12, 13 | 353 |
| Selby Bay Yacht Basin | 5 | 354 |
| Severn Marine Service | 5, 6 | 355 |
| Shad Landing (Pocomoke River State Park) | 12 | 356 |
| Shady Oaks Marina, Inc. | 5 | 357 |
| Sheltered Harbor Marina | 3 | 358 |
| Sheperd's Yacht Yard | 8, 9 | 359 |
| Sherman's Marina | 5 | 360 |
| Shipwright Harbor Marina | 5 | 361 |
| Shymansky's Marina & Restaurant | 16 | 362 |
| Skipjack Cove Yachting Resort | 1 | 363 |
| Skipjack Landing Marine Center | 4, 5, 6 | 364 |
| Skipper's Pier | 5 | 365 |
| Smallwood State Park | 17 | 366 |
| Smith Island Marina | 12, 13 | 367 |
| Smith Point Marina | 14 | 368 |
| Smith's Marina | 3 | 369 |
| Solomon's Pier Restaurant | 8, 9 | 370 |
| Solomon's Point Marina | 8, 9 | 371 |
| Solomon's Island Yacht Club | 8, 9 | 372 |
| Solomon's Yachting Center | 8, 9 | 373 |
| Somers Cove Marina | 12, 13 | 374 |
| South River Marina, Inc. | 5 | 375 |
| Spanish Main Motel | 19 | 376 |
| Spring Cove Marina (Rock Hall) | 2, 4 | 377 |
| Spring Cove Marina (Solomons) | 8, 9 | 378 |
| St. Clement's Island Museum | 15, 16 | 379 |
| St. Mary's Yachting Center | 14, 15 | 380 |
| St. Michaels Harbour Inn, Marina & Spa | 6, 7 | 381 |
| St. Michaels Marina | 6, 7 | 382 |
| Stanford's Marine Railway | 16 | 383 |
| Stansbury Yacht Basin, Inc. | 2, 3 | 384 |
| Stepp's Harbor View Marina | 16 | 385 |
| Steve's Yacht Repair at Annapolis Harbor Boat Yard | 3, 5, Inset-20 | 386 |
| Stine Marine Railway | 10, 11 | 387 |
| Stoney Creek Bridge Marina | 3 | 388 |
| Suicide Bridge Restaurant | 7 | 389 |
| Sun Marine, Inc. & Sue Island Yacht Basin | 2, 3 | 390 |
| Sunset Harbor Marina | 2, 3 | 391 |
| Sunset Marina | 19 | 392 |
| Swan Creek Marina, Inc. (Yard A) | 2, 4 | 393 |
| Swan Creek Marina, Inc. (Yard B) | 2, 4 | 394 |
| Swann's Pier | 15 | 395 |
| Sweden Point Marina | 17 | 396 |
| Talbot Street Pier | 19 | 397 |
| Tall Timbers Marina | 15 | 398 |
| Tantallon Marina | 18 | 399 |
| Taylor's Island Marina | 8 | 400 |
| Taylors Marina | 1 | 401 |
| Thames Point Marina | 3, Inset-10 | 402 |
| Thomas' Railway & Marina | 3 | 403 |
| Thursday's Steak & Crabhouse (Steamboat Landing) | 5 | 404 |
| Tidewater Marina (Havre de Grace) | 1 | 405 |
| Tidewater Yacht Service Center | 3, Inset-10 | 406 |
| Tilghman Island Inn | 5, 6 | 407 |
| Tilghman Island Marina | 5, 6 | 408 |
| Tilghman on Chesapeake Marina | 5, 6 | 409 |
| Tim's Rivershore Restaurant | 17, 18 | 410 |
| Tolchester Marina, Inc. | 2, 4 | 411 |
| Topside Inn | 5 | 412 |
| Town Creek Restaurant & Marina | 6, 7 | 413 |
| Town of Chesapeake City Docks | 1 | 414 |
| Tradewinds Marina, Inc. | 2, 3 | 415 |
| Tred Avon Yacht Club | 6, 7 | 416 |
| Triton Marina | 1 | 417 |
| Turkey Point Marina | 5 | 418 |
| Two Rivers Yacht Basin | 1 | 419 |
| Tyme N' Tyde Marina, Inc. | 17, 18 | 420 |
| Ventnor Marine Service | 3 | 421 |
| Vera's White Sands Restaurant & Marina | 8, 9 | 422 |
| W & P Nautical, Inc. | 3, 5, Inset-20 | 423 |
| Washburn's Boat Yard, Inc. | 8, 9 | 424 |
| Washington Marina Co. | 18 | 425 |
| Waterman's Crab House | 2, 4 | 426 |
| Waugh Point Marina, Inc. | 17 | 427 |
| Weaver's Marine Service | 3 | 428 |
| Webster's Cove Facility | 11 | 429 |
| Weeks Marina | 8, 9 | 430 |
| Wells Cove Marina | 4, 6 | 431 |
| West River Fuel Dock | 5 | 432 |
| West River Sailing Club | 5 | 433 |
| West River Yacht Harbor Condo Assoc. | 5 | 434 |
| West Shore Yacht Center | 2, 3 | 435 |
| Westmoreland State Park | 16 | 436 |
| Wharf at Handy's Point | 2 | 437 |
| White Marlin Marina | 19 | 438 |
| White Point Marina | 15 | 439 |
| White Rocks Marina & Yachting Center | 3 | 440 |
| Whitehall Marina | 3 | 441 |
| Whitehaven Marina | 11 | 442 |
| Wilkander's Marine Services, Inc. | 12 | 443 |
| Wilkerson's Seafood Restaurant | 16 | 444 |
| Willow Landing Marina | 17 | 445 |
| Windsor's Marina | 11,13 | 446 |
| Winkiedoodle Point Marina | 16 | 447 |
| Winpisinger Education Center at Placid Harbour | 8, 9 | 448 |
| Woodfield Fish & Oyster Co., Inc. | 5 | 449 |
| Worton Creek Marina | 2 | 450 |
| Yacht Basin Co. | 3, 5, Inset-20 | 451 |
| Yacht Maintenance Co., Inc. | 7 | 452 |
| Yeocomico Marina | 15 | 453 |
| Young's Boat Yard | 3 | 454 |
| Zahniser's Yachting Center | 8, 9 | 455 |

* ON SITE
\+ NEARBY

| CHART NUMBER | MARINA NUMBER | MARINA NAME | INTERNET ACCESS / WIRELESS | TELEPHONE | SLIPS | GASOLINE / DIESEL | GROCERIES / HARDWARE / ICE | ENGINE / HULL / PROPELLER | ELECTRICITY | RAMP | SEWAGE PUMPOUT | SNACKBAR / RESTAURANT | LODGING |
|---|---|---|---|---|---|---|---|---|---|---|---|---|---|
| | 12 | Anchor Marina | | 410-287-8280 | 45 | G | GHI | | E | R | SP | S+R* | |
| | 28 | Avalon Yacht Basin | | 410-287-6722 | 100 | | HI | EH | E | R | | R* | |
| | 40 | Bay Boat Works, Inc.* | | 410-287-8113 | 136 | GD | HI | EHP | E | R | SP | S+R* | L* |
| | 58 | Bohemia Anchorage, Inc. | | 410-275-8148 | 65 | | I | EHP | E | | SP | | |
| | 58 | Bohemia Bay Yacht Harbour | I | 410-885-2601 | 300 | GD | HI | EHP | E | | SP | S* | |
| | 60 | Bohemia Vista Yacht Basin | | 410-885-5402 | 145 | | HI | E | E | R | SP | S*R+ | L+ |
| | 91 | Charlestown Marina | | 410-287-8125 | 265 | G | HI | EHP | E | | SP | R* | L* |
| | 93 | Chesapeake Inn Restaurant & Marina | I/W | 410-885-2040 | 60 | | HI | | E | | | S*R+ | |
| | 112 | Cove | | 410-620-5505 | 96 | | HI | EH | E | | SP | | |
| | 132 | Duffy Creek Marina | | 410-275-2141 | 130 | GD | GHI | EH | E | R | SP | S+R* | L* |
| | 139 | Elk Neck State Park Rogues Harbor | | 410-287-5333 | | | HI | | | R | | S+ | L* |
| | 140 | Elk Point Marina | | 410-398-6600 | 50 | G | I | EH | E | R | | | |
| | 164 | Georgetown Yacht Basin | I/W | 410-648-5112 | 200 | GD | GHI | EHP | E | | SP | S+R+ | L* |
| | 170 | Granary Marina | I/W | 410-648-5112 | 150 | | HI | | E | | | S+R* | |
| | 175 | Gregg Neck Boat Yard | | 410-648-5360 | 80 | | HI | EHP | E | | SP | | |
| | 178 | Hall's Landing | | | S | | | | E | R | | R* | L* |
| | 182 | Hance's Point Yacht Club | | 410-287-6090 | | | I | | E | | SP | R* | |
| | 189 | Harbour North Marina | | 410-885-5656 | 150 | G | HI | EHP | E | | SP | S* | |
| | 197 | Havre De Grace City Yacht Basin | | 410-939-0015 | 275 | GD | I | | E | R | SP | S+R* | L* |
| | 198 | Havre De Grace Marina - Log Pond | | 410-939-2161 | 70 | GD | I | EH | E | | SP | S*R* | L* |
| | 199 | Havre De Grace Marina (Water Street) | | 410-939-2161 | 70 | GD | HI | EH | E | | SP | S*R* | L* |
| | 219 | Jackson Marine Sales/Shelter Cove Marina | | 410-287-9400 | 175 | GD | GHI | EHP | E | | SP | S+R* | L* |
| | 232 | Lee's Marina | | 410-287-5100 | 68 | | HI | EHP | E | | SP | S+R* | L* |
| | 240 | Locust Point Marina* | | 410-392-4994 | 90 | | HI | | E | R | SP | | |
| | 244 | Long Point Marina, Inc. | | 410-275-8181 | 138 | G | HI | EHP | E | | SP | S* | |
| | 245 | Losten Marina | | 410-275-8168 | 54 | | HI | EH | E | R | SP | S*R* | L* |
| | 248 | M.R. Props (at McDaniel Yacht Basin) | | 410-287-7453 | | | | P | | | | | |
| | 257 | McDaniel Yacht Basin, Inc. | I | 410-287-8121 | 200 | GD | HI | EHP | E | | SP | S+R* | L* |
| | 271 | North East River Marina | | 410-287-5298 | 89 | | HI | EH | E | | | S*R* | L* |
| | 272 | North East Yacht Sales | | 410-287-6660 | 100 | | I | | E | | | R* | |
| | 274 | Northeast River Yacht Club | | 410-287-6333 | 60 | | I | | | | | R* | |
| | 289 | Owens Marina | | 410-642-6646 | 200 | | HI | | E | R | SP | R* | |
| | 296 | Penn's Beach Marina | | 410-939-2060 | 140 | G | HI | EH | E | R | SP | S+R* | L* |
| | 297 | Perryville Yacht Club | | 410-642-6364 | 136 | G | I | EH | E | R | SP | S*R* | L* |
| | 329 | Richmond's Marina | | 410-275-2061 | 75 | | HI | EH | E | R | | | |
| | 342 | Sailing Associates, Inc. | | 410-275-8171 | 80 | | HI | EHP | E | | SP | S*R* | L* |
| | 346 | Sassafras Harbor Marina | I/W | 410-275-1144 | 200 | | GHI | EHP | E | | SP | S+R* | L* |
| | 347 | Schaefer's Canal House | | 410-885-2200 | S | GD | I | | E | | SP | R+ | |
| | 350 | Scotchman's Creek Marina | | 410-275-2631 | 32 | | | | E | | | | |
| | 363 | Skipjack Cove Yachting Resort | I/W | 410-275-2122 | 368 | GD | GHI | EHP | E | | SP | S+R* | L* |
| | 401 | Taylors Marina* | | 410-392-4994 | 74 | | HI | EH | E | R | | S*R* | L* |
| | 405 | Tidewater Marina (Havre de Grace)* | | 800-960-TIDE | 160 | GD | HI | EH | E | R | SP | S*R* | L* |
| | 414 | Town of Chesapeake City Docks | | 410-885-5298 | | | | | | | | R+ | |
| | 417 | Triton Marina | | 410-398-7515 | 220 | G | HI | EH | E | R | SP | S*R* | L* |
| | 419 | Two Rivers Yacht Basin | | 410-885-2257 | 150 | G | I | EH | E | | SP | S* | |
| | | | | | | | | | | | | | |
| | 7 | All Star Marine | | 410-574-8281 | | | I | EH | E | R | | R* | |
| | 37 | Baltimore Yacht Club* | | 410-682-2310 | S | G | HI | EH | E | R | | R* | |
| | 38 | Bar Harbor RV Park & Marina | | 410-679-0880 | 40 | | GI | | E | R | | S+ | |
| | 46 | Bayside Landing Park | | 410-639-2151 | S | | | | | | SP | | |
| | 47 | Beacon Light Marina | | 410-335-6489 | 90 | G | HI | E | E | R | SP | R* | |
| | 52 | Bill's Boats | | 410-477-5137 | 52 | | I | E | | R | SP | S*R* | L* |
| | 57 | Boating Center of Baltimore | | 410-687-2000 | 60 | | HI | EHP | E | | | R+ | |
| | 61 | Bowleys Marina (Coastal Properties)* | | 410-335-3553 | 505 | GD | HI | E | E | R | SP | S+R* | L+ |
| | 68 | Bush River Boat Works, Inc. | | 410-272-1882 | 80 | G | HI | EH | E | R | SP | R* | |
| | 95 | Chesapeake Yachting Center* | W | 410-335-4900 | 200 | GD | GHI | EHP | E | | SP | R+ | L+ |
| | 119 | Cutter Marine, Inc. | | 410-391-7245 | 125 | | HI | EHP | E | R | SP | S*R+ | L+ |
| | 122 | Deckelman's Boat Yard | | 410-391-6482 | 10 | | H | EHP | E | | | R+ | |
| | 133 | Dundee Creek Marina | | 410-335-9390 | 89 | | HI | | | R | SP | S+ | |
| | 138 | Edwards Boat Yard | | 410-335-2311 | 124 | GD | HI | | E | | SP | S*R* | |
| | 141 | Essex Marina & Boat Sales | I | 410-687-6149 | 80 | | GHI | EHP | E | | SP | R+ | L+ |
| | 154 | Flying Point Marina | | 410-676-7311 | 250 | G | GHI | EH | E | R | SP | | |
| | 158 | Galloway Creek Marina | | 410-335-3575 | S | | | EHP | E | | SP | | |
| | 169 | Goose Harbor Marina | | 410-335-7474 | 215 | G | HI | EHP | E | | SP | R+ | |
| | 171 | Gratitude Marina | | 410-639-7011 | 80 | GD | HI | EHP | E | | SP | R* | L* |
| | 172 | Gratitude Yachting Center | | 410-639-7111 | | | | | | | | R* | L* |
| | 173 | Great Oak Landing | I | 410-778-5007 | 350 | GD | GHI | EHP | E | | SP | R+ | L+ |
| | 174 | Green Point Landing | | 410-778-1615 | 57 | GD | HI | EHP | E | | SP | S+ | |
| | 176 | Gunpowder Cove Marina | | 410-679-5454 | 300 | G | HI | EH | E | R | SP | S+ | |
| | 196 | Haven Harbour Marina | I/W | 410-778-6697 | 217 | GD | GHI | EHP | E | | SP | R+ | L* |
| | 209 | Holly Neck Marina | | 410-574-9626 | 46 | | | EH | E | | | S*R* | |
| | 230 | Lankford Bay Marina | | 410-778-1414 | 103 | GD | Hi | EH | E | | SP | S+R* | L* |
| | 242 | Long Beach Marina | I/W | 410-335-8602 | 320 | GD | HI | EHP | E | | SP | R+ | L+ |
| | 252 | Markley's Marina, Inc. | | 410-687-5575 | 53 | | H | EHP | | | SP | R+ | |
| | 253 | Maryland Marina | | 410-335-8722 | 360 | | HI | HP | E | R | SP | R+ | |
| | 267 | Moonlight Bay Inn and Marina | | 410-639-2660 | 40 | | I | | E | | | R* | L* |
| | 273 | North Point Marina | | 410-639-2907 | 140 | GD | HI | | E | | SP | R+ | L+ |
| | 287 | Osprey Point Yacht Club | | 410-639-2194 | 160 | GD | I | | E | | SP | R* | L* |
| | 298 | Pete's Marina | | 410-477-1610 | | | I | | | R | | S+R+ | |
| | 321 | Porters Seneca Marina | | 410-335-6563 | 100 | G | HI | EHP | E | | SP | S*R+ | L+ |
| | 332 | River Watch Restaurant & Marina | | 410-687-1422 | 110 | GD | I | | E | | SP | S*R+ | L+ |

| CHART NUMBER | MARINA NUMBER | MARINA NAME | INTERNET ACCESS / WIRELESS | TELEPHONE | SLIPS | GASOLINE / DIESEL | GROCERIES / HARDWARE / ICE | ENGINE / HULL / PROPELLER | ELECTRICITY | RAMP | SEWAGE PUMPOUT | SNACKBAR / RESTAURANT | LODGING |
|---|---|---|---|---|---|---|---|---|---|---|---|---|---|
| | 335 | Rock Hall Landing Marina | I/W | 410-639-2224 | 75 | | I | | E | | SP | R* | L* |
| | 336 | Rock Hall Marine Railway | | 410-639-2263 | 25 | | | H | E | | | R+ | L+ |
| | 338 | Rocky Point Park | | 410-887-3780 | | | | | | R | | | |
| | 343 | Sailing Emporium, Inc.* | I | 410-778-1342 | 155 | GD | HI | EHP | E | | SP | S*R* | L* |
| | 377 | Spring Cove Marina (Rock Hall)* | W | 410-639-2110 | 193 | | | | E | | SP | | |
| | 390 | Sun Marine, Inc. & Sue Island Yacht Basin | | 410-574-7915 | 56 | | GHI | EH | E | R | SP | R* | L* |
| | 391 | Sunset Harbor Marina | | 410-786-7290 | 40 | | GHI | EHP | E | | SP | S* | |
| 2 | 393 | Swan Creek Marina, Inc. (Yard A) | | 410-639-7813 | 107 | | I | EHP | E | | SP | R* | L* |
| | 394 | Swan Creek Marina, Inc. (Yard B) | | 410-639-7813 | 107 | | I | EHP | E | | SP | R+ | L+ |
| | 411 | Tolchester Marina, Inc. | | 410-778-1400 | 260 | GD | HI | EHP | E | | SP | R+ | L* |
| | 415 | Tradewinds Marina, Inc. | | 410-335-7000 | 78 | | HI | EHP | E | R | SP | S*R+ | |
| | 426 | Waterman's Crab House | | 410-639-2261 | 25 | | I | | E | | | R+ | L+ |
| | 435 | West Shore Yacht Center | I/W | 410-686-6998 | 85 | G | HI | EHP | E | | SP | R+ | |
| | 438 | Wharf at Handy's Point | | 410-778-4363 | 55 | | GI | EH | E | | | | |
| | 450 | Worton Creek Marina | | 410-778-3282 | 110 | GD | GHI | EHP | E | | SP | R+ | |
| | | | | | | | | | | | | | |
| | 4 | Absolute Marine Services | | 410-647-4450 | 93 | | HI | EHP | E | | | | |
| | 7 | All Star Marine | | 410-574-8281 | | | I | EH | E | R | | R* | |
| | 9 | Anchor Bay East Marina* | I | 410-284-1044 | 70 | GD | HI | EHP | E | R | SP | S*R+ | L+ |
| | 10 | Anchor Bay Marina & Ship Store | | 410-574-0777 | 26 | | HI | | E | | SP | R* | |
| | 11 | Anchor Inn | | 410-437-0696 | S | | | | E | | | R+ | |
| | 15 | Anderson's Marine Service | | 410-255-1007 | 5 | | GHI | EHP | E | | SP | R+ | |
| | 27 | Atlantic Marina on the Magothy | | 410-360-2500 | 35 | GD | HI | EHP | E | | | S*R+ | |
| | 37 | Baltimore Yacht Club* | | 410-682-2310 | S | G | HI | EH | E | R | | R* | |
| | 38 | Bar Harbor RV Park & Marina | | 410-679-0880 | 44 | | H | EH | E | | | | |
| | 41 | Bay Boats Supply & Marina | | 410-574-0777 | 26 | | HI | | E | | SP | R+ | |
| | 42 | Bay Bridge Marina | | 410-643-3162 | 325 | GD | HI | EHP | E | | SP | S+R+ | L* |
| | 47 | Beacon Light Marina | | 410-335-6489 | 90 | G | HI | E | E | R | SP | R* | |
| | 52 | Bill's Boats | | 410-477-5137 | 52 | | I | E | | R | SP | S*R* | L* |
| | 57 | Boating Center of Baltimore | | 410-687-2000 | 60 | | HI | EHP | E | | | R+ | |
| | 61 | Bowleys Marina (Coastal Properties)* | | 410-335-3553 | 505 | GD | HI | E | E | R | SP | S+R* | L+ |
| | 65 | Buedal's Marina & Boatyard | | 410-687-3577 | 150 | GD | GHI | EH | E | | SP | R* | |
| | 95 | Chesapeake Yachting Center* | W | 410-335-4900 | 200 | GD | GHI | EHP | E | | SP | R+ | L+ |
| | 113 | Cox's Point Park Ramp | | 410-887-0255 | | | | | | R | | | |
| | 119 | Cutter Marine, Inc. | | 410-391-7245 | 125 | | HI | EHP | E | R | SP | S*R+ | L+ |
| | 120 | Cypress Marine | | 410-647-7940 | 40 | | | EHP | E | | | | |
| | 122 | Deckelman's Boat Yard | | 410-391-6482 | 10 | | H | EHP | E | | | R+ | |
| | 123 | Deep Creek Marina | | 410-974-1408 | 21 | GD | I | | E | | | S+R+ | |
| | 130 | Driftwood Inn, Inc. | | 410-391-3493 | 20 | | I | | | | | R+ | |
| | 138 | Edwards Boat Yard | | 410-335-2311 | 124 | GD | HI | | E | | SP | S*R* | |
| | 141 | Essex Marina & Boat Sales | I | 410-687-6149 | 80 | | GHI | EHP | E | | SP | R+ | L+ |
| | 145 | Fairview Marina* | I | 410-437-3400 | 112 | | HI | EHP | E | | SP | R+ | |
| | 146 | Fairwinds Marina | | 410-974-0758 | 100 | G | HI | EHP | E | R | | | |
| | 148 | Ferry Point Marina Yacht Yard | W | 410-544-6368 | 108 | | HI | EHP | E | | SP | S*R+ | |
| | 153 | Florida Marina & Boat Sales, Inc. | | 410-255-4365 | 60 | G | | | E | | SP | | |
| | 158 | Galloway Creek Marina | | 410-335-3575 | S | | | EHP | E | | SP | | |
| | 165 | Gibson Island Yacht Squadron | | 410-255-7632 | | | | | | | SP | R+ | L+ |
| | 169 | Goose Harbor Marina | | 410-335-7474 | 215 | G | HI | EHP | E | | SP | R+ | |
| 3 | 179 | Hamilton Harbour Marina | | 410-647-0733 | 22 | GD | I | EH | E | | SP | | |
| | 180 | Hammock Island Marina | | 410-437-1870 | 64 | | I | | E | | SP | | |
| | 209 | Holly Neck Marina | | 410-574-9626 | 46 | | | EH | E | | | S*R* | |
| | 214 | Iman's Boat Yard | | 410-477-1974 | 32 | | | EH | E | | | S*R* | L* |
| | 242 | Long Beach Marina | I/W | 410-335-8602 | 320 | GD | HI | EHP | E | | SP | R+ | L+ |
| | 250 | Magothy Marina* | I | 410-647-2356 | 182 | GD | I | E | E | R | SP | S*R+ | L+ |
| | 251 | Markel's Boatyard | | 410-477-3445 | 85 | G | HI | H | E | | SP | | |
| | 252 | Markley's Marina, Inc. | | 410-687-5575 | 53 | | H | EHP | E | | SP | R+ | |
| | 253 | Maryland Marina | | 410-335-8722 | 360 | | HI | HP | E | R | SP | R+ | |
| | 254 | Maryland Yacht Club | | 410-255-4444 | 125 | GD | I | | E | | SP | R+ | |
| | 256 | Maurgale Inn & Marina | | 410-437-0402 | 141 | | | EHP | E | | SP | R* | |
| | 261 | Middle Branch Moorings | | 410-539-2628 | 365 | GD | HI | EH | E | | SP | R* | L* |
| | 270 | Norman Creek Marina, Inc. | | 410-686-9343 | S | | I | | E | | SP | S*R* | L* |
| | 276 | Oak Harbor Marina* | | 410-255-4070 | 94 | | HI | EHP | E | | SP | R+ | |
| | 283 | Old Bay Marina | | 410-477-1488 | 84 | | | | E | | SP | | |
| | 293 | Pasadena Boatel & Beach Club | | 410-437-6926 | 60 | G | I | | E | | SP | R* | |
| | 294 | Pasadena Yacht Yard, Inc. | | 410-255-1771 | 53 | GD | H | EHP | E | | SP | R+ | L+ |
| | 298 | Pete's Marina | | 410-477-1610 | | | I | | | R | | S+R+ | |
| | 308 | Pleasure Cove Marina | | 410-437-6600 | 128 | GD | GHI | EHP | E | | SP | R* | |
| | 310 | Podickory Point | | 410-757-8000 | 117 | | I | | E | | SP | S+R* | L* |
| | 321 | Porter's Seneca Marina | | 410-335-6563 | 100 | G | HI | EHP | E | | SP | S*R+ | L+ |
| | 330 | Riley's Marina Sales & Service, Inc. | | 410-686-0771 | 98 | G | H | EHP | E | | SP | R+ | |
| | 332 | River Watch Restaurant & Marina | | 410-687-1422 | 110 | GD | I | | E | | SP | S*R+ | L+ |
| | 333 | Riverside Marine, Inc. | | 410-686-1500 | 100 | | HI | EH | E | R | SP | S+R+ | |
| | 338 | Rocky Point Park | | 410-887-3780 | | | | | | R | | | |
| | 341 | Rudy's Marina | | 410-477-3276 | S | G | HI | EH | E | R | SP | | |
| | 344 | Sandy Point State Park | | 410-974-2772 | 8 | GD | I | | | R | SP | S+ | |
| | 351 | Scott Marine Sales & Service | | 410-827-8150 | 14 | | | EH | E | | | S*R* | L* |
| | 358 | Sheltered Harbor Marina | | 410-288-4100 | 172 | | | EHP | E | | | R+ | |
| | 369 | Smith's Marina | | 410-923-3444 | 65 | G | HI | EH | E | R | SP | S+ | |
| | 384 | Stansbury Yacht Basin, Inc. | | 410-686-3909 | 85 | G | HI | EHP | E | R | SP | R+ | |
| | 388 | Stoney Creek Bridge Marina | | 410-255-5566 | 70 | G | I | E | E | R | | S*R* | L* |
| | 390 | Sun Marine, Inc. & Sue Island Yacht Basin | | 410-574-7915 | 56 | | GHI | EH | E | R | SP | R* | L* |

These marinas meet the rigorous pollution prevention standards established by the Maryland Clean Marina Committee and the Department of Natural Resources. The operators have voluntarily adopted measures to control pollution associated with marina operations and stand as notable examples of the conservation ethic: individual responsibility for healthy land and water.

* ON SITE
\+ NEARBY

| CHART NUMBER | MARINA NUMBER | MARINA NAME | INTERNET ACCESS / WIRELESS | TELEPHONE | SLIPS | GASOLINE / DIESEL | GROCERIES / HARDWARE / ICE | ENGINE / HULL / PROPELLER | ELECTRICITY | RAMP | SEWAGE PUMPOUT | SNACKBAR / RESTAURANT | LODGING |
|---|---|---|---|---|---|---|---|---|---|---|---|---|---|
| | 391 | Sunset Harbor Marina | | 410-786-7290 | 40 | | GHI | EHP | E | | SP | S* | |
| | 403 | Thomas' Railway & Marina | | 410-255-3101 | 56 | | H | EH | E | | | R* | |
| | 415 | Tradewinds Marina, Inc. | | 410-335-7000 | 78 | | HI | EHP | E | R | SP | S*R+ | |
| | 421 | Ventnor Marine Service | | 410-255-4100 | 130 | GD | HI | EH | E | R | SP | | |
| 3 | 428 | Weaver's Marine Service | | 410-686-4944 | 85 | G | HI | EH | E | R | | S*R* | L* |
| | 436 | West Shore Yacht Center | I/W | 410-686-6998 | 85 | G | HI | EHP | E | | SP | R+ | |
| | 440 | White Rocks Marina & Yachting Center | | 410-255-3800 | 360 | | HI | | E | R | SP | S*R+ | |
| | 441 | Whitehall Marina | | 410-757-4819 | 120 | | H | EHP | E | | | | |
| | 454 | Young's Boat Yard* | | 410-477-8607 | 110 | | H | | E | | SP | | |
| | 14 | Anchorage Marina | I/W | 410-522-7200 | 590 | | GI | EP | E | | SP | S*R+ | |
| | 33 | Baltimore Inner Harbor Marine Center | I/W | 410-837-5339 | 135 | GD | GHI | | E | | SP | R* | L+ |
| | 34 | Baltimore Marine Center at Lighthouse Point | | 410-675-8888 | 500 | GD | GHI | EHP | E | | SP | S*R+ | L+ |
| | 35 | Baltimore Marine Center-Pier 7 | | 410-675-8888 | | GD | GHI | EHP | E | | SP | S*R+ | L+ |
| | 36 | Baltimore Yacht Basin | | 410-539-8895 | 175 | | I | EH | E | | SP | R* | |
| INSET 10 PAGE A | 98 | City of Baltimore Public Docks/Inner Harbor | | 410-396-3174 | 150 | | | | E | | | R+ | L+ |
| | 186 | Harbor View Marina (Coastal Properties) | I | 410-752-1122 | 300 | | GI | | E | | SP | R+ | L+ |
| | 200 | Henderson Wharf Marina | | 410-732-1049 | 200 | | I | | E | | SP | R+ | L+ |
| | 216 | Inner Harbor East Marina | | 410-625-1700 | 188 | | GI | | E | | SP | R+ | L+ |
| | 316 | Port Covington Maritime Center | | 410-625-4992 | 40 | | GH | EHP | E | | SP | R+ | L+ |
| | 402 | Thames Point Marina | | 410-522-7368 | 50 | | | | E | | | | |
| | 406 | Tidewater Yacht Service Center | | 410-625-4992 | 25 | GD | HI | EHP | E | | SP | S*R+ | L+ |
| | 2 | A & B Yachtsmen, Inc. | | 410-263-9073 | | | H | EHP | | | | | |
| | 18 | Annapolis City Dock | I/W | 410-263-7973 | 31 | | HI | | E | | SP | S*R* | L* |
| | 19 | Annapolis City Marina, Ltd. | W | 410-268-0660 | 85 | GD | GHI | | E | | SP | R+ | L+ |
| | 20 | Annapolis Landing Marina | I/W | 410-263-0090 | 120 | GD | HI | | E | | SP | S*R+ | L+ |
| | 21 | Annapolis Maryland Capital Yacht Club | W | 410-269-5219 | 81 | | I | HP | E | | SP | R+ | L+ |
| | 22 | Annapolis Waterfront Marriott/ Pusser's Landing | | 410-263-7837 | | | | | E | | | S+R* | L* |
| | 23 | Annapolis Yacht Club | I | 410-263-9279 | 120 | | | | | | | R+ | L+ |
| | 24 | Annapolis Yacht Sales & Services, Inc. | | 410-267-8181 | S | | | EHP | | | | R+ | |
| | 30 | Back Creek Marina | | 410-280-6417 | 48 | | | | E | | | S*R* | L* |
| | 51 | Bert Jabin's Yacht Yard* | I | 410-268-9667 | 200 | | GHI | EHP | E | | SP | S*R+ | L+ |
| | 90 | Chandlery Dock (at Fawcett) | | 41-268-9041 | 5 | | H | | E | | | R+ | L+ |
| INSET 20 PAGE B | 92 | Chesapeake Harbour Marina* | I/W | 410-268-1969 | 200 | | I | | E | | SP | R+ | L+ |
| | 136 | Eastport Yacht Club | | 410-267-9549 | 34 | | | | E | | | R+ | L+ |
| | 137 | Eastport Yacht Yard | | 410-280-9888 | 100 | | I | EHP | E | | SP | R+ | L+ |
| | 147 | Fawcett Boat Supplies, Inc. | | 410-267-8681 | | | H | | | | | S+R+ | L+ |
| | 212 | Horn Point Harbor Marina (CPM) | | 410-269-0933 | 60 | | | EH | E | | SP | S*R+ | |
| | 258 | Mears Marina* | I/W | 410-268-8282 | 232 | | I | EH | E | | SP | R+ | L+ |
| | 285 | Olde Towne Marina, Ltd. | | 410-263-9277 | 35 | | | | E | | | R+ | L+ |
| | 299 | Petrini Shipyard, Inc. | I | 410-263-4278 | 45 | | | EHP | E | | | R+ | L+ |
| | 315 | Port Annapolis Marina* | I | 410-269-1990 | 290 | | HI | EHP | E | | SP | S*R+ | |
| | 345 | Sarles Boat & Engine Shop, Inc. | | 888-837-6526 | 48 | | I | EHP | E | R | | S*R+ | L+ |
| | 386 | Steve's Yacht Repair at Annapolis Harbor Boat Yard | | 410-268-0092 | | | | EHP | E | | | R* | |
| | 423 | W & P Nautical, Inc. | | 410-268-7700 | 50 | | | | E | | | S*R* | L* |
| | 451 | Yacht Basin Co. | I/W | 410-263-3544 | 107 | GD | I | | E | | SP | R+ | L* |
| | 17 | Angler's Restaurant & Marina | | 410-827-6717 | 60 | | HI | | E | | | R+ | L+ |
| | 46 | Bayside Landing Park | | 410-639-2151 | S | | | | | | SP | | |
| | 85 | Castle Harbor Marina | | 410-643-5599 | 350 | GD | GHI | | E | | SP | S+R+ | |
| | 89 | Centerville Public Landing | | 410-758-0835 | 22 | | | | | R | | | |
| | 96 | Chestertown Marina | I | 410-778-3616 | 60 | GD | HI | E | E | R | SP | S+R* | L* |
| | 134 | Eastern Bay Marina, Inc./Crab Alley Marina | | 410-643-7339 | 38 | | I | EH | E | R | | S*R* | |
| | 150 | Fisherman's Inn & Crabdeck Restaurants | | 410-827-8807 | 18 | | I | | | | | R* | L+ |
| | 171 | Gratitude Marina* | | 410-639-7011 | 80 | GD | HI | EH | E | | SP | R* | L* |
| | 172 | Gratitude Yachting Center | | 410-639-7111 | | | | | | | | R* | L* |
| | 191 | Harris Crab House | | 410-827-9500 | S | | | | | | | R* | |
| | 192 | Harrison Yacht Sales | | 410-827-7800 | | | | | | | SP | R* | L* |
| | 196 | Haven Harbour Marina* | | 410-778-6697 | 217 | GD | GHI | EH | E | | SP | R+ | L* |
| | 217 | Island View Marina | | 410-643-2842 | 42 | | I | EH | E | | SP | | |
| | 223 | Kennersley Point Marina | | 410-758-2394 | 55 | | HI | EH | E | R | SP | S+R+ | L+ |
| | 224 | Kent Island Yacht Club | | 410-643-4101 | 70 | | | | | | | | |
| 4 | 225 | Kent Narrows Yacht Yard | | 410-643-4400 | | | H | EHP | | | | | |
| | 230 | Lankford Bay Marina | | 410-778-1414 | 106 | GD | HI | EHP | E | | SP | S+R* | L* |
| | 238 | Lippincott Marine* | | 410-827-9300 | 200 | | HI | EHP | E | | SP | R+ | L+ |
| | 243 | Long Cove Marina | | 410-778-6777 | 104 | GD | HI | EHP | E | | SP | S+ | |
| | 259 | Mears Point Marina* | | 410-827-8888 | 535 | GD | GHI | EHP | E | | SP | R+ | L+ |
| | 267 | Moonlight Bay Inn and Marina | | 410-639-2660 | | | GHI | | E | | | S+R* | L* |
| | 273 | North Point Marina | | 410-639-2907 | 130 | GD | HI | E | E | | SP | S*R+ | L* |
| | 287 | Osprey Point Yacht Club | | 410-639-2663 | 157 | GD | HI | EH | E | | SP | S+R* | L* |
| | 305 | Piney Narrows Yacht Haven* | I | 410-643-6600 | 278 | GD | HI | EHP | E | R | SP | R+ | L+ |
| | 336 | Rock Hall Marine Railway | | 410-639-2263 | 25 | | H | H | E | | | R* | L* |
| | 340 | Rolph's Wharf Marina | W | 410-778-6389 | 40 | GD | HI | HP | E | | SP | R* | L* |
| | 343 | Sailing Emporium, Inc.* | | 410-778-1342 | 155 | GD | HI | EH | E | | SP | S*R* | L* |
| | 351 | Scott Marine Sales & Service | | 410-827-8150 | 84 | | HI | EH | E | | SP | R* | L* |
| | 352 | Scott's Point Marina | | 410-778-2959 | 34 | | I | | E | | | S*R* | L* |
| | 364 | Skipjack Landing Marine Center* | | 410-643-2694 | 75 | G | HI | EHP | E | | SP | S+R+ | L+ |
| | 377 | Spring Cove Marina (Rock Hall)* | W | 410-639-2110 | 193 | | | | E | | SP | | |

| CHART NUMBER | MARINA NUMBER | MARINA NAME | INTERNET ACCESS / WIRELESS | TELEPHONE | SLIPS | GASOLINE / DIESEL | GROCERIES / HARDWARE / ICE | ENGINE / HULL / PROPELLER | ELECTRICITY | RAMP | SEWAGE PUMPOUT | SNACKBAR / RESTAURANT | LODGING |
|---|---|---|---|---|---|---|---|---|---|---|---|---|---|
| | 393 | Swan Creek Marina, Inc. (Yard A) | | 410-639-7813 | 107 | | I | EH | E | | | R* | L |
| | 394 | Swan Creek Marina, Inc. (Yard B) | | 410-639-7813 | S | | | EH | E | | | | |
| 4 | 411 | Tolchester Marina, Inc. | | 410-778-1400 | 260 | GD | HI | EH | E | | SP | | L |
| | 426 | Waterman's Crab House | | 410-639-2261 | 25 | | I | | E | | | R+ | L |
| | 431 | Wells Cove Marina | | 410-827-3870 | 76 | | | | E | | SP | R+ | L |
| | 13 | Anchor Yacht Basin | | 410-269-6674 | 125 | GD | HI | EHP | E | | SP | S*R+ | |
| | 31 | Backyard Boats | | 410-867-3119 | 56 | GD | HI | EHP | E | R | SP | S*R+ | |
| | 42 | Bay Bridge Marina | | 410-643-3162 | 325 | GD | HI | EHP | E | | SP | S+R+ | L |
| | 43 | Bay Harbour Boatyard | | 410-867-2392 | 15 | | | EHP | | | | | |
| | 44 | Bay Hundred Restaurant | | 410-886-2126 | S | | | | | | | R* | |
| | 45 | Bay View Marina | | 410-798-6060 | 154 | G | I | EH | E | | SP | S*R* | |
| | 55 | Blue Water Marina | | 410-798-6733 | 63 | | | HP | E | | SP | | |
| | 67 | Burr Yacht Sales | | 410-798-5900 | 20 | | | | E | | | | |
| | 71 | Cadle Creek Marina | | 410-798-1915 | 50 | GD | HI | EHP | E | | SP | S*R+ | |
| | 84 | Casa Rio Marina, Inc.* | | 301-261-7111 | 39 | | HI | EHP | E | R | SP | S*R+ | |
| | 85 | Castle Harbor Marina | | 410-643-5599 | 350 | GD | GHI | | E | | SP | S+R+ | |
| | 99 | Clark's Landing Shadyside | | 410-867-6111 | S | | | EHP | E | R | | R+ | |
| | 134 | Eastern Bay Marina, Inc./Crab Alley Marina | | 410-643-7339 | 38 | | I | EH | E | R | | S*R* | |
| | 151 | Fishing Creek Landings* | | 301-855-3572 | 99 | G | HI | | E | R | SP | S*R+ | L |
| | 157 | Galesville Yacht Yard, Inc. | | 410-867-7517 | | GD | HI | EHP | E | | SP | S*R+ | L |
| | 160 | Gates Marine | | 410-867-9666 | 88 | | HI | EHP | E | | SP | R+ | |
| | 184 | Harbor Hills Yacht Club | | 410-956-4606 | | | | | E | | SP | | |
| | 187 | Harbour Cove Marina | | 301-261-9500 | 84 | G | HI | EHP | E | R | SP | S*R+ | |
| | 193 | Harrison's Country Inn | | 410-886-2121 | 25 | | I | | E | | | R+ | L |
| | 195 | Hartge Yacht Yard* | I/W | 410-867-2188 | 275 | GD | HI | EHP | E | | SP | R+ | L |
| | 201 | Herrington Harbour North* | I/W | 410-867-4343 | 575 | | HI | EHP | E | | SP | R+ | L |
| | 202 | Herrington Harbour South* | I/W | 410-741-5100 | 580 | GD | GHI | EHP | E | | SP | S*R* | L |
| | 206 | Holiday Hill Marina | | 443-871-3909 | 145 | | I | EH | E | | SP | R+ | |
| | 208 | Holiday Point Marina | | 410-956-2208 | 160 | | | EHP | E | | SP | R+ | |
| | 217 | Island View Marina | | 410-643-2842 | 42 | | I | EH | E | | SP | | |
| | 226 | Kentmorr Harbour Marina | | 410-643-0029 | 100 | GD | I | EHP | E | R | SP | S+R+ | |
| | 228 | Knapps Narrows Marina and Inn | I | 800-322-5181 | 130 | GD | HI | EHP | E | | SP | R+ | L |
| | 231 | Leatherbury Point Marina | | 301-261-5599 | 15 | | | | | | SP | | |
| | 237 | Liberty Yacht Club & Marina | | 800-971-1300 | 425 | GD | HI | EHP | E | | SP | S*R+ | L |
| | 239 | Little Island Marina* | | 410-798-0276 | 41 | | | | E | | SP | S*R* | |
| 5 | 247 | Lowes Wharf Marina Inn | W | 410-745-6684 | 22 | GD | HI | | E | | SP | S+R* | L |
| | 263 | Mike's Restaurant & Crab House | | 410-956-2847 | 66 | | GI | | E | | SP | S+R+ | |
| | 275 | Oak Grove Marine Center* | | 410-266-6696 | 140 | GD | I | EHP | E | R | SP | R* | |
| | 292 | Parrish Creek Marina & Boatyard | | 41--867-0393 | 110 | | I | EH | E | | SP | S*R* | L |
| | 301 | Phipps Marine Railway | | 410-867-2737 | 18 | | | H | E | | | | |
| | 302 | Pier 7 Marina | | 410-956-2288 | 200 | | I | | E | R | SP | R* | |
| | 306 | Pirates Cove Restaurant | I/W | 410-867-2300 | 80 | | I | | E | | SP | R* | L |
| | 325 | Queen Anne Marina | | 410-643-2021 | 124 | GD | GHI | EH | E | R | SP | S+R* | L |
| | 328 | Rhode River Marina | | 410-798-1658 | 110 | G | HI | EHP | E | | SP | S*R+ | |
| | 337 | Rockhold Creek Marina & Yacht Repair | | 410-867-7919 | 50 | | GHI | EHP | E | | SP | R+ | L |
| | 339 | Rod & Reel | | 301-855-8450 | 125 | GD | I | | E | | SP | S*R* | L |
| | 341 | Londontowne Marina* | | 410-956-5077 | 55 | G | I | EHP | E | | SP | S*R+ | |
| | 354 | Selby Bay Yacht Basin* | | 410-798-0232 | 100 | GD | I | | E | | SP | R+ | |
| | 355 | Severn Marine Service | | 410-886-2159 | 48 | | H | EHP | E | | SP | R+ | L |
| | 357 | Shady Oaks Marina, Inc. | | 410-867-7700 | 65 | | | EHP | E | | SP | R* | |
| | 360 | Sherman's Marina | | 301-261-5013 | 32 | GD | HI | | E | | SP | S*R+ | L |
| | 361 | Shipwright Harbor Marina* | I | 410-867-7686 | 250 | | I | EHP | E | | SP | R+ | L |
| | 364 | Skipjack Landing Marine Center* | | 410-643-2694 | 75 | G | HI | EH | E | | SP | S+ | |
| | 365 | Skipper's Pier | | 410-867-7110 | 10 | GD | I | | | | | S*R* | |
| | 375 | South River Marina, Inc. | | 410-798-1717 | 156 | | HI | EHP | E | R | SP | S*R+ | |
| | 404 | Thursday's Steak & Crabhouse (Steamboat Landing) | | 410-867-7200 | 26 | | | | | | | R* | |
| | 407 | Tilghman Island Inn | | 410-886-2141 | 21 | | | | | | | R* | L |
| | 408 | Tilghman Island Marina | I | 410-886-2500 | 41 | | GHI | | E | | SP | R+ | L |
| | 409 | Tilghman on Chesapeake Marina | | 410-886-2389 | 55 | | I | | E | | SP | R+ | L |
| | 412 | Topside Inn | | 410-867-4433 | | | I | | | | | R* | L |
| | 418 | Turkey Point Marina | | 410-798-1369 | 103 | G | HI | EHP | E | R | SP | S*R+ | |
| | 432 | West River Fuel Dock | I/W | 410-867-1444 | 185 | GD | HI | | E | | SP | S*R+ | L+ |
| | 433 | West River Sailing Club | | 410-867-WRSC | | | | | | | | S+R+ | L+ |
| | 434 | West River Yacht Harbor Condo Assoc. | | 410-867-4065 | 180 | GD | GHI | EHP | E | | SP | S*R+ | L+ |
| | 449 | Woodfield Fish & Oyster Co., Inc. | | 410-867-3421 | 23 | | I | | E | | | R+ | |
| | 3 | A & M Marine Service Inc. | | 410-827-7409 | | | | EHP | E | | | R+ | |
| | 17 | Angler's Restaurant & Marina | | 410-827-6717 | 60 | | HI | | E | | | R+ | L* |
| | 42 | Bay Bridge Marina | | 410-643-3162 | 325 | GD | HI | EHP | E | | SP | S+R+ | L* |
| | 44 | Bay Hundred Restaurant | | 410-886-2126 | S | | | | | | | R* | |
| | 74 | Campbell's Bachelor Point Yacht Co.* | | 410-226-5592 | 80 | | HI | E | E | | SP | R+ | L+ |
| | 75 | Campbell's Boatyard at Jack's Point | I | 410-226-5105 | 54 | GD | GHI | EHP | E | | SP | R+ | L+ |
| 6 | 76 | Campbell's Town Creek Boatyard | | 410-226-0213 | 42 | | I | EH | E | | SP | R+ | L+ |
| | 85 | Castle Harbor Marina | | 410-643-5599 | 350 | GD | GHI | | E | | SP | S+R+ | |
| | 94 | Chesapeake Maritime Museum | I | 410-745-2916 | 20 | | I | | E | | SP | R+ | L+ |
| | 114 | Crab Claw Restaurant | | 410-745-2900 | 12 | | | | | | | R* | |
| | 118 | Cuts & Case Inc. | | 410-226-5416 | 35 | | | EHP | E | | | R+ | L+ |
| | 125 | Dickerson Harbor | | 410-822-8556 | 50 | | | EHP | E | | | | |
| | 134 | Eastern Bay Marina, Inc./Crab Alley Marina | | 410-643-7339 | 38 | | I | EH | E | R | | S*R* | |

* ON SITE
+ NEARBY

| CHART NUMBER | MARINA NUMBER | MARINA NAME | INTERNET ACCESS / WIRELESS | TELEPHONE | SLIPS | GASOLINE / DIESEL | GROCERIES / HARDWARE / ICE | ENGINE / HULL / PROPELLER | ELECTRICITY | RAMP | SEWAGE PUMPOUT | SNACKBAR / RESTAURANT | LODGING |
|---|---|---|---|---|---|---|---|---|---|---|---|---|---|
| | 135 | Easton Point Marina | | 410-822-1201 | 24 | GD | HI | EHP | E | R | SP | S*R+ | L+ |
| | 150 | Fisherman's Inn & Crabdeck Restaurants | | 410-827-8807 | 18 | | I | | | | | R* | L+ |
| | 191 | Harris Crab House | | 410-827-9500 | S | | | | | | | R* | |
| | 192 | Harrison Yacht Sales | | 410-827-7800 | | | | | | | SP | R* | L* |
| | 193 | Harrison's Country Inn | | 410-886-2121 | 25 | | I | | E | | | R+ | L+ |
| | 203 | Higgins Yacht Yard | W | 410-745-9303 | 30 | | HI | EHP | E | | SP | R+ | L+ |
| | 204 | Hinckley Yacht Services | W | 410-226-5113 | 66 | | HI | EHP | E | | SP | S+R+ | L+ |
| | 215 | Inn at Perry Cabin | I | 410-745-2200 | 3 | | | | | | | R+ | L* |
| | 217 | Island View Marina | | 410-643-2842 | 42 | | I | EH | E | | SP | | |
| | 224 | Kent Island Yacht Club | | 410-643-4101 | 70 | | | | | | | | |
| | 225 | Kent Narrows Yacht Yard | | 410-643-4400 | | | H | EHP | | | | | |
| | 226 | Kentmorr Harbour Marina | | 410-643-0029 | 100 | GD | I | EHP | E | R | SP | S+R+ | |
| | 228 | Knapps Narrows Marina and Inn | I | 800-322-5181 | 130 | GD | HI | EHP | E | | SP | R+ | L* |
| | 238 | Lippincott Marine* | | 410-827-9300 | 195 | | HI | EH | E | | SP | S*R* | L* |
| | 247 | Lowes Wharf Marina Inn | W | 410-745-6684 | 22 | GD | HI | | E | | SP | S+R* | L+ |
| | 255 | Masthead Restaurant at Pier Street Marina | | 410-226-5171 | 65 | GD | | | E | R | | R+ | L+ |
| | 259 | Mears Point Marina* | | 410-827-8888 | 535 | GD | GHI | EHP | E | | SP | R+ | L* |
| 6 | 260 | Mears Yacht Haven (Coastal Properties)* | I | 410-226-5450 | 95 | GD | HI | | E | | SP | R+ | L+ |
| | 265 | Miles River Yacht Club | | 410-745-9511 | 60 | | I | | E | | | R+ | |
| | 290 | Oxford Boat Yard (Coastal Properties) | I | 410-226-5101 | 76 | | GHI | EHP | E | | SP | R+ | L+ |
| | 291 | Oxford Yacht Agency | | 410-2226-5454 | 20 | | | EHP | E | | | R+ | L+ |
| | 305 | Piney Narrows Yacht Haven* | | 410-643-6600 | 278 | GD | HI | EH | E | R | SP | S+R* | L* |
| | 325 | Queen Anne Marina | W | 410-643-2021 | 110 | GD | GHI | EH | E | R | SP | S*R+ | |
| | 349 | Schooners Landing Restaurant | | 410-226-0160 | 32 | | | | E | | | R* | L+ |
| | 351 | Scott Marine Sales & Service | | 410-827-8150 | 84 | | HI | EH | E | | SP | R* | L* |
| | 355 | Severn Marine Service | | 410-886-2159 | 48 | | H | EHP | E | | SP | R+ | L+ |
| | 364 | Skipjack Landing Marine Center* | | 410-643-2694 | 75 | G | HI | EH | E | | SP | S+ | |
| | 381 | St. Michaels Harbour Inn, Marina & Spa | I | 410-745-9001 | 50 | | HI | | E | | SP | S+R+ | L+ |
| | 382 | St. Michaels Marina* | I/W | 410-745-2400 | 50 | GD | GHI | | E | | SP | S+R+ | L* |
| | 407 | Tilghman Island Inn | | 410-886-2141 | 21 | | | | | | | R* | L+ |
| | 408 | Tilghman Island Marina | I | 410-886-2500 | 41 | | GHI | | E | | SP | R+ | L+ |
| | 409 | Tilghman on Chesapeake Marina | | 410-886-2389 | 55 | | I | | E | | SP | R+ | L+ |
| | 413 | Town Creek Restaurant & Marina | | 410-226-5131 | 25 | | I | | E | | | S+R+ | |
| | 416 | Tred Avon Yacht Club | | 410-226-5269 | 6 | | GHI | | E | | | R+ | L+ |
| | 431 | Wells Cove Marina | | 410-827-3870 | 76 | | | | E | | SP | R+ | L+ |
| | | | | | | | | | | | | | |
| | 53 | Black Dog Boat Works | | 410-479-3355 | 6 | | | H | E | | | S*R* | L* |
| | 73 | Cambridge Municipal Yacht Basin | | 410-228-4031 | 196 | | I | | E | | SP | R* | L* |
| | 74 | Campbell's Bachelor Point Yacht Co.* | | 410-226-5592 | 80 | | HI | E | E | | SP | R+ | L+ |
| | 75 | Campbell's Boatyard at Jack's Point | I | 410-226-5105 | 54 | GD | GHI | EHP | E | | SP | R+ | L+ |
| | 76 | Campbell's Town Creek Boatyard | | 410-226-0213 | 42 | | I | EH | E | | SP | R+ | L+ |
| | 94 | Chesapeake Maritime Museum | I | 410-745-2916 | 20 | | I | | E | | SP | R+ | L+ |
| | 97 | Choptank-Towne Yacht Basin | | 410-479-3731 | S | G | | | E | R | SP | | |
| | 114 | Crab Claw Restaurant | | 410-745-2900 | 12 | | | | | | | R* | |
| | 118 | Cuts & Case Inc. | | 410-226-5416 | 35 | | | EHP | E | | | R+ | L+ |
| | 125 | Dickerson Harbor | | 410-822-8556 | 50 | | | EHP | E | | | | |
| | 135 | Easton Point Marina | | 410-822-1201 | 24 | GD | HI | EHP | E | R | SP | S*R+ | L+ |
| | 161 | Gateway Marina & Ship's Store | | 410-476-3304 | 112 | GD | HI | EHP | E | | SP | S+R* | L* |
| | 162 | Generation III Marina | | 410-228-2520 | 10 | | H | EHP | E | | SP | S*R+ | L+ |
| | 203 | Higgins Yacht Yard | W | 410-745-9303 | 30 | | HI | EHP | E | | SP | R+ | L+ |
| | 204 | Hinckley Yacht Services | W | 410-226-5113 | 66 | | HI | EHP | E | | SP | S+R+ | L+ |
| 7 | 213 | Hyatt Regency Chesapeake Bay Golf Resort Spa & Marina | I/W | 410-901-1234 | 150 | GD | GHI | | E | | SP | S*R* | L* |
| | 215 | Inn at Perry Cabin | I | 410-745-2200 | 3 | | | | | | | R+ | L* |
| | 249 | Madison Bay Marina & Campground | | 410-228-4111 | 45 | | | | E | | SP | S+R+ | |
| | 255 | Masthead Restaurant at Pier Street Marina | | 410-226-5171 | 65 | GD | | | E | R | | R+ | L+ |
| | 260 | Mears Yacht Haven (Coastal Properties)* | I | 410-226-5450 | 95 | GD | HI | | E | | SP | R+ | L+ |
| | 262 | Mid-Shore Electronics | | 410-228-7335 | 6 | | | | E | | | R+ | |
| | 265 | Miles River Yacht Club | | 410-745-9511 | 60 | | I | | E | | | R+ | |
| | 290 | Oxford Boat Yard (Coastal Properties) | I | 410-226-5101 | 76 | | GHI | EHP | E | | SP | R+ | L+ |
| | 291 | Oxford Yacht Agency | | 410-2226-5454 | 20 | | | EHP | E | | | R+ | L+ |
| | 349 | Schooners Landing Restaurant | | 410-226-0160 | 32 | | | | E | | | R* | L+ |
| | 381 | St. Michaels Harbour Inn, Marina & Spa | I | 410-745-9001 | 50 | | HI | | E | | SP | S+R+ | L+ |
| | 382 | St. Michaels Marina* | I/W | 410-745-2400 | 50 | GD | GHI | | E | | SP | S+R+ | L* |
| | 389 | Suicide Bridge Restaurant | | 410-943-4689 | 54 | G | | | E | R | SP | R+ | |
| | 413 | Town Creek Restaurant & Marina | | 410-226-5131 | 25 | | I | | E | | | S+R+ | |
| | 416 | Tred Avon Yacht Club | | 410-226-5269 | 6 | | GHI | | E | | | R+ | L+ |
| | 452 | Yacht Maintenance Co., Inc. | | 410-228-8878 | 14 | | H | EHP | E | | SP | R+ | L+ |
| | | | | | | | | | | | | | |
| | 29 | Back Creek Inn Bed & Breakfast | | 410-326-2022 | 2 | | | | | | | | L* |
| | 54 | Blackstone Marina | | 301-373-2015 | 65 | | HI | EHP | E | | | | |
| | 56 | Boatel California | | 301-737-1400 | 75 | | | E | E | R | SP | R* | |
| | 63 | Breezy Point Marina | | 301-855-9894 | 225 | GD | GHI | EH | E | R | SP | S* | |
| | 64 | Broomes Island Marina | | 410-586-0304 | 49 | | | | E | | SP | S*R+ | |
| | 66 | Bunky's Charter Boats | | 410-326-3241 | | GD | GI | | | | | S+R+ | L+ |
| 8 | 72 | Calvert Marina | | 410-326-4251 | 450 | GD | GHI | EHP | E | | SP | S*R+ | L+ |
| | 86 | Catamarans | | 410-326-8399 | 10 | | | | | | | R+ | L+ |
| | 100 | Clarke's Landing (Hollywood) | | 301-373-9819 | 8 | G | I | | E | R | | R+ | |
| | 109 | Comfort Inn/Beacon Marina | | 410-326-6303 | 186 | | | | E | R | SP | R* | L* |
| | 126 | DiGiovanni's Dock of the Bay | | 410-394-6400 | | | | | | | | R* | L+ |
| | 138 | Dockside, LLC | | 410-320-9790 | 16 | | | | E | | | S+R+ | L+ |

* ON SITE
+ NEARBY

| CHART NUMBER | MARINA NUMBER | MARINA NAME | INTERNET ACCESS / WIRELESS | TELEPHONE | SLIPS | GASOLINE / DIESEL | GROCERIES / HARDWARE / ICE | ENGINE / HULL / PROPELLER | ELECTRICITY | RAMP | SEWAGE PUMPOUT | SNACKBAR / RESTAURANT | LODGING |
|---|---|---|---|---|---|---|---|---|---|---|---|---|---|
| | 152 | Flag Harbor Condo Marina | | 410-586-0070 | 168 | G | I | EH | E | | SP | R+ | L+ |
| | 185 | Harbor Island Marina, Inc. | | 410-326-3441 | 250 | GD | HI | EHP | E | | SP | S+R+ | L+ |
| | 207 | Holiday Inn Select Solomons | I | 410-326-1052 | 80 | | I | | E | | SP | R* | L* |
| | 222 | K.B. Derr and Son | | 410-326-7089 | 100 | | H | E | E | | SP | | |
| | 249 | Madison Bay Marina & Campground | | 410-228-4111 | 45 | | | | E | | SP | S+R+ | |
| | 295 | Patuxent Beach Marina | | 301-862-3553 | 40 | | I | | E | R | | S+R+ | |
| | 304 | Pine Cove Marina | | 410-326-2817 | 106 | | I | EH | E | R | | | |
| | 359 | Sheperd's Yacht Yard | | 410-326-3939 | 300 | | HI | EH | E | | | R* | |
| | 370 | Solomon's Pier Restaurant | | 410-326-2424 | | | | | | | | R* | L+ |
| | 371 | Solomon's Point Marina | | 410-326-4258 | 22 | | HI | EH | E | | | R* | |
| 8 | 372 | Solomon's Island Yacht Club | | 410-326-3718 | 30 | | | | E | | | R+ | L+ |
| | 373 | Solomon's Yachting Center | I/W | 410-326-2401 | 110 | GD | HI | EHP | E | | SP | S*R+ | L+ |
| | 378 | Spring Cove Marina (Solomons)* | I/W | 410-326-2161 | 235 | GD | GHI | EHP | E | | SP | S*R+ | L+ |
| | 400 | Taylor's Island Marina | | 410-397-3454 | 105 | GD | HI | | E | | SP | S+R+ | L* |
| | 422 | Vera's White Sands Restaurant & Marina | | 410-586-1182 | 64 | | | | E | | SP | R* | |
| | 424 | Washburn's Boat Yard, Inc. | I | 410-326-6701 | | | H | EHP | | | | R+ | L+ |
| | 430 | Weeks Marina | | 301-373-5124 | 60 | | HI | EH | E | | SP | R* | L* |
| | 448 | Winpisinger Education Center at Placid Harbour | | 301-373-3300 | 35 | | | | E | | | | |
| | 455 | Zahniser's Yachting Center* | W | 410-326-2166 | 300 | | HI | EHP | E | | SP | R* | L+ |
| | | | | | | | | | | | | | |
| | 29 | Back Creek Inn Bed & Breakfast | | 410-326-2022 | 2 | | | | | | | | L* |
| | 50 | Benedict Marina | | 301-274-4429 | S | G | I | E | E | R | | R+ | |
| | 54 | Blackstone Marina | | 301-373-2015 | 65 | | HI | EHP | E | | | | |
| | 56 | Boatel California | | 301-737-1400 | 75 | | | E | E | R | SP | R* | |
| | 63 | Breezy Point Marina | | 301-855-9894 | 225 | GD | GHI | EH | E | R | SP | S* | |
| | 64 | Broomes Island Marina | | 410-586-0304 | 49 | | | | E | | SP | S*R+ | |
| | 66 | Bunky's Charter Boats | | 410-326-3241 | | GD | GI | | | | | S+R+ | L+ |
| | 72 | Calvert Marina | | 410-326-4251 | 450 | GD | GHI | EHP | E | | SP | S*R+ | L+ |
| | 77 | Cape St. Mary's Marina | | 301-373-2001 | 120 | GD | HI | EH | E | R | SP | S+R+ | L+ |
| | 86 | Catamarans | | 410-326-8399 | 10 | | | | | | | R+ | L+ |
| | 100 | Clarke's Landing (Hollywood) | | 301-373-9819 | 8 | G | I | | E | R | | R+ | |
| | 109 | Comfort Inn/Beacon Marina | | 410-326-6303 | 186 | | | | E | R | SP | R* | L* |
| | 126 | DiGiovanni's Dock of the Bay | | 410-394-6400 | | | | | | | | R* | L+ |
| | 128 | Dockside, LLC | | 410-320-9790 | 16 | | | | E | | | S+R+ | L+ |
| | 152 | Flag Harbor Condo Marina | | 410-586-0070 | 168 | G | I | EH | E | | SP | R+ | L+ |
| | 185 | Harbor Island Marina, Inc. | | 410-326-3441 | 250 | GD | HI | EHP | E | | SP | S+R+ | L+ |
| 9 | 207 | Holiday Inn Select Solomons | I | 410-326-1052 | 80 | | I | | E | | SP | R* | L* |
| | 222 | K.B. Derr and Son | | 410-326-7089 | 100 | | H | E | E | | SP | | |
| | 295 | Patuxent Beach Marina | | 301-862-3553 | 40 | | I | | E | R | | S+R+ | |
| | 304 | Pine Cove Marina | | 410-326-2817 | 106 | | I | EH | E | R | | | |
| | 327 | Ray's Pier Restaurant | | 301-274-3733 | S | | | | E | | | S+R+ | |
| | 359 | Sheperd's Yacht Yard | | 410-326-3939 | 300 | | HI | EH | E | | | R* | |
| | 370 | Solomon's Pier Restaurant | | 410-326-2424 | | | | | | | | R* | L+ |
| | 371 | Solomon's Point Marina | | 410-326-4258 | 22 | | HI | EH | E | | | R* | |
| | 372 | Solomon's Island Yacht Club | | 410-326-3718 | 30 | | | | E | | | R+ | L+ |
| | 373 | Solomon's Yachting Center | I/W | 410-326-2401 | 110 | GD | HI | EHP | E | | SP | S*R+ | L+ |
| | 378 | Spring Cove Marina (Solomons)* | I/W | 410-326-2161 | 235 | GD | GHI | EHP | E | | SP | S*R+ | L+ |
| | 422 | Vera's White Sands Restaurant & Marina | | 410-586-1182 | 64 | | | | E | | SP | R* | |
| | 424 | Washburn's Boat Yard, Inc. | I | 410-326-6701 | | | H | EHP | | | | R+ | L+ |
| | 430 | Weeks Marina | | 301-373-5124 | 60 | | HI | EH | E | | SP | R* | L* |
| | 448 | Winpisinger Education Center at Placid Harbour | | 301-373-3300 | 35 | | | | E | | | | |
| | 455 | Zahniser's Yachting Center* | W | 410-326-2166 | 300 | | HI | EHP | E | | SP | R* | L+ |
| | | | | | | | | | | | | | |
| | 70 | Buzz's Marina | | 301-872-5887 | 10 | GD | I | EH | E | | | S* | |
| | 110 | Courtney Boat Yard | | 301-872-4202 | 12 | | | EH | E | | | S*R+ | L* |
| | 131 | Drury's Marina | | 301-872-5887 | | GD | HI | E | E | | | S* | |
| | 300 | Phil's Marina | | 301-872-5838 | 50 | | GI | EH | E | | | S | |
| | 312 | Point Lookout Boating Facility | | 301-872-5688 | 8 | G | HI | | | | SP | | |
| 10 | 313 | Point Lookout Marina | W | 301-872-5000 | 160 | GD | HI | EH | E | | SP | S*R+ | L* |
| | 314 | Point Lookout State Park | | 301-872-5688 | | G | GI | | | | SP | R+ | |
| | 323 | Powley Marina | | 410-397-8188 | 36 | | | EH | E | R | | | |
| | 331 | Rippons Harbor | | 410-397-3200 | 40 | GD | I | H | E | R | | S+R* | L* |
| | 387 | Stine Marine Railway | | 410-397-8574 | 16 | | | H | E | R | | | |
| | | | | | | | | | | | | | |
| | 318 | Port of Salisbury Marina (CPM) | | 410-548-3176 | 86 | GD | I | | E | | SP | S*R* | L* |
| | 323 | Powley Marina | | 410-397-8188 | 36 | | | EH | E | R | | | |
| | 387 | Stine Marine Railway | | 410-397-8574 | 16 | | | H | E | R | | | |
| 11 | 429 | Webster's Cove Facility | | 410-651-1930 | S | G | I | | | | SP | R+ | |
| | 442 | Whitehaven Marina | | 410-873-2662 | 35 | G | | | E | | SP | S*R* | L* |
| | 446 | Windsor's Marina | | 410-784-2692 | 40 | | | | | R | | S*R* | |
| | | | | | | | | | | | | | |
| | 115 | Crisfield Fishing Center | | 410-968-3162 | 40 | GD | GHI | | E | | | S+ | |
| | 116 | Crisfield Propeller & Seamark Marine | | 410-968-0800 | | | | EH | | | | R+ | |
| | 117 | Crockett's Marina & Boatyard | | 410-968-3169 | 20 | | H | EH | E | | | S*R* | L* |
| | 167 | Goldsborough's Marine | | 410-968-0852 | | | H | E | | | | S+R+ | L+ |
| 12 | 221 | Jane's Island State Park | | 410-968-1565 | | | | | | | | | |
| | 264 | Milburn Landing | | 410-632-2566 | | | | | | R | | | |
| | 309 | Pocomoke City Municipal Marina | | 410-957-1333 | 50 | | GI | | E | | SP | S+R* | L* |
| | 353 | Sea Mark Marine | I | 410-968-0800 | 29 | | H | EH | E | | | S*R* | L* |

* ON SITE + NEARBY

| CHART NUMBER | MARINA NUMBER | MARINA NAME | INTERNET ACCESS / WIRELESS | TELEPHONE | SLIPS | GASOLINE / DIESEL | GROCERIES / HARDWARE / ICE | ENGINE / HULL / PROPELLER | ELECTRICITY | RAMP | SEWAGE PUMPOUT | SNACKBAR / RESTAURANT | LODGING |
|---|---|---|---|---|---|---|---|---|---|---|---|---|---|
| 12 | 356 | Shad Landing (Pocomoke River State Park) | I | 410-632-2566 | 25 | G | GI | | E | R | SP | S+ | |
| | 367 | Smith Island Marina | I | 410-425-4220 | 6 | | | | | | | | |
| | 374 | Somers Cove Marina | | 410-968-0925 | 485 | GD | I | | E | | SP | S*R* | L* |
| | 443 | Wilkander's Marine Services, Inc. | | 410-749-9521 | 12 | | | EH | E | | SP | | |
| 13 | 115 | Crisfield Fishing Center | | 410-968-3162 | 40 | GD | GHI | | E | | | S+ | |
| | 116 | Crisfield Propeller & Seamark Marine | | 410-968-0800 | | | | EH | | | | R+ | |
| | 117 | Crockett's Marina & Boatyard | | 410-968-3169 | 20 | | H | EH | E | | | S*R* | L* |
| | 167 | Goldsborough's Marine | | 410-968-0852 | | | H | E | | | | S+R+ | |
| | 221 | Jane's Island State Park | | 410-968-1565 | | | | | | | | | |
| | 353 | Sea Mark Marine | I | 410-968-0800 | 29 | | H | EH | E | | | S*R* | L* |
| | 367 | Smith Island Marina | I | 410-425-4220 | 6 | | | | | | | | |
| | 374 | Somers Cove Marina | | 410-968-0925 | 485 | GD | I | | E | | SP | S*R* | L* |
| | 446 | Windsor's Marina | | 410-784-2692 | 40 | | | | | R | | S*R* | |
| 14 | 70 | Buzz's Marina | | 301-872-5887 | 10 | GD | I | EH | E | | | S* | |
| | 101 | Coan River Marina | | 804-529-6767 | 55 | GD | GHI | EH | E | | SP | S*R+ | |
| | 103 | Cockrell Marine Railway | | 804-453-3560 | S | GD | H | EH | E | | | | |
| | 110 | Courtney Boat Yard | | 301-872-4202 | 12 | | | EH | E | | | S*R+ | L* |
| | 111 | Courtney's Restaurant & Seafood | | 301-872-4403 | 3 | | I | | | | | S+R+ | L* |
| | 124 | Dennis Point Marina, Inc. | | 301-994-2288 | 115 | GD | GHI | EH | E | | SP | S+R+ | L* |
| | 131 | Drury's Marina | | 301-872-5887 | | GD | HI | E | E | | | S* | |
| | 235 | Leroy's Marina | | 804-453-6806 | 26 | GD | GI | E | E | | SP | R+ | L+ |
| | 236 | Lewisetta Marina | | 804-529-7299 | 19 | GD | GHI | EH | | | SP | S* | |
| | 300 | Phil's Marina | | 301-872-5838 | 50 | | GI | EH | E | | | S | |
| | 312 | Point Lookout Boating Facility | | 301-872-5688 | 8 | G | HI | | | | SP | | |
| | 313 | Point Lookout Marina | W | 301-872-5000 | 160 | GD | HI | EH | E | | SP | S*R+ | L* |
| | 314 | Point Lookout State Park | | 301-872-5688 | | G | GI | | | | SP | R+ | |
| | 348 | Scheible's Fishing Center. Inc. | | 301-872-5185 | 5 | GD | I | | E | | | S*R+ | L+ |
| | 368 | Smith Point Marina | I/W | 804-453-4077 | 98 | GD | HI | E | E | | | S+R* | L* |
| | 380 | St. Mary's Yachting Center | | 301-994-2288 | 115 | GD | GHI | EH | E | | SP | S*R+ | |
| 15 | 62 | Branson Cove Marina | | 804-472-3866 | 6 | GD | GHI | | E | | SP | S*R+ | |
| | 87 | Cather Marine, Inc. | | 301-769-3335 | 70 | G | GHI | E | E | | SP | S+ | |
| | 88 | Cedar Cove Marina | I | 301-994-1155 | 66 | G | GHI | EH | E | | SP | S*R* | L+ |
| | 101 | Coan River Marina | | 804-529-6767 | 55 | GD | GHI | EH | E | | SP | S*R+ | |
| | 104 | Cole's Point Plantation | | 804-472-3955 | 140 | GD | GHI | EH | E | | SP | S*R+ | L+ |
| | 106 | Colton's Point Marina | | 301-769-3121 | 95 | GD | HI | EH | E | | SP | S*R+ | L+ |
| | 108 | Comb's Creek Marina | | 301-475-2017 | 45 | | GH | EH | E | | SP | R+ | L+ |
| | 124 | Dennis Point Marina, Inc. | | 301-994-2288 | 115 | GD | GHI | EH | E | | SP | S+R+ | L* |
| | 127 | Dock O' The Bay | | 301-475-3129 | S | G | I | | E | | | R+ | |
| | 194 | Harry Hogan Machine Shop | | 804-529-6800 | S | | | EH | E | | | | |
| | 227 | Kinsale Harbor Yacht Club | | 804-472-2514 | 99 | | I | | E | | SP | S*R+ | |
| | 229 | Krentz Marine Railway | | 804-529-6800 | S | GD | HI | EH | E | | | | |
| | 234 | Leonardtown Wharf | | | S | | | I | | | | R+ | |
| | 236 | Lewisetta Marina | | 804-529-7299 | 19 | GD | GHI | EH | | | SP | S* | |
| | 246 | Lower Machodoc Marine, Inc. | | 804-472-4038 | | | H | E | E | | SP | | |
| | 286 | Olverson's Lodge Creek Marina | I | 800-529-5071 | 195 | GD | GI | | E | | SP | S+R* | L+ |
| | 317 | Port Kinsale Marina & Resort | I/W | 804-472-2044 | 116 | GD | GHI | EH | E | | SP | S*R+ | L+ |
| | 326 | Ragged Point Marina | | 804-472-3955 | S | GD | GHI | E | E | | | S+R+ | |
| | 379 | St. Clement's Island Museum | | 301-769-2222 | 6 | | | | | | | S+ | |
| | 380 | St. Mary's Yachting Center | | 301-994-2288 | 115 | GD | GHI | EH | E | | SP | S*R+ | |
| | 395 | Swann's Pier | | 301-994-0774 | 10 | GD | GHI | | | | | R+ | |
| | 398 | Tall Timbers Marina | | 301-994-1508 | 170 | GD | HI | EH | E | | SP | R+ | L* |
| | 439 | White Point Marina | I | 804-472-2977 | 50 | GD | GHI | EH | E | | SP | S*R+ | L* |
| | 453 | Yeocomico Marina | | 804-472-2971 | S | GD | GHI | EH | E | | SP | R+ | L+ |
| 16 | 25 | Aqua-Land Marina | | 301-259-0572 | 150 | GD | GHI | EH | E | | | S+R* | |
| | 80 | Captain Billy's Crabhouse | | 301-932-4323 | 15 | | H | | E | | | R+ | |
| | 82 | Captain John's Crabhouse & Marina | | 301-259-2315 | 40 | G | GHI | | E | | SP | S*R* | |
| | 87 | Cather Marine, Inc. | | 301-769-3335 | 70 | G | GHI | E | E | | SP | S+ | |
| | 102 | Cobb Island Marina | | 301-259-2879 | 100 | | HI | EH | E | | SP | S+R+ | |
| | 105 | Colonial Beach Yacht Center | I | 804-224-7230 | 150 | GD | HI | EH | E | | SP | R+ | L+ |
| | 106 | Colton's Point Marina | | 301-769-3121 | 95 | GD | HI | EH | E | | SP | S*R+ | L+ |
| | 121 | Dahlgren Marine Works | | 540-663-2741 | 68 | GD | GHI | E | E | | SP | S*R+ | |
| | 163 | George L. Quade's Store & Boat Rentals | | 301-769-3903 | | G | GI | | | | | S*R* | |
| | 166 | Gilligan's Pier | | 301-259-4514 | 20 | | I | | E | | | S*R+ | |
| | 168 | Goose Bay Marina, Inc. | | 301-932-0885 | 250 | GD | GHI | E | E | | SP | S* | |
| | 177 | H. C. Parker Marina | | 804-224-0895 | 40 | | | | | | SP | | |
| | 183 | Happy Clam | | 804-224-9279 | S | | I | | | | | R+ | |
| | 211 | Hop's Marina | | 804-224-0022 | S | GD | | | | | SP | | |
| | 266 | Monroe Bay Landing | | 804-227-7360 | 15 | | | | E | | | R+ | |
| | 269 | Nightingale Motel & Marina | | 804-224-7956 | 36 | | H | | E | | SP | S*R+ | L+ |
| | 288 | Outdoor World Harbor View | | 804-224-8161 | S | G | GHI | EH | E | | SP | S+ | |
| | 307 | Pirate's Den Marina | | 301-259-2879 | S | GD | | | E | | SP | | |
| | 319 | Port Tobacco Marina & Restaurant | | 301-653-3873 | 30 | G | HI | | | | SP | S*R+ | |
| | 320 | Port Tobacco Marina, Inc. | | 301-932-1407 | 400 | G | HI | EH | E | | SP | S+R* | |
| | 334 | Robertson's Crab House | | 301-934-9234 | S | | I | | | | | S+R+ | |
| | 362 | Shymansky's Marina & Restaurant | | 301-259-2221 | 110 | GD | GHI | EH | E | | SP | S*R+ | |
| | 379 | St. Clement's Island Museum | | 301-769-2222 | 6 | | | | | | | S+ | |
| 16 | 383 | Stanford's Marine Railway | | 804-224-7644 | 30 | | H | EH | E | | | | R |
| | 385 | Stepp's Harbor View Marina | | 804-224-9265 | 144 | G | GHI | EH | E | | SP | S*R+ | L |
| | 437 | Westmoreland State Park | | 800-933-PARK | | G | GHI | | | | | R+ | L |
| | 444 | Wilkerson's Seafood Restaurant | | 804-224-7117 | S | | I | | E | | SP | R* | |
| | 447 | Winkiedoodle Point Marina | | 804-224-9560 | 65 | | G | | E | | SP | R+ | L |
| 17 | 26 | Aquia Creek Marina & Boatyard | | 540-720-7437 | S | G | H | EH | E | | | | |
| | 49 | Belmont Bay Harbor (Coastal Properties) | | 703-490-5088 | 155 | GD | I | | E | | SP | S*R* | L |
| | 81 | Captain John Beach Marina | | 703-339-6726 | S | G | HI | | E | | SP | | |
| | 121 | Dahlgren Marine Works | | 540-663-2741 | 68 | GD | GHI | E | E | | SP | S*R+ | |
| | 142 | E-Z Cruz Marina | | 703-670-8111 | 200 | G | GHI | E | E | | | S*R+ | |
| | 143 | Fairview Beach Tim's II | | 540-775-7500 | | | | | | | | R* | |
| | 144 | Fairview Beach Yacht Club, Inc. | | 540-775-5971 | S | G | GI | EH | E | | | | |
| | 168 | Goose Bay Marina, Inc. | | 301-932-0885 | 250 | GD | GHI | E | E | | SP | S* | |
| | 181 | Hampton's Landing Marina | | 703-221-4915 | | GD | I | EH | E | | SP | | |
| | 205 | Hoffmaster's Marina | | 703-494-7161 | 141 | G | HI | EH | E | | | S+R* | |
| | 210 | Hope Springs Marina | | 540-659-1128 | 180 | GD | | | E | | SP | R+ | L+ |
| | 233 | Leesylvania State Park | | 703-670-0372 | | G | GHI | | | | | | |
| | 277 | Occoquan Harbor Marina, Inc. | | 703-494-3600 | S | GD | GHI | EH | E | | | R+ | L+ |
| | 303 | Pilot House Marina & Boat Sales | | 703-670-6900 | 175 | D | HI | EH | E | | SP | S*R+ | |
| | 311 | Pohick Bay Regional Park | | 703-339-6104 | | | GI | | | | SP | | |
| | 322 | Potomac Marine & Canvas Co. | | 703-670-2265 | S | G | HI | EH | | | | R+ | |
| | 324 | Prince William Marine Sales | | 703-550-9808 | S | GD | HI | EH | E | | | R+ | |
| | 366 | Smallwood State Park | | 301-743-7613 | 50 | G | | | E | | SP | | |
| | 396 | Sweden Point Marina | | 301-743-7613 | 50 | G | GHI | EH | E | | SP | R+ | L+ |
| | 410 | Tim's Rivershore Restaurant | | 703-441-1375 | | | I | | | | | R* | |
| | 420 | Tyme N' Tyde Marina, Inc. | | 703-491-5116 | 12 | G | HI | EH | E | | SP | S+R* | |
| | 427 | Waugh Point Marina, Inc. | | 540-775-7121 | 80 | G | H | EH | E | | SP | R* | |
| | 445 | Willow Landing Marina | | 540-659-2653 | 89 | G | HI | EH | | | SP | | |
| 18 | 6 | Alexandria City Marina | W | 703-838-4265 | 40 | | | | | | SP | S+R+ | L+ |
| | 8 | Anacostia Marina, Inc. | | 202-544-5191 | S | | HI | EH | E | | | | |
| | 48 | Belle Haven Marina, Inc. | | 703-768-0018 | | | I | | | | | S* | L+ |
| | 49 | Belmont Bay Harbor (Coastal Properties) | | 703-490-5088 | 155 | GD | I | | E | | SP | S*R* | L* |
| | 69 | Buzzard Point Marina | | 202-488-8400 | 90 | | I | | E | | SP | S*R* | |
| | 78 | Capital Yacht Club | I/W | 202-488-8110 | 88 | | I | | E | | | R+ | L+ |
| | 81 | Captain John Beach Marina | | 703-339-6726 | S | G | HI | | E | | SP | | |
| | 107 | Columbia Island Marina | | 202-347-0173 | 386 | G | I | | E | | SP | R+ | |
| | 142 | E-Z Cruz Marina | | 703-670-8111 | 200 | G | GHI | E | E | | | S*R+ | |
| | 155 | Fort Belvoir Marina | | 703-781-8282 | | | | | | | | | |
| | 156 | Fort Washington Marina | | 301-292-7700 | 300 | GD | I | | E | | SP | S*R+ | |
| | 159 | Gangplank Marina (Coastal Properties) | W | 202-554-5000 | 305 | | I | | E | | SP | S*R* | L* |
| | 205 | Hoffmaster's Marina | | 703-494-7161 | 141 | G | HI | EH | E | | | S+R* | |
| | 218 | Jack's Boat House | | 202-337-9642 | | | | | | | | | |
| | 220 | James Creek Marina | | 202-554-8844 | 297 | GD | GHI | | E | | SP | S*R* | L* |
| | 233 | Leesylvania State Park | | 703-670-0372 | | G | GHI | | | | | | |
| | 268 | National Harbor Marina (CPM) | | 410-269-0933 | 64 | GD | | | | | | | |
| | 277 | Occoquan Harbor Marina, Inc. | | 703-494-3600 | S | GD | GHI | EH | E | | | R+ | L+ |
| | 303 | Pilot House Marina & Boat Sales | | 703-670-6900 | 175 | D | HI | EH | E | | SP | S*R+ | |
| | 311 | Pohick Bay Regional Park | | 703-339-6104 | | | GI | | | | SP | | |
| | 322 | Potomac Marine & Canvas Co. | | 703-670-2265 | S | G | HI | EH | | | | R+ | |
| | 324 | Prince William Marine Sales | | 703-550-9808 | S | GD | HI | EH | E | | | R+ | |
| | 399 | Tantallon Marina | | 301-203-4858 | 125 | GD | I | | E | | SP | | |
| | 410 | Tim's Rivershore Restaurant | | 703-441-1375 | | | I | | | | | R* | |
| | 420 | Tyme N' Tyde Marina, Inc. | | 703-491-5116 | 12 | G | HI | EH | E | | SP | S+R* | |
| | 425 | Washington Marina Co. | | 202-554-0222 | 150 | D | HI | EH | E | | SP | S*R* | L* |
| 19 | 1 | 54th Street Marina | | 410-524-1948 | 40 | | | | E | | | | |
| | 5 | Advanced Marina | | 410-723-2124 | 15 | G | GHI | EH | E | | SP | S*R* | L* |
| | 16 | Angler Marina | | 410-289-7424 | 7 | GD | I | | E | | | R+ | L+ |
| | 32 | Bahia Marina | | 410-289-7438 | 75 | GD | GHI | E | E | | | S*R* | L* |
| | 39 | Barnacle Bill's Marine | | 410-723-5632 | 15 | G | HI | EH | E | | | S+R* | L* |
| | 79 | Captain Bill Bunting | | 410-289-7424 | 16 | GD | I | | | | | R+ | L* |
| | 83 | Captain's Galley | | 410-213-2525 | S | | I | | | | | R+ | L+ |
| | 129 | Dorchester Street Dock | | 410-289-6720 | 20 | GD | I | | E | | | R+ | L* |
| | 149 | Fisherman's Marina | | 410-289-7468 | 45 | GD | I | | E | | | R+ | |
| | 188 | Harbour Island Marina | | 410-289-3511 | 60 | GD | I | | E | | SP | S*R+ | L+ |
| | 190 | Hargis Marina | | 410-632-0800 | S | GD | HI | EH | E | | | | |
| | 278 | Ocean City Fisherman's Marina | | 410-213-2478 | 50 | GD | I | E | E | | | S*R+ | L+ |
| | 279 | Ocean City Fishing Center | W | 800-322-3065 | 170 | GD | HI | E | E | | SP | S*R+ | L* |
| | 280 | Ocean City Fishing Center Bayside | | 410-213-1121 | 50 | G | I | | E | | SP | S*R* | L* |
| | 281 | Ocean City Yacht Club | | 410-213-2474 | 110 | G | I | E | E | | | S*R* | L* |
| | 282 | Ocean Pines Marina | | 410-641-7447 | 81 | G | I | | E | | SP | R+ | L+ |
| | 284 | Old Town Marina | I | 410-289-6470 | 15 | GD | I | | E | | | S*R+ | L+ |
| | 376 | Spanish Main Motel | | 410-289-9155 | S | G | I | | E | | | R* | L+ |
| | 392 | Sunset Marina | I/W | 877-514-3474 | 74 | GD | GHI | | E | | SP | S*R+ | |
| | 397 | Talbot Street Pier | | 410-289-9125 | 8 | GD | I | | E | | | S*R+ | L+ |
| | 439 | White Marlin Marina | I | 410-289-6470 | 50 | GD | GI | E | E | | | S*R* | L+ |

# NAVIGATIONAL AIDS

Buoys are the road signs of the sea, marking the channel. If you stay on the correct side of these channel markers, you won't run aground.

Channel buoys are distinguished by shape, color, and numbers. To determine on which side you should pass them depends on whether you are going up or down a bay, river, creek, or channel. **Remember:**

**G.P.O.E. or Greatest People on Earth Green — Port on Entering**

**R.R.R. Red Right Returning (From the sea)**

Buoys are numbered from the entrance of a bay, river, or channel. The first red buoy is number 2, the second red 4, and the third 6, etc. Red buoys always have even numbers. Black or green buoys, on the other hand, have odd numbers and from the entrance are numbered 1, 3, 5, etc.

Channel buoys come in two shapes. One that looks like an inverted cone is called a "Nun" and is always red while the other one, looking like a can, is known as a "Can" and is always black or green.

Reflector material is being used on buoys so that they are easier to see at night. Most unlighted aids will have red reflector material on red buoys, green or white on black ones, and white on green ones.

Day beacons are mainly used in tributaries of the Bay. These unlighted markers are known as "Major Aids to Navigation". Red-Orange beacons have the same meaning as red buoys and are numbered in the same manner. They are triangular in shape with red numbes. To mark the port side of a channel from seaward, day beacons are square and have the same meaning and are numbered in the same manner as black or green buoys. These beacons are usually light green with dark green numbers. Some are still black but are being changed to green. On a chart green and red day beacons are marked by triangles. The triangle for red beacons is red, for green ones it is a green square. Some black day beacons may not have been changed as yet on the charts.

Therefore, you can tell on which side of a channel buoy the deep water lies by either color, number, or shape.

Buoys at important points in a channel are lighted. A white light is used on either a red or a black buoy but a red light is used only on a red buoy, and a green light only on a black or green one.

Beacons may also be lighted with green lights showing a green or white light and red beacons with a red or white light. These lights can be either:

**FIXED** (a steady light).
**FLASHING** (the period of darkness longer than the period of light).
**OCCULTING** (the period of light longer than the period of darkness).
**ISO PHASE** (the period of light and darkness the same).

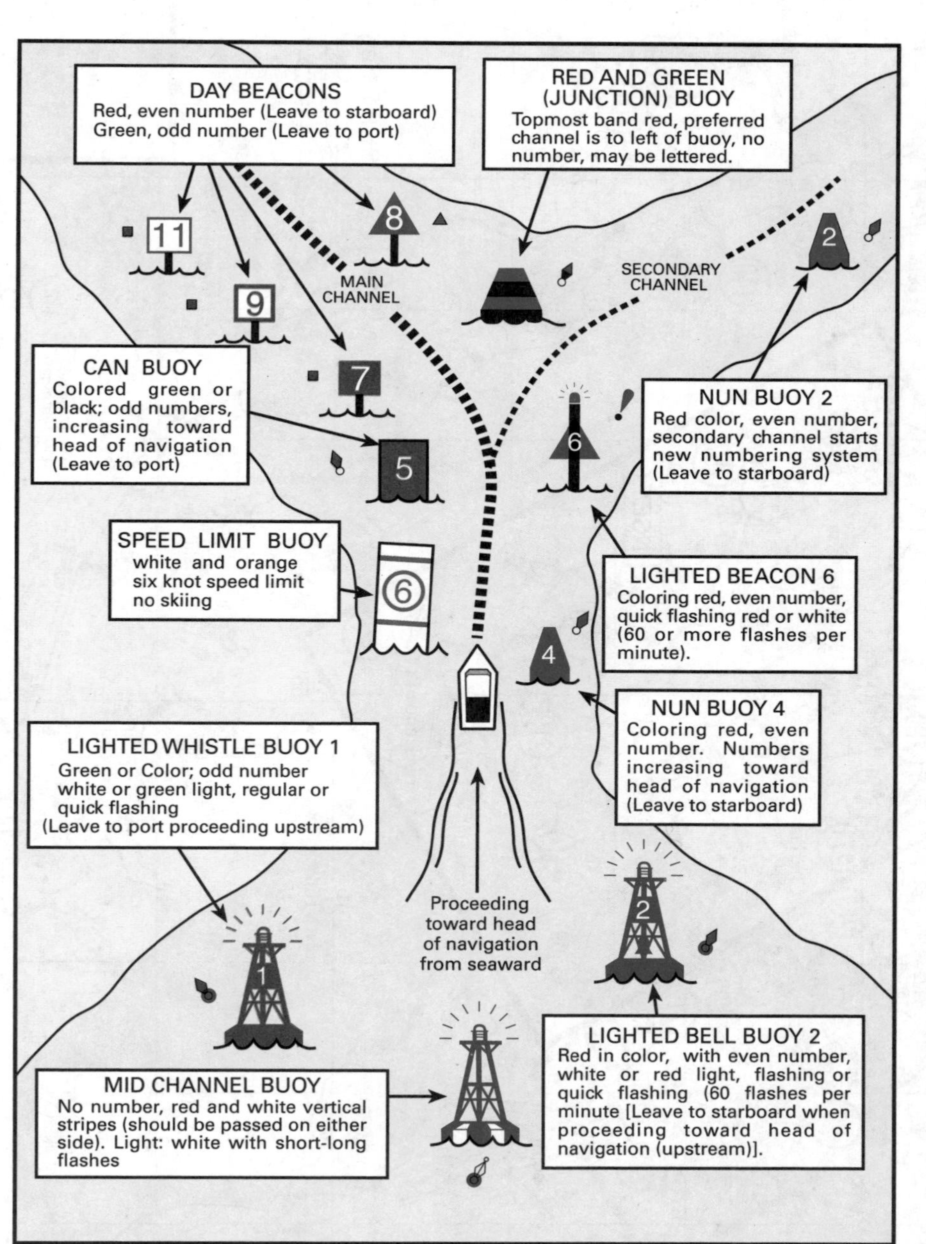


## SYMBOLS AND ABBREVIATIONS

**DEPTHS IN FEET AT MEAN LOW WATER**
**HEIGHTS IN FEET AT MEAN HIGH WATER**

(For complete list of Symbols and Abbreviations, see N.O.S. Chart No. 1)

**NOTE:** New Symbol for buoys. Circle is used instead of dot to indicate position is approximate "PA".

**Navigation aids:**

Light (on fixed structure) — Landmark — AERO, aeronautical
Daybeacon (Unlighted) — Mid-channel buoy
Unlighted buoy (C. can, N. nun, S. spar, Bell, Gong, Horn, Whistle)
Danger or junction buoy — Anchorage buoy — Mooring buoy
Lighted buoy — R. Bn. radiobeacon

**Bottom characteristics:**

| | | | | |
|---|---|---|---|---|
| Cl. clay | M. mud | Oys. oyster | stk. sticky | gn. green |
| Co. coral | Rk. rock | hrd. hard | bk black | gy. gray |
| G. gravel | S. sand | rky. rocky | br. brown | wh. white |
| Grs. grass | Sh. shells | sft. soft | bu. blue | yl. yellow |

**Light characteristics:** (Lights are white unless otherwise indicated.)

| | | | |
|---|---|---|---|
| F. fixed | I. Qk. interrupted quick | G. green | M. nautical miles |
| Fl. flashing | Iso Isophase | R. Red | DIA. diaphone |
| Bn. Beacon | Occ. occulting | m. minutes | WHIS. whistle |
| Alt. alternating | Mo. (A) morse code | sec. seconds | OBSC. obscured |
| Qk. quick | Rot. rotating | ft. feet | SEC. sector |

**Dangers:**

Sunken wreck — Visible wreck — Rocks
21 Wreck, rock, obstruction, or shoal swept clear to the depth indicated.
(2) Rocks that cover and uncover, with heights in feet above datum of soundings
AUTH authorized; Obstr. obstruction; P.A. position approximate; E.D. existence doubtful

Virginia's Measured 1/2 Miles
(position as shown on chart approx.)
*MEASURED*
*1/2 Naut. Mile*

CAUTION
Mariners are warned to stay clear of the protective riprap surrounding navigational light structures, shown thus:

*RESTRICTED AREAS*
*Watercraft shall upon being warned, immediately vacate the area designated unless given other instructions relative to navigating these areas.*

**NOTE A**

**Navigation regulations are published in Chapter 2, U.S. Coast Pilot 3, or weekly Notice to Mariners which include new or revised regulations. Information concerning the regulations may be obtained at the Office of the District Engineer, Corps of Engineers in Baltimore, Maryland.**

**Anchorage regulations may be obtained at the Office of the Commander, 5th Coast Guard District in Portsmouth, Va.**

**Refer to section numbers shown with area designation.**

**Additional general instructions supplementing 207.100 may be found in Chapter 7, U.S. Coast Pilot 3.**

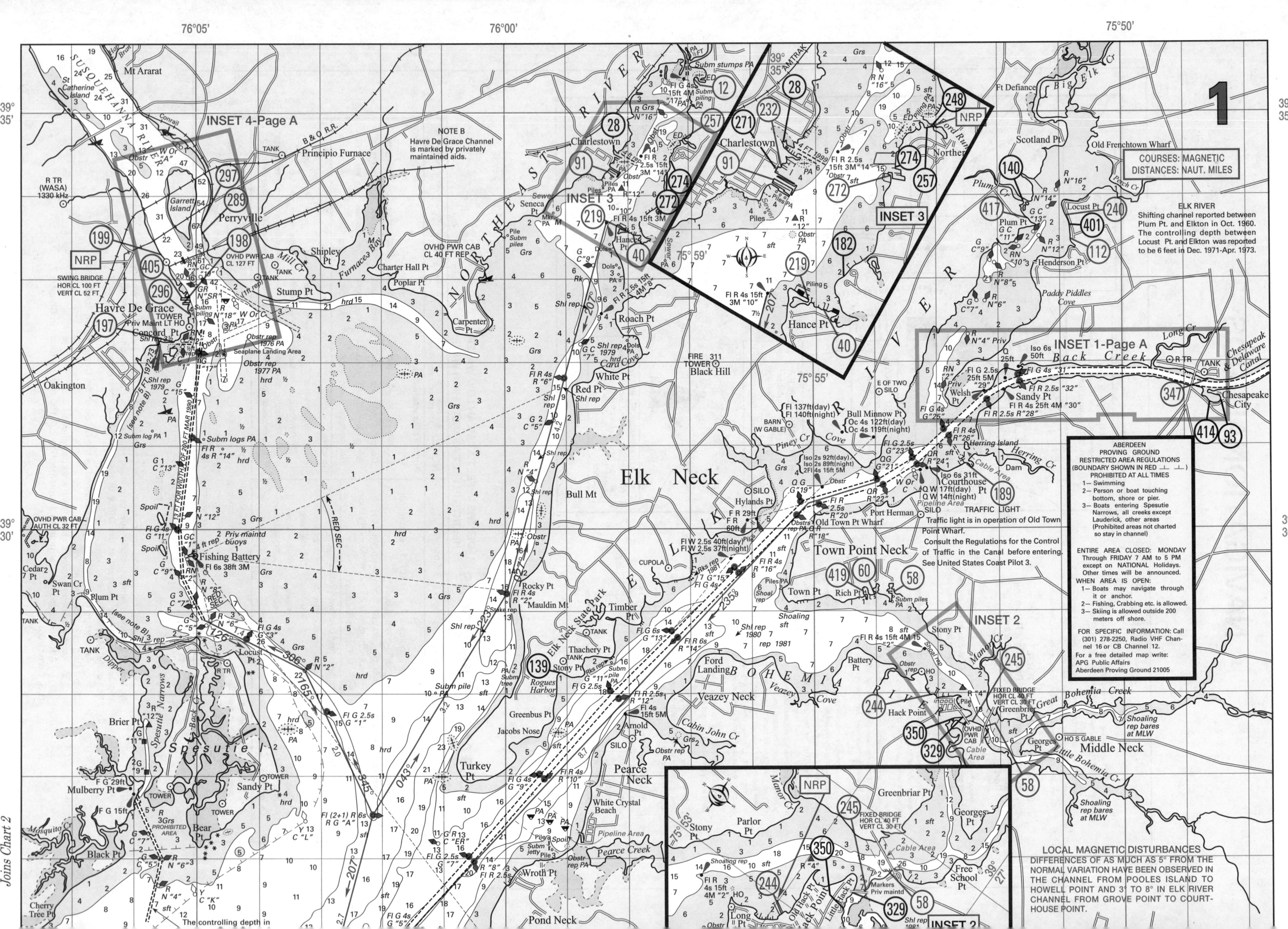
1
COURSES: MAGNETIC
DISTANCES: NAUT. MILES
ELK RIVER
Shifting channel reported between Plum Pt. and Elkton in Oct. 1960. The controlling depth between Locust Pt. and Elkton was reported to be 6 feet in Dec. 1971-Apr. 1973.
NOTE B
Havre De Grace Channel is marked by privately maintained aids.
INSET 4-Page A
INSET 3
INSET 1-Page A
INSET 2
ABERDEEN PROVING GROUND RESTRICTED AREA REGULATIONS (BOUNDARY SHOWN IN RED)
PROHIBITED AT ALL TIMES
1— Swimming
2— Person or boat touching bottom, shore or pier.
3— Boats entering Spesutie Narrows, all creeks except Lauderick, other areas (Prohibited areas not charted so stay in channel)
ENTIRE AREA CLOSED: MONDAY Through FRIDAY 7 AM to 5 PM except on NATIONAL Holidays. Other times will be announced.
WHEN AREA IS OPEN:
1— Boats may navigate through it or anchor.
2— Fishing, Crabbing etc. is allowed.
3— Skiing is allowed outside 200 meters off shore.
FOR SPECIFIC INFORMATION: Call (301) 278-2250, Radio VHF Channel 16 or CB Channel 12.
For a free detailed map write: APG Public Affairs Aberdeen Proving Ground 21005
TRAFFIC LIGHT
Traffic light is in operation of Old Town Point Wharf.
Consult the Regulations for the Control of Traffic in the Canal before entering. See United States Coast Pilot 3.
LOCAL MAGNETIC DISTURBANCES
DIFFERENCES OF AS MUCH AS 5° FROM THE NORMAL VARIATION HAVE BEEN OBSERVED IN THE CHANNEL FROM POOLES ISLAND TO HOWELL POINT AND 3° TO 8° IN ELK RIVER CHANNEL FROM GROVE POINT TO COURTHOUSE POINT.
Elk Neck
Town Point Neck
Middle Neck
Havre De Grace
Perryville
Charlestown
Chesapeake City
Chesapeake & Delaware Canal
Back Creek
Susquehanna River
Northeast River
Elk River
Bohemia River
Spesutie I
Joins Chart 2
76°05'
76°00'
75°50'
39° 35'
39° 30'

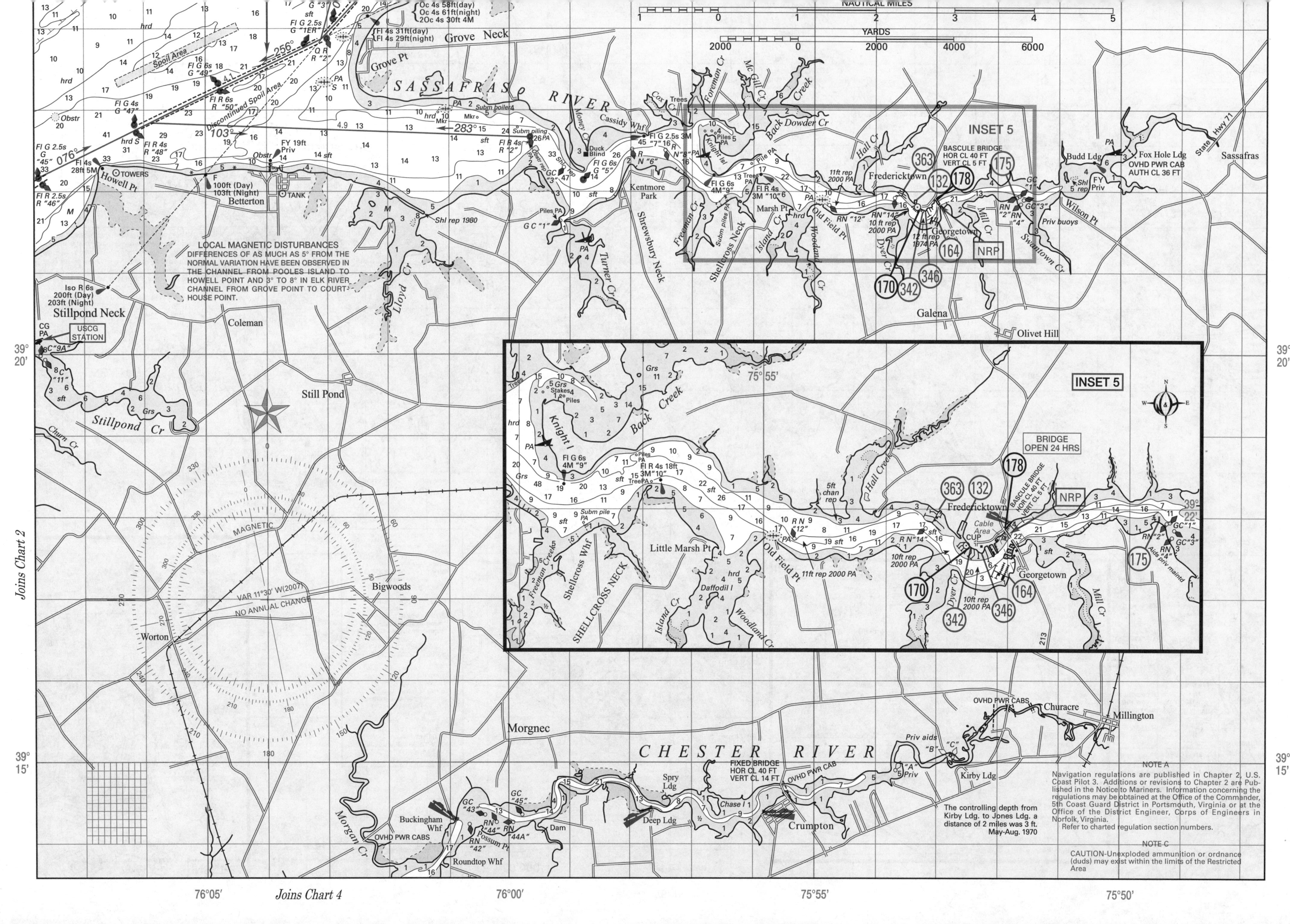
NAUTICAL MILES
YARDS
SASSAFRAS RIVER
Grove Neck
Grove Pt
Stillpond Neck
Howell Pt
Betterton
Kentmore Park
Shrewsbury Neck
Fredericktown
Georgetown
Galena
Olivet Hill
Sassafras
Fox Hole Ldg
OVHD PWR CAB AUTH CL 36 FT
Budd Ldg
Wilson Pt
BASCULE BRIDGE HOR CL 40 FT VERT CL 5 FT
INSET 5
LOCAL MAGNETIC DISTURBANCES
DIFFERENCES OF AS MUCH AS 5° FROM THE NORMAL VARIATION HAVE BEEN OBSERVED IN THE CHANNEL FROM POOLES ISLAND TO HOWELL POINT AND 3° TO 8° IN ELK RIVER CHANNEL FROM GROVE POINT TO COURT-HOUSE POINT.
USCG STATION
Coleman
Still Pond
Stillpond Cr
Bigwoods
Worton
VAR 11°30' W(2007)
NO ANNUAL CHANGE
BRIDGE OPEN 24 HRS
Knight I
Back Creek
Little Marsh Pt
Old Field Pt
SHELLCROSS NECK
Shellcross Whf
Freeman Creek
Daffodil I
Island Cr
Woodland Cr
Hall Creek
Mill Cr
CHESTER RIVER
Morgnec
Churacre
Millington
OVHD PWR CABS
Kirby Ldg
FIXED BRIDGE HOR CL 40 FT VERT CL 14 FT
Spry Ldg
Deep Ldg
Crumpton
Buckingham Whf
Roundtop Whf
Morgan Cr
The controlling depth from Kirby Ldg. to Jones Ldg. a distance of 2 miles was 3 ft. May-Aug. 1970
NOTE A
Navigation regulations are published in Chapter 2, U.S. Coast Pilot 3. Additions or revisions to Chapter 2 are published in the Notice to Mariners. Information concerning the regulations may be obtained at the Office of the Commander, 5th Coast Guard District in Portsmouth, Virginia or at the Office of the District Engineer, Corps of Engineers in Norfolk, Virginia.
Refer to charted regulation section numbers.
NOTE C
CAUTION-Unexploded ammunition or ordnance (duds) may exist within the limits of the Restricted Area
Joins Chart 2
Joins Chart 4

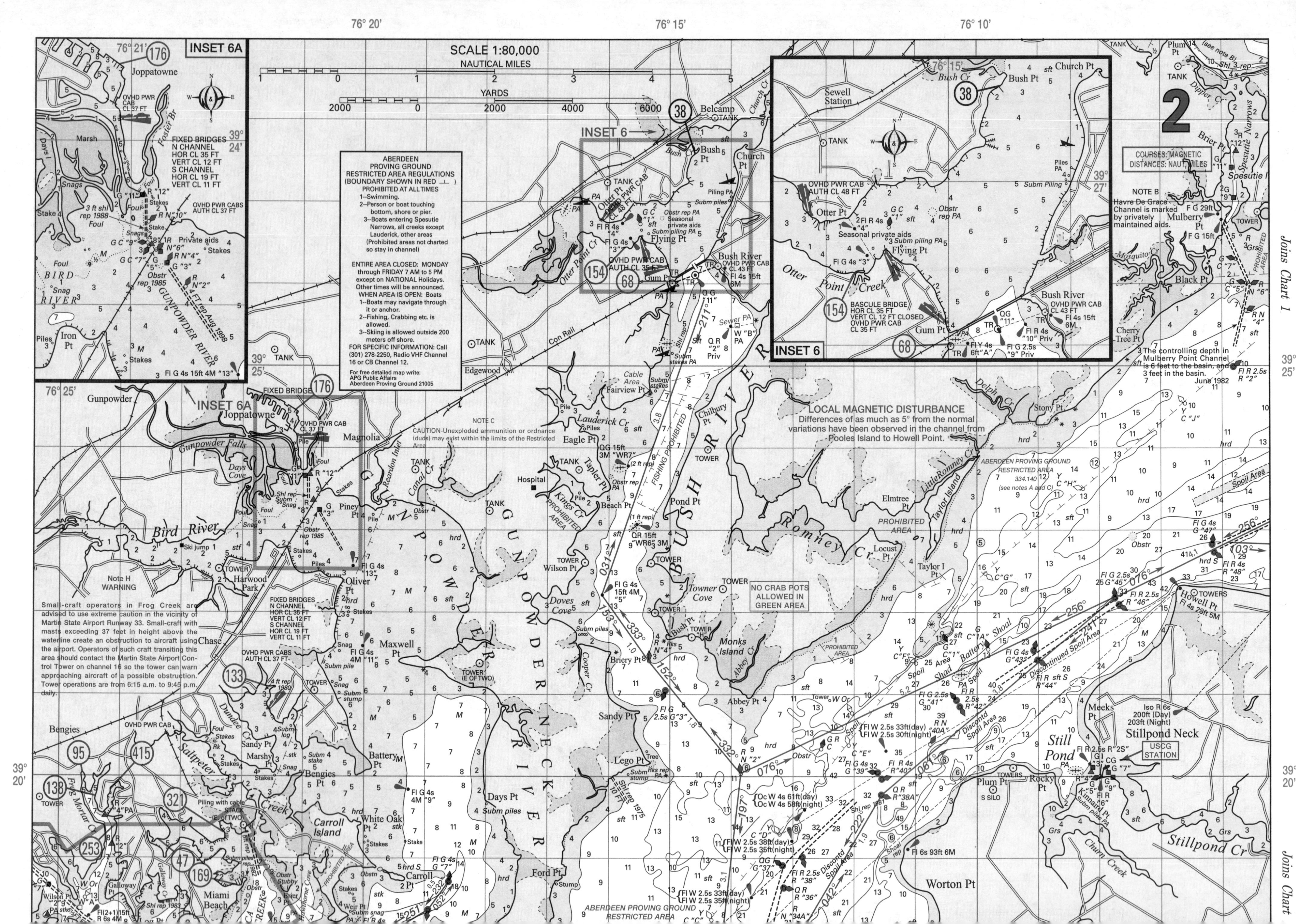

Joins Chart 1
2
SCALE 1:80,000
NAUTICAL MILES
YARDS
COURSES: MAGNETIC
DISTANCES: NAUT MILES
INSET 6
INSET 6A
ABERDEEN PROVING GROUND RESTRICTED AREA REGULATIONS (BOUNDARY SHOWN IN RED)
PROHIBITED AT ALL TIMES
1–Swimming.
2–Person or boat touching bottom, shore or pier.
3–Boats entering Spesutie Narrows, all creeks except Lauderick, other areas (Prohibited areas not charted so stay in channel)
ENTIRE AREA CLOSED: MONDAY through FRIDAY 7 AM to 5 PM except on NATIONAL Holidays. Other times will be announced.
WHEN AREA IS OPEN: Boats
1–Boats may navigate through it or anchor.
2–Fishing, Crabbing etc. is allowed.
3–Skiing is allowed outside 200 meters off shore.
FOR SPECIFIC INFORMATION: Call (301) 278-2250, Radio VHF Channel 16 or CB Channel 12.
For free detailed map write: APG Public Affairs Aberdeen Proving Ground 21005
NOTE C
CAUTION-Unexploded ammunition or ordnance (duds) may exist within the limits of the Restricted Area
NOTE B
Havre De Grace Channel is marked by privately maintained aids.
3 The controlling depth in Mulberry Point Channel is 6 feet to the basin, and 3 feet in the basin. June 1982
LOCAL MAGNETIC DISTURBANCE
Differences of as much as 5° from the normal variations have been observed in the channel from Pooles Island to Howell Point.
NO CRAB POTS ALLOWED IN GREEN AREA
Note H
WARNING
Small-craft operators in Frog Creek are advised to use extreme caution in the vicinity of Martin State Airport Runway 33. Small-craft with masts exceeding 37 feet in height above the waterline create an obstruction to aircraft using the airport. Operators of such craft transiting this area should contact the Martin State Airport Control Tower on channel 16 so the tower can warn approaching aircraft of a possible obstruction. Tower operations are from 6:15 a.m. to 9:45 p.m. daily.
FIXED BRIDGES
N CHANNEL
HOR CL 35 FT
VERT CL 12 FT
S CHANNEL
HOR CL 19 FT
VERT CL 11 FT
BASCULE BRIDGE
HOR CL 35 FT
VERT CL 12 FT CLOSED
OVHD PWR CAB
CL 35 FT
ABERDEEN PROVING GROUND RESTRICTED AREA
BUSH RIVER
GUNPOWDER RIVER
GUNPOWDER NECK
Bird River
Romney Cr
Stillpond Neck
Still Pond
Stillpond Cr
USCG STATION
Worton Pt
Howell Pt
Joppatowne
Edgewood
Magnolia
Belcamp
Bengies
Chase
Carroll Island
Spesutie I
Mulberry Pt

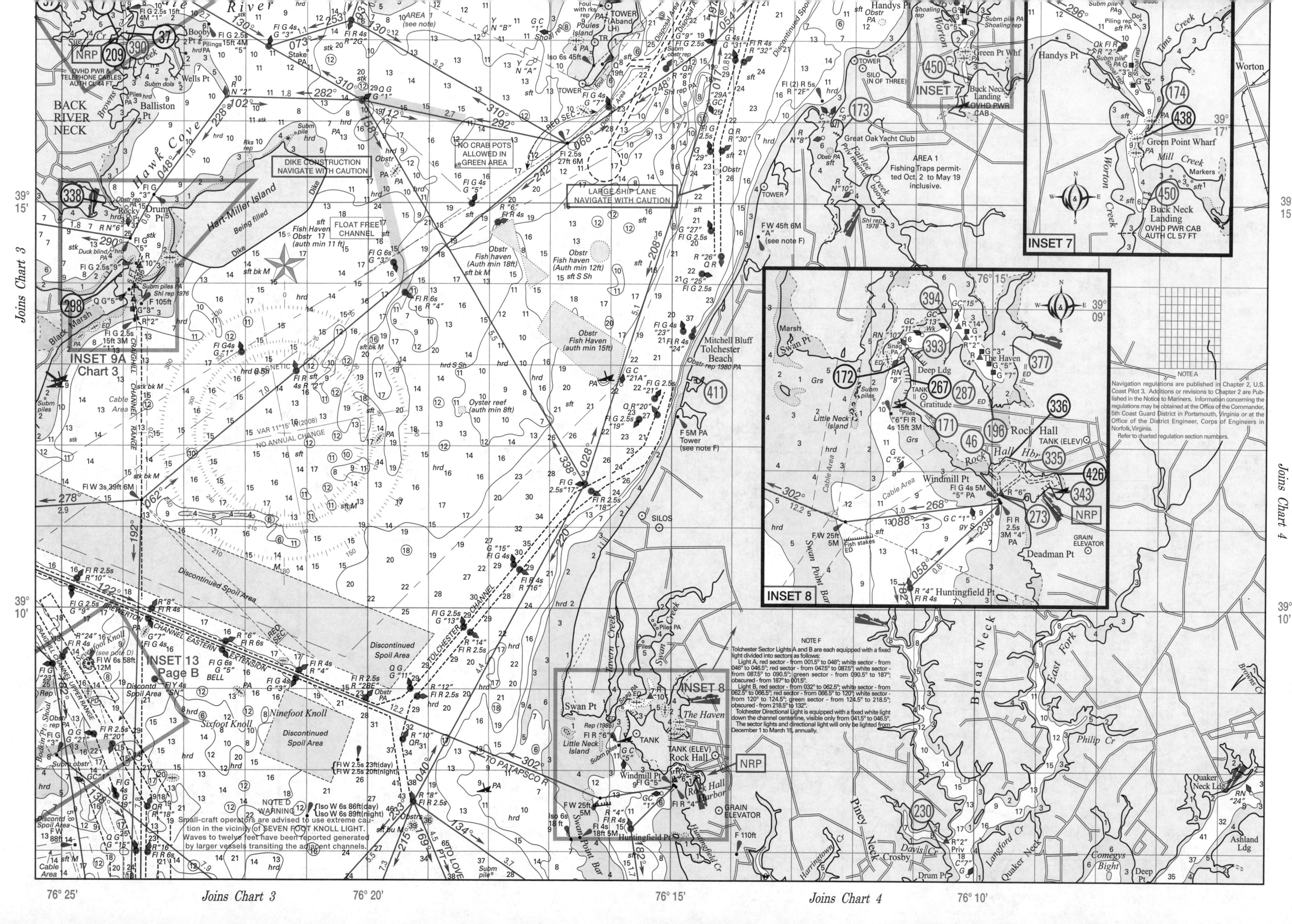

Joins Chart 3
Joins Chart 4
INSET 7
INSET 8
INSET 9A Chart 3
INSET 13 Page B
Worton Creek
Mill Creek
Green Point Wharf
Buck Neck Landing
OVHD PWR CAB AUTH CL 57 FT
Handys Pt
Rock Hall
The Haven
Swan Pt
Swan Point Bar
Windmill Pt
Huntingfield Pt
Deadman Pt
Little Neck Island
Mitchell Bluff
Tolchester Beach
Great Oak Yacht Club
Fairlee Creek
Hart-Miller Island
Being filled
BACK RIVER NECK
Hawk Cove
Sixfoot Knoll
Ninefoot Knoll
Discontinued Spoil Area
Broad Neck
Piney Neck
Langford Cr
East Fork
Philip Cr
Quaker Neck
TOLCHESTER CHANNEL
CRAIGHILL CHANNEL RANGE
BREWERTON CHANNEL EASTERN EXTENSION
TO PATAPSCO R
TO LOVE PT
DIKE CONSTRUCTION NAVIGATE WITH CAUTION
LARGE SHIP LANE NAVIGATE WITH CAUTION
FLOAT FREE CHANNEL
NO CRAB POTS ALLOWED IN GREEN AREA
AREA 1 Fishing Traps permitted Oct. 2 to May 19 inclusive.
NOTE A
Navigation regulations are published in Chapter 2, U.S. Coast Pilot 3. Additions or revisions to Chapter 2 are Published in the Notice to Mariners. Information concerning the regulations may be obtained at the Office of the Commander, 5th Coast Guard District in Portsmouth, Virginia or at the Office of the District Engineer, Corps of Engineers in Norfolk, Virginia.
Refer to charted regulation section numbers.
NOTE F
Tolchester Sector Lights A and B are each equipped with a fixed light divided into sectors as follows:
Light A, red sector - from 001.5° to 046°; white sector - from 046° to 046.5°; red sector - from 047.5° to 087.5°; white sector - from 087.5° to 090.5°; green sector - from 090.5° to 187°; obscured - from 187° to 001.5°.
Light B, red sector - from 032° to 062.5°; white sector - from 062.5° to 066.5°; red sector - from 066.5° to 120°; white sector - from 120° to 124.5°; green sector - from 124.5° to 218.5°; obscured - from 218.5° to 132°.
Tolchester Directional Light is equipped with a fixed white light down the channel centerline, visible only from 041.5° to 046.5°.
The sector lights and directional light will only be lighted from December 1 to March 15, annually.
NOTE D
WARNING
Small-craft operators are advised to use extreme caution in the vicinity of SEVEN FOOT KNOLL LIGHT. Waves to twelve feet have been reported generated by larger vessels transiting the adjacent channels.

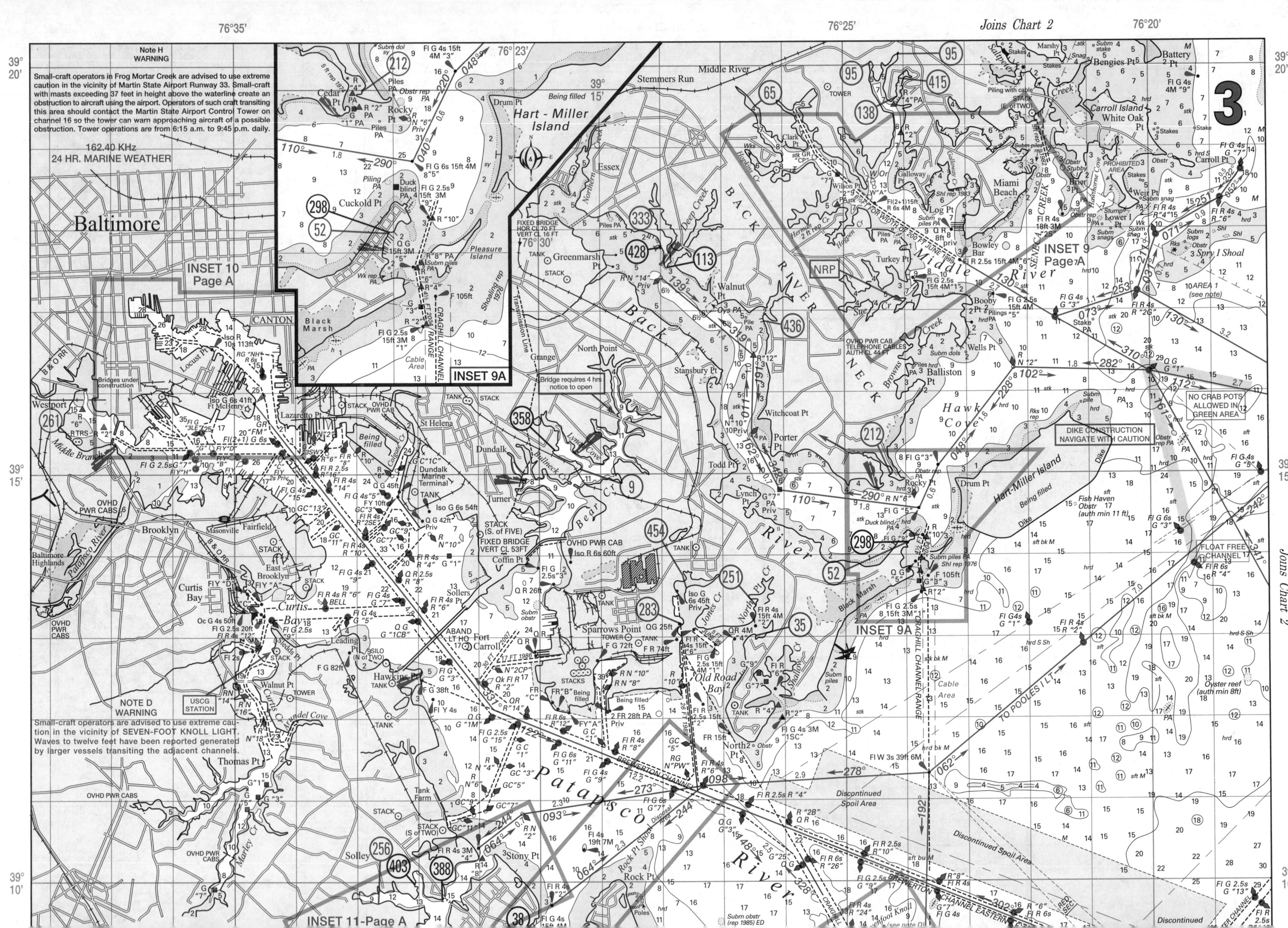
3
Joins Chart 2
Note H
WARNING
Small-craft operators in Frog Mortar Creek are advised to use extreme caution in the vicinity of Martin State Airport Runway 33. Small-craft with masts exceeding 37 feet in height above the waterline create an obstruction to aircraft using the airport. Operators of such craft transiting this area should contact the Martin State Airport Control Tower on channel 16 so the tower can warn approaching aircraft of a possible obstruction. Tower operations are from 6:15 a.m. to 9:45 p.m. daily.
162.40 KHz
24 HR. MARINE WEATHER
NOTE D
WARNING
Small-craft operators are advised to use extreme caution in the vicinity of SEVEN-FOOT KNOLL LIGHT. Waves to twelve feet have been reported generated by larger vessels transiting the adjacent channels.
Baltimore
INSET 10
Page A
INSET 9A
INSET 9
Page A
INSET 11-Page A
Hart - Miller Island
CRAGHILL CHANNEL RANGE
BREWERTON CHANNEL
Patapsco River
Back River
Middle River
BACK RIVER NECK
Hawk Cove
NO CRAB POTS ALLOWED IN GREEN AREA
DIKE CONSTRUCTION NAVIGATE WITH CAUTION
Bridge requires 4 hrs notice to open
FLOAT FREE CHANNEL
TO POOLES I LT
Discontinued Spoil Area
Curtis Bay
Fort Carroll
Sparrows Point
Old Road Bay
Dundalk
Essex
Stemmers Run
Seneca Creek
Bengies Pt
Carroll Island
Pleasure Island
Cuckold Pt
Rocky Pt
Drum Pt
North Point
Stony Pt
Rock Pt
Solley
Brooklyn
Fairfield
Canton
Westport
Baltimore Highlands
USCG STATION

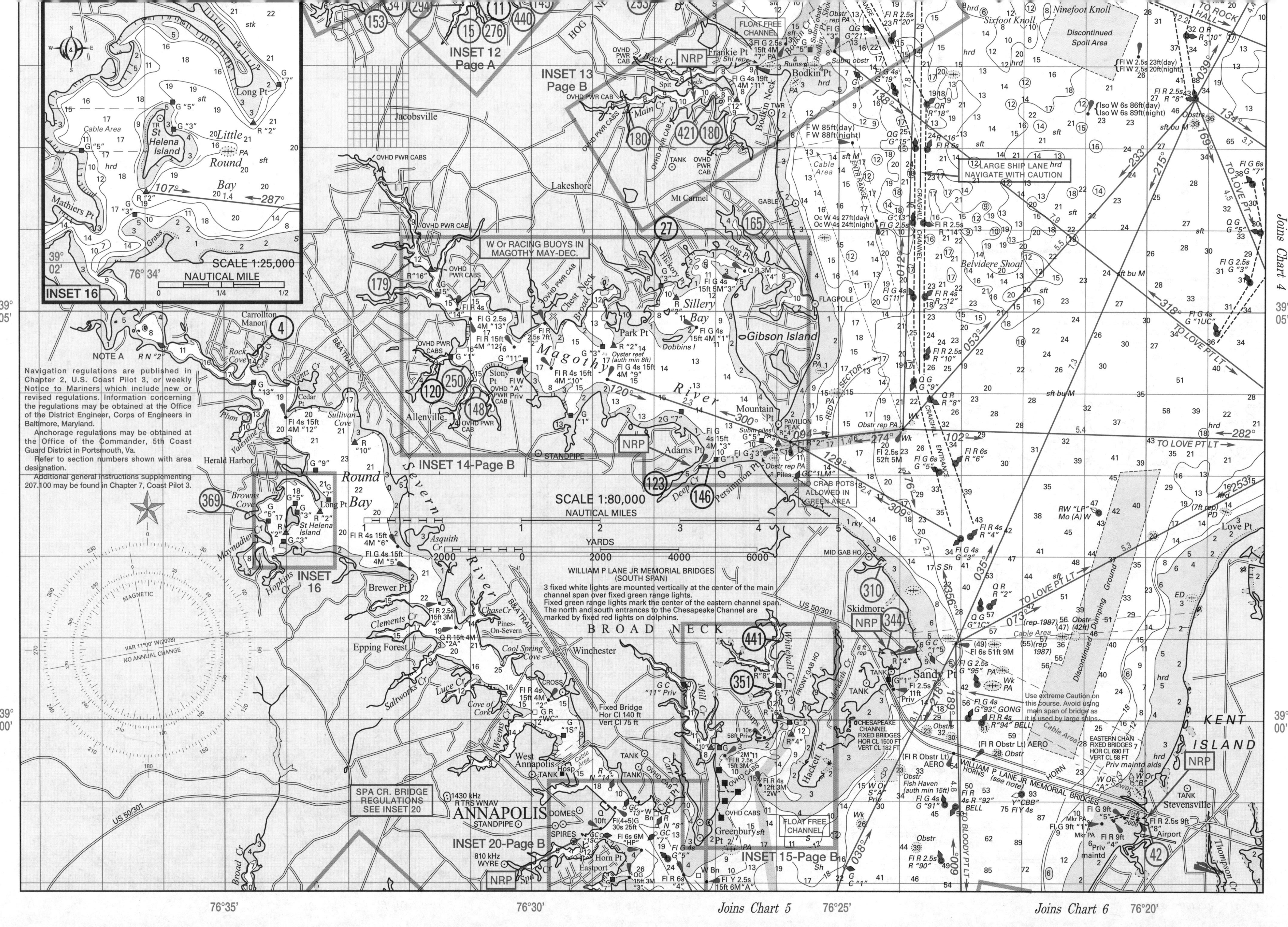

Joins Chart 4
Joins Chart 5
Joins Chart 6
39° 05'
39° 00'
76°35'
76°30'
76°25'
76°20'
INSET 16
SCALE 1:25,000
NAUTICAL MILE
St Helena Island
Little Round Bay
Long Pt
Mathiers Pt
Cable Area
INSET 12 Page A
INSET 13 Page B
INSET 14-Page B
INSET 15-Page B
INSET 20-Page B
Jacobsville
Lakeshore
Mt Carmel
Bodkin Neck
Bodkin Pt
Frankie Pt
Gibson Island
Sillery Bay
Magothy River
Mountain Pt
Hickory Pt
Park Pt
Dobbins I
Chest Neck
Broad Cr
Stony Pt
Allenville
Adams Pt
Deep Cr
Persimmon Pt
W Or RACING BUOYS IN MAGOTHY MAY-DEC.
LARGE SHIP LANE NAVIGATE WITH CAUTION
CRAIGHILL CHANNEL
CRAIGHILL ENTRANCE
Belvidere Shoal
Sixfoot Knoll
Ninefoot Knoll
Discontinued Spoil Area
Discontinued Dumping Ground
TO ROCK HALL
TO LOVE PT
TO LOVE PT LT
TO BLOODY PT LT
Love Pt
KENT ISLAND
Stevensville
Thompson Cr
NO CRAB POTS ALLOWED IN GREEN AREA
SCALE 1:80,000
NAUTICAL MILES
YARDS
WILLIAM P LANE JR MEMORIAL BRIDGES (SOUTH SPAN)
3 fixed white lights are mounted vertically at the center of the main channel span over fixed green range lights.
Fixed green range lights mark the center of the eastern channel span.
The north and south entrances to the Chesapeake Channel are marked by fixed red lights on dolphins.
NOTE A
Navigation regulations are published in Chapter 2, U.S. Coast Pilot 3, or weekly Notice to Mariners which include new or revised regulations. Information concerning the regulations may be obtained at the Office of the District Engineer, Corps of Engineers in Baltimore, Maryland.
Anchorage regulations may be obtained at the Office of the Commander, 5th Coast Guard District in Portsmouth, Va.
Refer to section numbers shown with area designation.
Additional general instructions supplementing 207.100 may be found in Chapter 7, Coast Pilot 3.
Carrollton Manor
Rock Cove
Cedar Pt
Sullivan Cove
Herald Harbor
Browns Cove
Round Bay
Severn River
Asquith Cr
Brewer Pt
Clements Cr
Epping Forest
Pines-On-Severn
Cool Spring Cove
Saltworks Cr
Luce Cr
Cove of Cork
Weems Cr
West Annapolis
BROAD NECK
Winchester
Whitehall Cr
Mill Cr
Meredith Cr
Hackett Pt
Sharps Pt
Greenbury Pt
Skidmore
Sandy Pt
Fixed Bridge Hor Cl 140 ft Vert Cl 75 ft
CHESAPEAKE CHANNEL FIXED BRIDGES HOR CL 1500 FT VERT CL 182 FT
EASTERN CHAN FIXED BRIDGES 7 HOR CL 690 FT VERT CL 58 FT
WILLIAM P LANE JR MEMORIAL BRIDGES (see note)
Use extreme Caution on this course. Avoid using main span of bridge as it is used by large ships.
ANNAPOLIS
Eastport
Horn Pt
SPA CR. BRIDGE REGULATIONS SEE INSET 20
FLOAT FREE CHANNEL
US 50/301
B&A TRAIL
MAGNETIC
VAR 11°00' W(2008) NO ANNUAL CHANGE

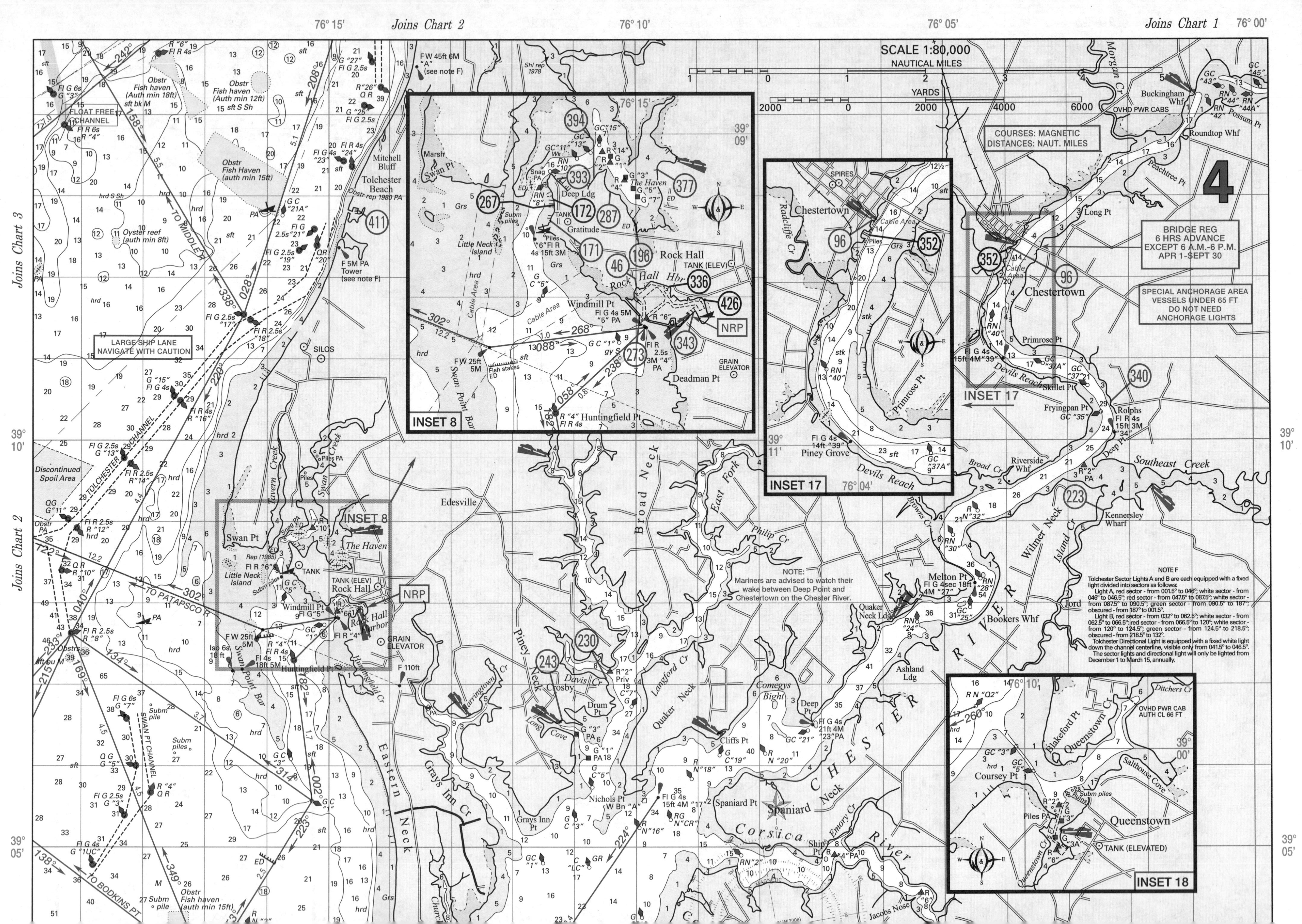
Joins Chart 2
Joins Chart 1
Joins Chart 3
Joins Chart 2
76° 15'
76° 10'
76° 05'
76° 00'
39° 10'
39° 05'
4
SCALE 1:80,000
NAUTICAL MILES
YARDS
COURSES: MAGNETIC
DISTANCES: NAUT. MILES
BRIDGE REG
6 HRS ADVANCE
EXCEPT 6 A.M.-6 P.M.
APR 1-SEPT 30
SPECIAL ANCHORAGE AREA
VESSELS UNDER 65 FT
DO NOT NEED
ANCHORAGE LIGHTS
LARGE SHIP LANE
NAVIGATE WITH CAUTION
FLOAT FREE CHANNEL
TOLCHESTER CHANNEL
SWAN PT CHANNEL
TO MIDDLE R
TO PATAPSCO R
TO BODKINS PT
Discontinued Spoil Area
Obstr Fish haven (Auth min 18ft)
Obstr Fish haven (Auth min 12ft)
Obstr Fish Haven (auth min 15ft)
Oyster reef (auth min 8ft)
F W 45ft 6M "A" (see note F)
F 5M PA Tower (see note F)
Mitchell Bluff
Tolchester Beach
Obstr rep 1980 PA
SILOS
Swan Pt
Little Neck Island
Tavern Creek
Swan Creek
The Haven
Rock Hall
Rock Hall Harbor
Windmill Pt
Huntingfield Pt
Huntingfield Cr
Swan Point Bar
GRAIN ELEVATOR
NRP
Edesville
Eastern Neck
Grays Inn Cr
Grays Inn Pt
Piney Neck
Harringtown Cr
Long Cove
Crosby
Davis Cr
Drum Pt
Broad Neck
East Fork
Philip Cr
Langford Cr
Quaker Neck
Quaker Neck Ldg
Comegys Bight
Deep Pt
Cliffs Pt
Nichols Pt
Spaniard Pt
Spaniard Neck
Corsica River
Emory Cr
Ship Pt
Jacobs Nose
Ashland Ldg
Melton Pt
Bookers Whf
CHESTER RIVER
Wilmer Neck
Island Cr
Jord
Browns Cr
Broad Cr
Riverside Whf
Southeast Creek
Kennersley Wharf
Deep Pt
Rolphs
Fryingpan Pt
Skillet Pt
Devils Reach
Primrose Pt
Chestertown
Long Pt
Peachtree Pt
Morgan Cr
Buckingham Whf
Roundtop Whf
Possum Pt
OVHD PWR CABS
NOTE:
Mariners are advised to watch their wake between Deep Point and Chestertown on the Chester River.
NOTE F
Tolchester Sector Lights A and B are each equipped with a fixed light divided into sectors as follows:
Light A, red sector - from 001.5° to 046°; white sector - from 046° to 046.5°; red sector - from 047.5° to 087.5°; white sector - from 087.5° to 090.5°; green sector - from 090.5° to 187°; obscured - from 187° to 001.5°.
Light B, red sector - from 032° to 062.5°; white sector - from 062.5° to 066.5°; red sector - from 066.5° to 120°; white sector - from 120° to 124.5°; green sector - from 124.5° to 218.5°; obscured - from 218.5° to 132°.
Tolchester Directional Light is equipped with a fixed white light down the channel centerline, visible only from 041.5° to 046.5°.
The sector lights and directional light will only be lighted from December 1 to March 15, annually.
INSET 8
Marsh
Deep Ldg
Gratitude
Deadman Pt
Cable Area
Fish stakes
INSET 17
Radcliffe Cr
SPIRES
Piney Grove
INSET 18
Ditchers Cr
OVHD PWR CAB AUTH CL 66 FT
Blakeford Pt
Queenstown Cr
Salthouse Cove
Coursey Pt
Queenstown
TANK (ELEVATED)

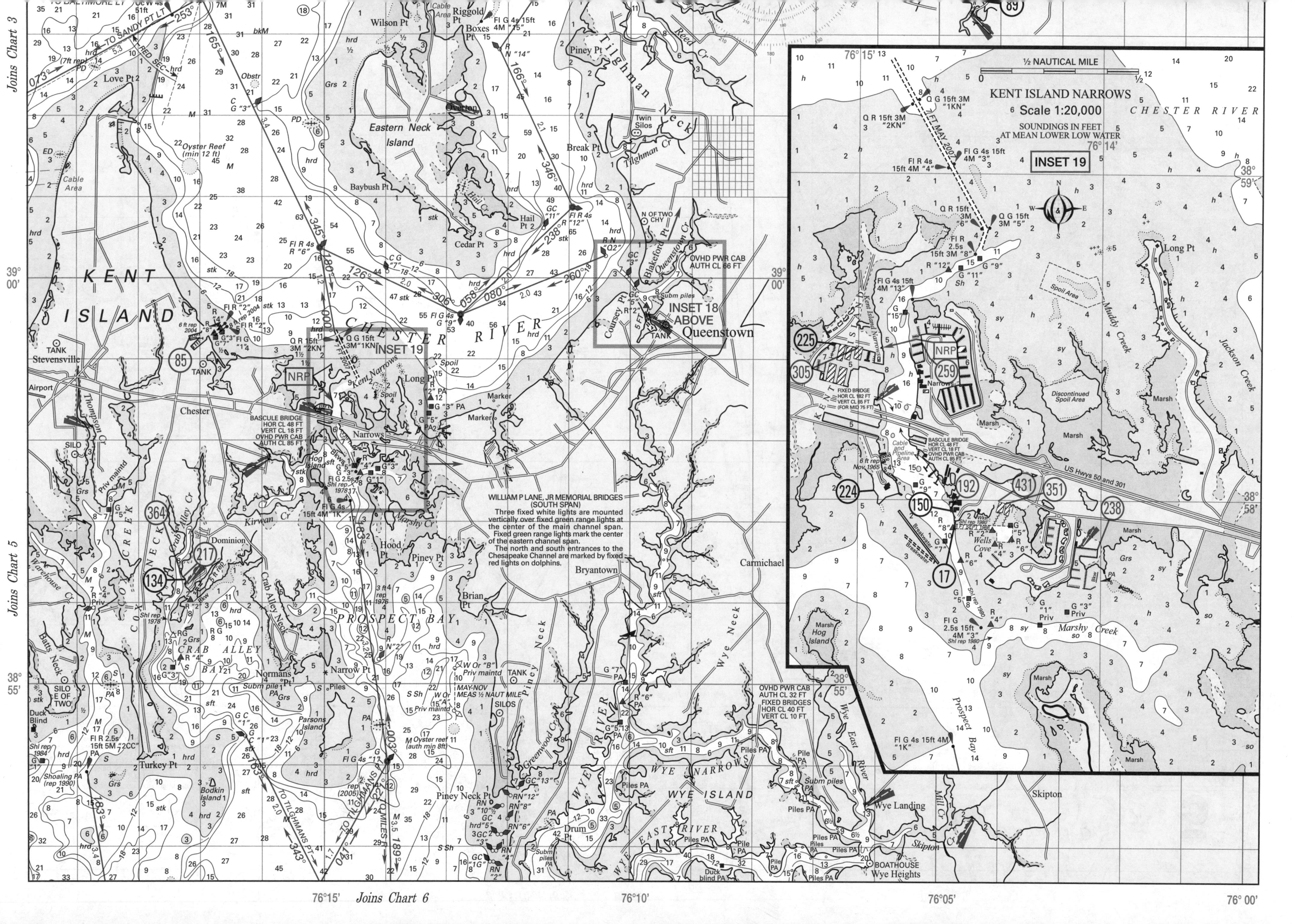

Joins Chart 3
Joins Chart 5
Joins Chart 6
KENT ISLAND
CHESTER RIVER
Eastern Neck Island
Tilghman Neck
Queenstown
INSET 18 ABOVE
INSET 19
Kent Narrows
Chester
Stevensville
Airport
Love Pt
Wilson Pt
Riggold Pt
Boxes Pt
Piney Pt
Break Pt
Baybush Pt
Cedar Pt
Hail Pt
Overton
Twin Silos
Tilghman Cr
Reed Cr
Hail Cr
Blakeford Pt
Queenstown Cr
Coursey Pt
OVHD PWR CAB AUTH CL 66 FT
BASCULE BRIDGE HOR CL 48 FT VERT CL 18 FT OVHD PWR CAB AUTH CL 85 FT
WILLIAM P LANE, JR MEMORIAL BRIDGES (SOUTH SPAN)
Three fixed white lights are mounted vertically over fixed green range lights at the center of the main channel span. Fixed green range lights mark the center of the eastern channel span.
The north and south entrances to the Chesapeake Channel are marked by fixed red lights on dolphins.
Oyster Reef (min 12 ft)
Cable Area
Thompson Cr
Kirwan Cr
Cox Neck
Cox Creek
Crab Alley Cr
Crab Alley Neck
Crab Alley Bay
Dominion
Warehouse Cr
Batts Neck
Prospect Bay
Hood Pt
Piney Pt
Brian Pt
Marshy Cr
Narrow Pt
Normans Pt
Parsons Island
Turkey Pt
Bodkin Island
Piney Neck
Piney Neck Pt
Greenwood Cr
Bryantown
Carmichael
Wye Neck
Wye River
Wye Narrows
Wye Island
Wye East River
Drum Pt
Wye Landing
Wye Heights
BOATHOUSE
Skipton
Skipton Cr
Mill Cr
OVHD PWR CAB AUTH CL 32 FT FIXED BRIDGES HOR CL 40 FT VERT CL 10 FT
TO TILGHMANS PT
TO SANDY PT LT
RED SEC
KENT ISLAND NARROWS
Scale 1:20,000
SOUNDINGS IN FEET AT MEAN LOWER LOW WATER
½ NAUTICAL MILE
INSET 19
7 FT MAY 2007
Long Pt
Muddy Creek
Jackson Creek
Spoil Area
Discontinued Spoil Area
Marsh
US Hwys 50 and 301
FIXED BRIDGE HOR CL 182 FT VERT CL 65 FT (FOR MID 75 FT)
Cable and Pipeline Area
Breakwater
Wells Cove
Marshy Creek
Hog Island
Prospect Bay
Q G 15ft 3M "1KN"
Q R 15ft 3M "2KN"
Fl G 4s 15ft 4M "1K"
76°15'
76°10'
76°05'
76°00'
39° 00'
38° 55'

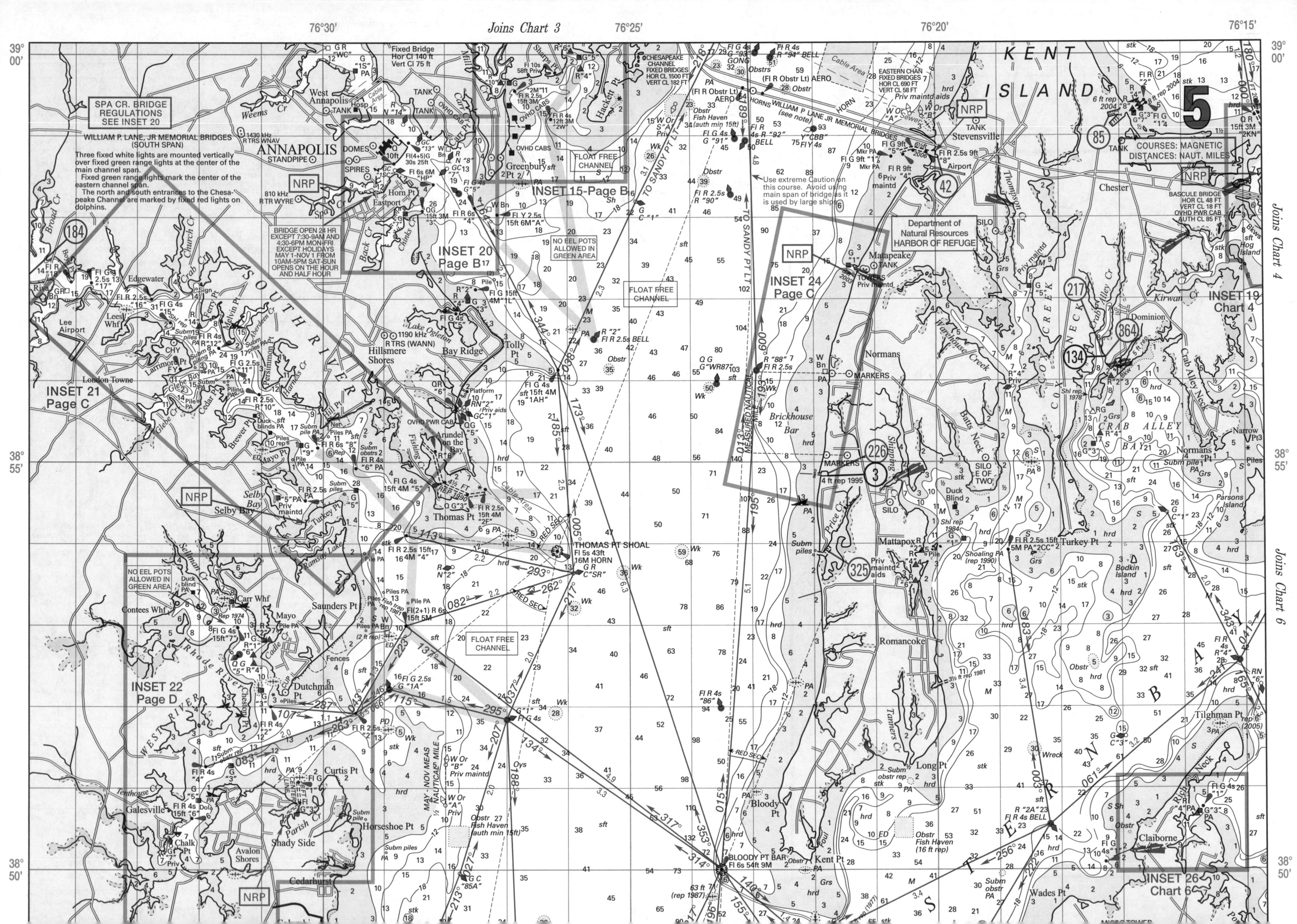

Joins Chart 3
Joins Chart 4
Joins Chart 6
76°30'
76°25'
76°20'
76°15'
39° 00'
38° 55'
38° 50'
5
KENT ISLAND
COURSES: MAGNETIC
DISTANCES: NAUT. MILES
SPA CR. BRIDGE REGULATIONS SEE INSET 20
WILLIAM P. LANE, JR MEMORIAL BRIDGES (SOUTH SPAN)
Three fixed white lights are mounted vertically over fixed green range lights at the center of the main channel span.
Fixed green range lights mark the center of the eastern channel span.
The north and south entrances to the Chesapeake Channel are marked by fixed red lights on dolphins.
BRIDGE OPEN 24 HR EXCEPT 7:30-9AM AND 4:30-6PM MON-FRI EXCEPT HOLIDAYS MAY 1-NOV 1 FROM 10AM-5PM SAT-SUN OPENS ON THE HOUR AND HALF HOUR
Use extreme Caution on this course. Avoid using main span of bridge as it is used by large ships.
Department of Natural Resources HARBOR OF REFUGE
FLOAT FREE CHANNEL
NO EEL POTS ALLOWED IN GREEN AREA
MEASURED NAUTICAL MILE
MAY - NOV MEAS NAUTICAL MILE
TO SANDY PT LT
THOMAS PT SHOAL
Fl 5s 43ft 16M HORN
BLOODY PT BAR
Fl 6s 54ft 9M
CHESAPEAKE CHANNEL FIXED BRIDGES HOR CL 1500 FT VERT CL 182 FT
EASTERN CHAN FIXED BRIDGES HOR CL 690 FT VERT CL 58 FT
BASCULE BRIDGE HOR CL 48 FT VERT CL 18 FT OVHD PWR CAB AUTH CL 85 FT
Fixed Bridge Hor Cl 140 ft Vert Cl 75 ft
INSET 15-Page B
INSET 19 Chart 4
INSET 20 Page B
INSET 21 Page C
INSET 22 Page D
INSET 24 Page C
INSET 26 Chart 6
NRP
ANNAPOLIS
SOUTH RIVER
Rhode River
WEST RIVER
CRAB ALLEY BAY
COX CREEK
COX NECK
Crab Alley Neck
Stevensville
Chester
Matapeake
Romancoke
Mattapox
Kent Pt
Bloody Pt
Long Pt
Turkey Pt
Tilghman Pt
Claiborne
Wades Pt
Thomas Pt
Tolly Pt
Bay Ridge
Hillsmere Shores
Arundel on the Bay
Horn Pt
Eastport
Greenbury Pt
Saunders Pt
Dutchman Pt
Curtis Pt
Horseshoe Pt
Cheston Pt
Mayo
Galesville
Shady Side
Avalon Shores
Cedarhurst
Edgewater
London Towne
Lee Airport
Contees Whf
Carr Whf
Selby Bay
Sellman Cr
Batts Neck
Shipping Cr
Tanners Cr
Warehouse Creek
Thompson Cr
Brickhouse Bar
Bodkin Island
Parsons Island
Hog Island
Normans
Dominion
Kirwan Cr
West Annapolis
Weems Cr
Hackett Pt
Sharps Pt
Lake Ogleton
Fishing Cr
Price Cr
Parish Cr
Chalk Pt

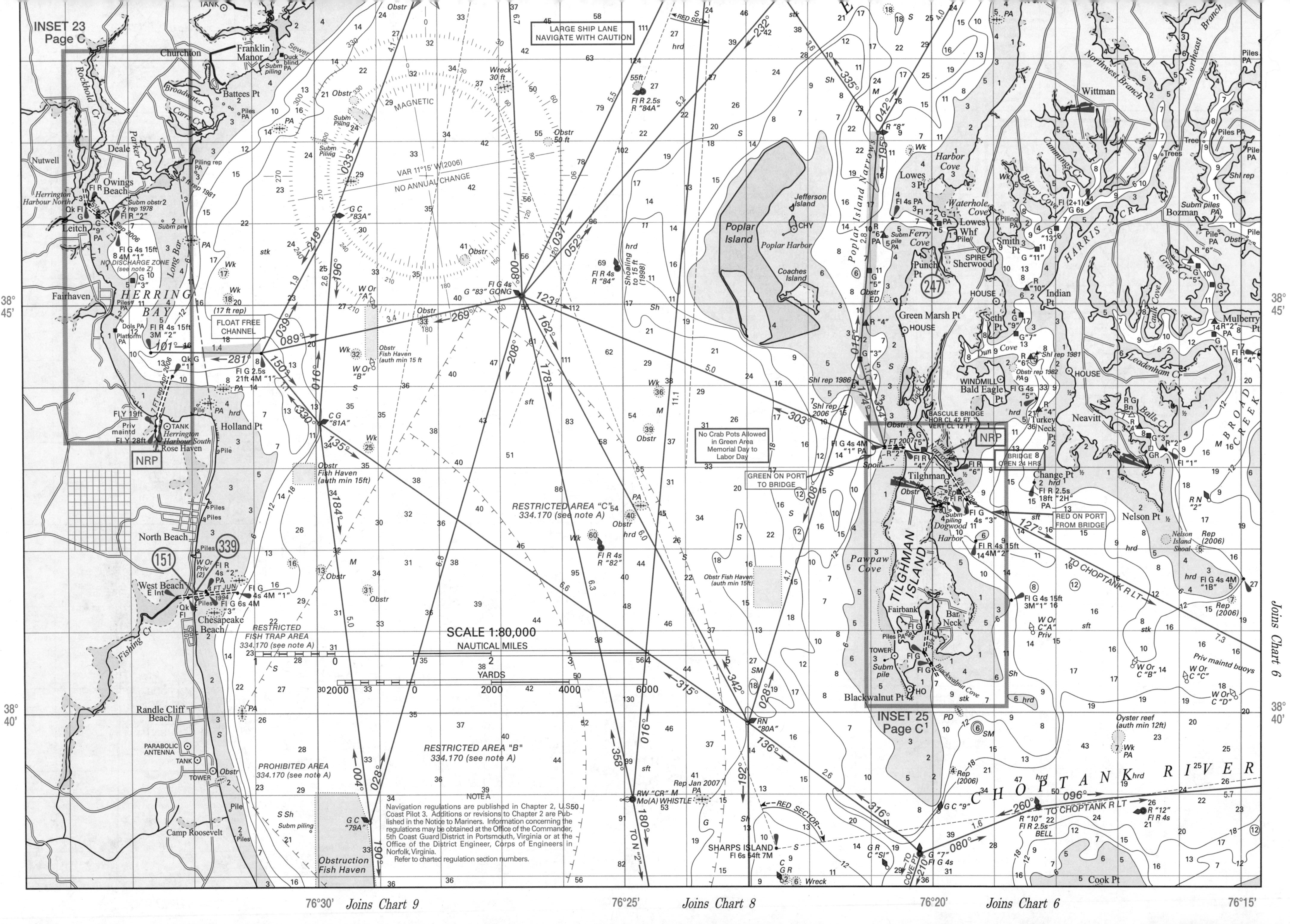

INSET 23
Page C
INSET 25
Page C1
LARGE SHIP LANE
NAVIGATE WITH CAUTION
FLOAT FREE
CHANNEL
No Crab Pots Allowed
in Green Area
Memorial Day to
Labor Day
GREEN ON PORT
TO BRIDGE
RED ON PORT
FROM BRIDGE
BASCULE BRIDGE
HOR CL 42 FT
VERT CL 12 FT
BRIDGE 8
OPEN 24 HRS
NRP
VAR 11°15' W(2006)
NO ANNUAL CHANGE
MAGNETIC
SCALE 1:80,000
NAUTICAL MILES
YARDS
RESTRICTED AREA "C"
334.170 (see note A)
RESTRICTED AREA "B"
334.170 (see note A)
PROHIBITED AREA
334.170 (see note A)
RESTRICTED
FISH TRAP AREA
334.170 (see note A)
NO DISCHARGE ZONE
(see note Z)
NOTE A
Navigation regulations are published in Chapter 2, U.S. Coast Pilot 3. Additions or revisions to Chapter 2 are published in the Notice to Mariners. Information concerning the regulations may be obtained at the Office of the Commander, 5th Coast Guard District in Portsmouth, Virginia or at the Office of the District Engineer, Corps of Engineers in Norfolk, Virginia.
Refer to charted regulation section numbers.
HERRING BAY
Poplar Island
Poplar Harbor
Jefferson Island
Coaches Island
Poplar Island Narrows
TILGHMAN ISLAND
CHOPTANK RIVER
HARRIS CR
BROAD CREEK
TO CHOPTANK R LT
TO N "2"
Churchton
Franklin Manor
Battees Pt
Deale
Owings Beach
Leitch
Fairhaven
Nutwell
Holland Pt
Rose Haven
North Beach
West Beach
Chesapeake Beach
Randle Cliff Beach
Camp Roosevelt
Rockhold Cr
Parker Cr
Carrs Cr
Broadwater Cr
Fishing Cr
Long Bar
Herrington Harbour North
Herrington Harbour South
Wittman
Bozman
Northwest Branch
Northeast Branch
Cummings Cr
Briary Cove
Harbor Cove
Lowes Pt
Waterhole Cove
Lowes Whf
Ferry Cove
Punch Pt
Sherwood
Indian Pt
Green Marsh Pt
Seth Pt
Dun Cove
Bald Eagle Pt
Grace Cr
Caulk Cove
Leadenham Cr
Mulberry Pt
Neavitt
Balls Cr
Turkey Neck Pt
Change Pt
Nelson Pt
Nelson Island Shoal
Tilghman
Knapps Narrows
Dogwood Harbor
Pawpaw Cove
Fairbank
Bar Neck
Blackwalnut Cove
Blackwalnut Pt
Cook Pt
SHARPS ISLAND
Fl 6s 54ft 7M
Oyster reef
(auth min 12ft)
Priv maintd buoys
Obstruction
Fish Haven
Obstr
Fish Haven
(auth min 15ft)
Obstr Fish Haven
(auth min 15ft)
Shoaling
to 15 ft
(1998)
G "83" GONG
Fl G 4s
RW "CR" Mo(A) WHISTLE
RN "80A"
CG "81A"
GC "83A"
GC "79A"
Fl R 2.5s R "84A"
Fl R 4s R "84"
Fl R 4s R "82"
RED SECTOR
Joins Chart 6
Joins Chart 8
Joins Chart 9
38° 45'
38° 40'
76°30'
76°25'
76°20'
76°15'

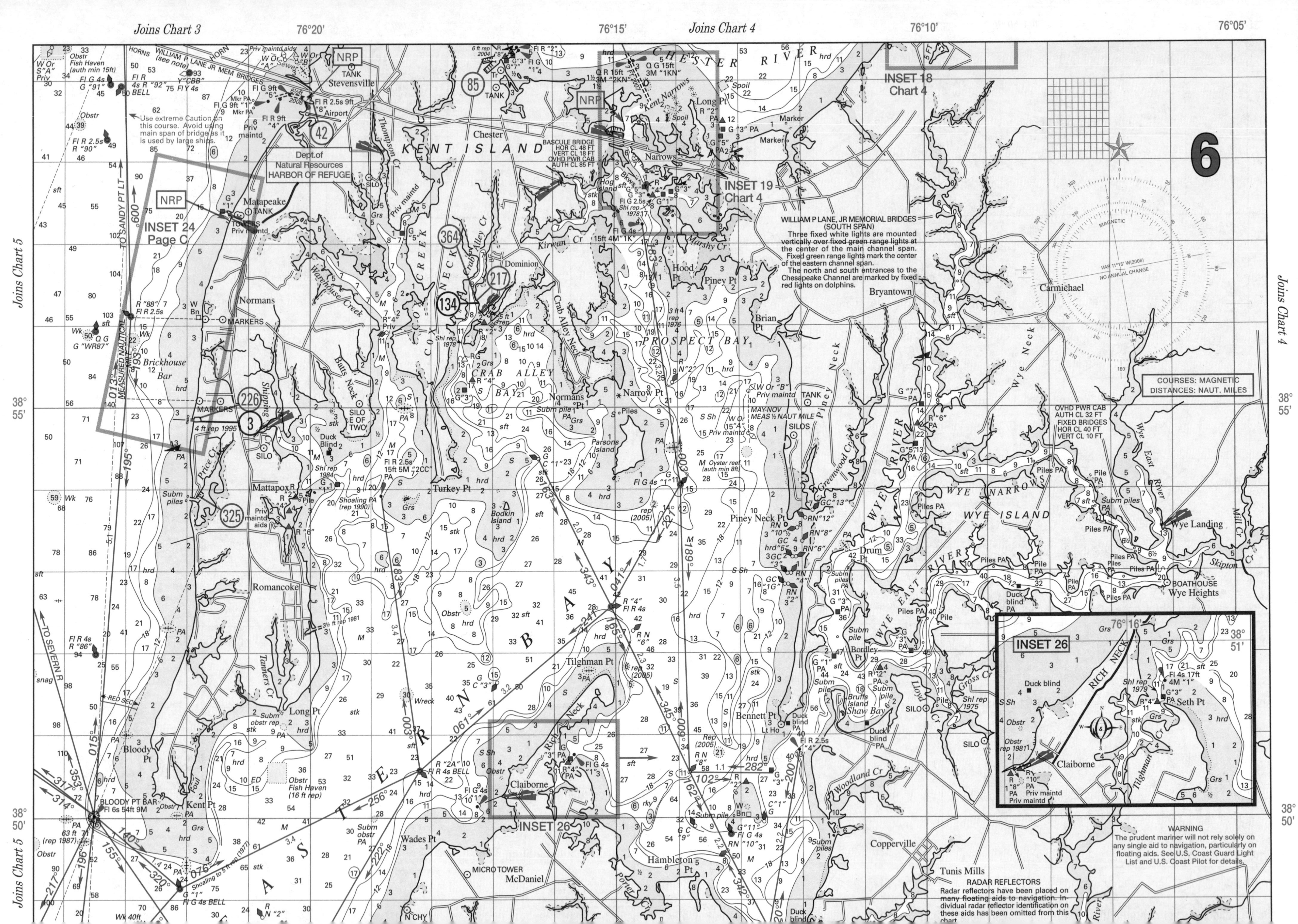

Joins Chart 3
Joins Chart 4
Joins Chart 5
76°20'
76°15'
76°10'
76°05'
38° 55'
38° 50'
6
CHESTER RIVER
KENT ISLAND
PROSPECT BAY
CRAB ALLEY BAY
COX NECK
EASTERN BAY
WYE RIVER
WYE EAST RIVER
WYE NARROWS
WYE ISLAND
RICH NECK
INSET 18
Chart 4
INSET 19
Chart 4
INSET 24
Page C
INSET 26
Stevensville
Chester
Narrows
Kent Narrows
Dominion
Bryantown
Carmichael
Wye Landing
Wye Heights
Matapeake
Normans
Batts Neck
Romancoke
Mattapex
Claiborne
Copperville
Tunis Mills
McDaniel
Kent Pt
Bloody Pt
Long Pt
Turkey Pt
Piney Neck Pt
Bennett Pt
Tilghman Pt
Hambleton Pt
Wades Pt
Drum Pt
Bordley Pt
Seth Pt
Narrow Pt
Hood Pt
Piney Pt
Brian Pt
Bodkin Island
Parsons Island
Bruffs Island
Shaw Bay
Brickhouse Bar
Thompson Cr
Warehouse Creek
Shipping Cr
Price Cr
Tanners Cr
Kirwan Cr
Marshy Cr
Crab Alley Cr
Crab Alley Neck
Greenwood Cr
Lloyd Cr
Gross Cr
Woodland Cr
Mill Cr
Skipton Cr
Porter Cr
Tilghman Cr
Piney Neck
Wye Neck
Dept.of Natural Resources HARBOR OF REFUGE
BASCULE BRIDGE HOR CL 48 FT VERT CL 18 FT OVHD PWR CAB AUTH CL 85 FT
WILLIAM P LANE JR MEM BRIDGES
Use extreme Caution on this course. Avoid using main span of bridge as it is used by large ships.
WILLIAM P LANE, JR MEMORIAL BRIDGES (SOUTH SPAN)
Three fixed white lights are mounted vertically over fixed green range lights at the center of the main channel span. Fixed green range lights mark the center of the eastern channel span. The north and south entrances to the Chesapeake Channel are marked by fixed red lights on dolphins.
OVHD PWR CAB AUTH CL 32 FT
FIXED BRIDGES HOR CL 40 FT VERT CL 10 FT
COURSES: MAGNETIC
DISTANCES: NAUT. MILES
VAR 11°15' W(2006)
NO ANNUAL CHANGE
MEASURED NAUTICAL MILE
TO SANDY PT LT
TO SEVERN R
BLOODY PT BAR
Fl 6s 54ft 9M
MICRO TOWER
WARNING
The prudent mariner will not rely solely on any single aid to navigation, particularly on floating aids. See U.S. Coast Guard Light List and U.S. Coast Pilot for details.
RADAR REFLECTORS
Radar reflectors have been placed on many floating aids to navigation. Individual radar reflector identification on these aids has been omitted from this chart.

Joins Chart 7
Joins Chart 5
Joins Chart 9
Joins Chart 8
38° 45'
38° 40'
76°20'
76°15'
76°10'
76°05'
POLLUTION REPORTS
Report all spills of oil and hazardous substances to the National Response Center via 800-424-8802 (toll free) or to the nearest U.S. Coast Guard facility if telephone communication is impossible (33 CFR 153)
BASCULE BRIDGE HOR CL 40 FT VERT CL 18 FT
BRIDGE OPENS SUNRISE TO SUNSET SIX HOURS NOTICE AT OTHER TIMES
FIXED BRIDGE HOR CL 24 FT VERT CL 24 FT OVHD PWR CABS AUTH CL 36 FT
TOWN CREEK
The controlling depth from the entrance to the upper end of the improvement was 5 1/2 feet centerline in April 1972
INSET 27 Chart 7
INSET 28 Chart 7
INSET 29 CHART 7
INSET 25 Page C
No Crab Pots Allowed in Green Area Memorial Day to Labor Day
GREEN ON PORT TO BRIDGE
RED ON PORT FROM BRIDGE
BASCULE BRIDGE HOR CL 42 FT VERT CL 12 FT
BRIDGE 8 OPEN 24 HRS
SCALE 1:80,000
NAUTICAL MILES
YARDS
CHOPTANK RIVER
MILES RIVER
HARRIS CR
BROAD CREEK
TRED AVON
TILGHMAN ISLAND
Poplar Island
Poplar Island Narrows
Poplar Harbor
Jefferson Island
Coaches Island
St Michaels
Oxford
Tilghman
Wittman
Bozman
Sherwood
Neavitt
Royal Oak
Newcomb
Kirkham
Bloomfield
Easton Pt
Edmundson Neck
Deep Neck
Ferry Neck
Baileys Neck
Island Neck
Grubin Neck
Island Creek
Bellevue
Double Mills Pt
Long Pt
Neck Pt
Camden Pt
Watermelon Pt
Green Marsh Pt
Blackwalnut Pt
Bar Neck
Fairbank
Pawpaw Cove
Harbor Cove
Lowes Pt
Lowes Whf
Waterhole Cove
Ferry Cove
Punch Pt
Smith Pt
Indian Pt
Seth Pt
Dun Cove
Bald Eagle Pt
Turkey Neck Pt
Change Pt
Nelson Pt
Nelson Island Shoal
Holland Pt
Lucy Pt
Benoni Pt
Bachelor Pt
Peck Pt
Deepwater Pt
Chlora Pt
Martin Pt
Castle Haven
Cook Pt
Todds Pt
Dickinson Bay
Sawmill Cove
Lowry Cove
Trappe Ldg
La Trappe Cr
Boone Cr
Town Cr
Goldsborough Cr
Trippe Creek
Plaindealing Cr
Peachblossom Cr
Le Gates Cove
Maxmore Cr
Dixon Cr
Glebe Cr
Hunting Cr
Long Pt
Oak Cr
Solitude Cr
Elberts Cove
Edge Cr
Drum Pt
Cedar Pt
Deep Neck Pt
Bridge Creek
Irish Cr
Leadenham Cr
Balls Cr
Grace Cr
Cummings Cr
Briary Cove
Caulk Cove
Mulberry Pt
Hambleton Island
San Domingo Cr
Fairview Pt
Haul Cr
Northwest Branch
Knapps Narrows
Dogwood Harbor
SHARPS ISLAND Fl 6s 54ft 7M
CHOPTANK RIVER Fl 4s 35ft 8M
TO CAMBRIDGE
TO COVE PT
RED SECTOR
Priv maintd buoys
Oyster reef (auth min 12ft)
Obstr Fish Haven (auth min 15ft)

76°10' *Joins Chart 6* 75°55'

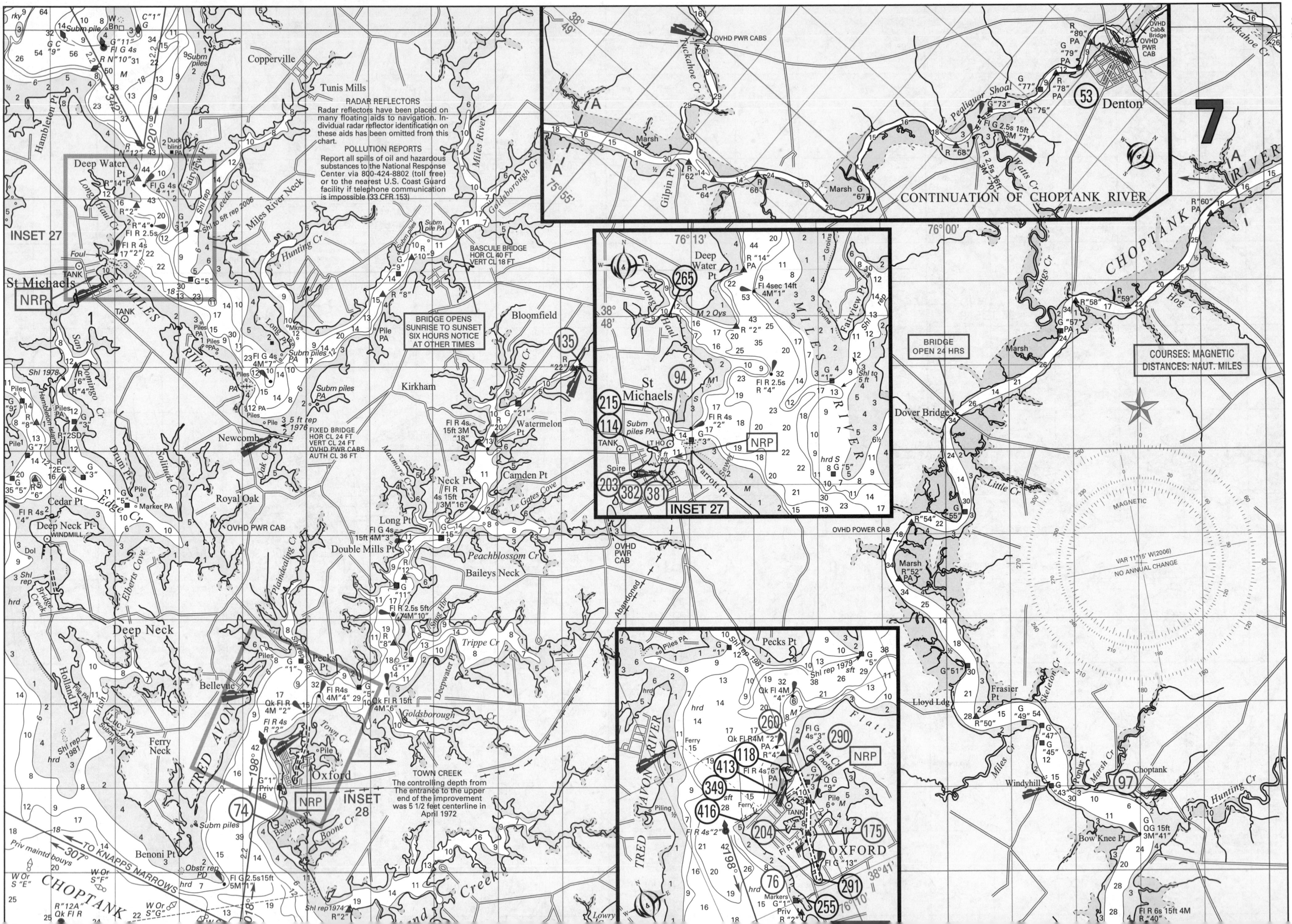
7
CONTINUATION OF CHOPTANK RIVER
Denton
53
RADAR REFLECTORS
Radar reflectors have been placed on many floating aids to navigation. Individual radar reflector identification on these aids has been omitted from this chart.
POLLUTION REPORTS
Report all spills of oil and hazardous substances to the National Response Center via 800-424-8802 (toll free) or to the nearest U.S. Coast Guard facility if telephone communication is impossible (33 CFR 153)
BASCULE BRIDGE
HOR CL 40 FT
VERT CL 18 FT
BRIDGE OPENS
SUNRISE TO SUNSET
SIX HOURS NOTICE
AT OTHER TIMES
FIXED BRIDGE
HOR CL 24 FT
VERT CL 24 FT
OVHD PWR CABS
AUTH CL 36 FT
BRIDGE
OPEN 24 HRS
COURSES: MAGNETIC
DISTANCES: NAUT. MILES
VAR 11°15' W(2006)
NO ANNUAL CHANGE
MAGNETIC
TOWN CREEK
The controlling depth from The entrance to the upper end of the improvement was 5 1/2 feet centerline in April 1972
INSET 27
INSET 28
St Michaels
Copperville
Tunis Mills
Miles River Neck
Miles River
MILES RIVER
Kirkham
Bloomfield
Newcomb
Royal Oak
Camden Pt
Watermelon Pt
Neck Pt
Long Pt
Double Mills Pt
Baileys Neck
Peachblossom Cr
Deep Neck
Bellevue
Ferry Neck
Oxford
OXFORD
TRED AVON RIVER
Benoni Pt
CHOPTANK
TO KNAPPS NARROWS
CHOPTANK RIVER
Dover Bridge
Lloyd Ldg
Frasier Pt
Windyhill
Choptank
Bow Knee Pt
Tuckahoe Cr
Gilpin Pt
Watts Cr
Kings Cr
Hog Cr
Little Cr
Miles Cr
Skeleton Cr
Marsh Cr
Hunting Cr
Hambleton Pt
Hambleton Island
Deep Water Pt
Fairview Pt
Long Haul Cr
Leeds Cr
Goldsborough Cr
Dixon Cr
Le Gates Cove
Maxmore Cr
Oak Cr
Solitude Cr
Edge Cr
Drum Pt
Cedar Pt
Deep Neck Pt
Elberts Cove
Bridge Creek
Plaindealing Cr
Tripps Cr
Deepwater Pt
Peck Pt
Town Cr
Boone Cr
Holland Pt
Irish Cr
Lucy Pt
OVHD PWR CAB
OVHD POWER CAB
NRP
135
265
94
215
114
203
382
381
260
290
118
413
349
416
204
175
76
291
255
74
97

38° 50' 38° 45' 38° 40' *Joins Chart 6*

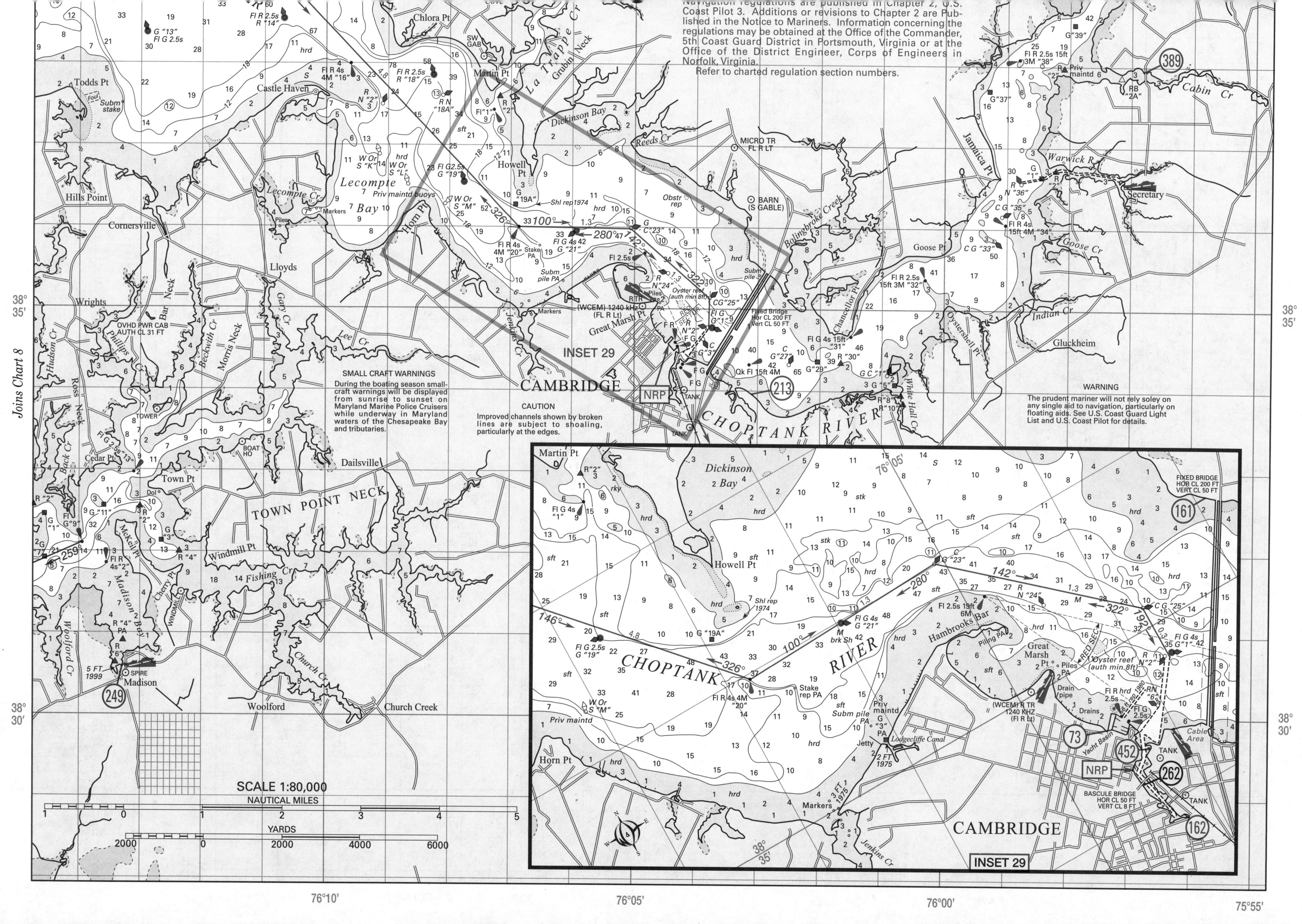

Navigation regulations are published in Chapter 2, U.S. Coast Pilot 3. Additions or revisions to Chapter 2 are published in the Notice to Mariners. Information concerning the regulations may be obtained at the Office of the Commander, 5th Coast Guard District in Portsmouth, Virginia or at the Office of the District Engineer, Corps of Engineers in Norfolk, Virginia.
Refer to charted regulation section numbers.
SMALL CRAFT WARNINGS
During the boating season small-craft warnings will be displayed from sunrise to sunset on Maryland Marine Police Cruisers while underway in Maryland waters of the Chesapeake Bay and tributaries.
CAUTION
Improved channels shown by broken lines are subject to shoaling, particularly at the edges.
WARNING
The prudent mariner will not rely soley on any single aid to navigation, particularly on floating aids. See U.S. Coast Guard Light List and U.S. Coast Pilot for details.
Joins Chart 8
CAMBRIDGE
CHOPTANK RIVER
INSET 29
TOWN POINT NECK
Lecompte Bay
Dickinson Bay
Chlora Pt
Martin Pt
Castle Haven
Todds Pt
Hills Point
Cornersville
Lloyds
Wrights
Howell Pt
Horn Pt
Great Marsh Pt
Hambrooks Bar
Goose Pt
Jamaica Pt
Secretary
Gluckheim
Dailsville
Town Pt
Cedar Pt
Windmill Pt
Madison
Woolford
Church Creek
SCALE 1:80,000
NAUTICAL MILES
YARDS
FIXED BRIDGE HOR CL 200 FT VERT CL 50 FT
BASCULE BRIDGE HOR CL 50 FT VERT CL 8 FT
76°10'
76°05'
76°00'
75°55'
38° 35'
38° 30'

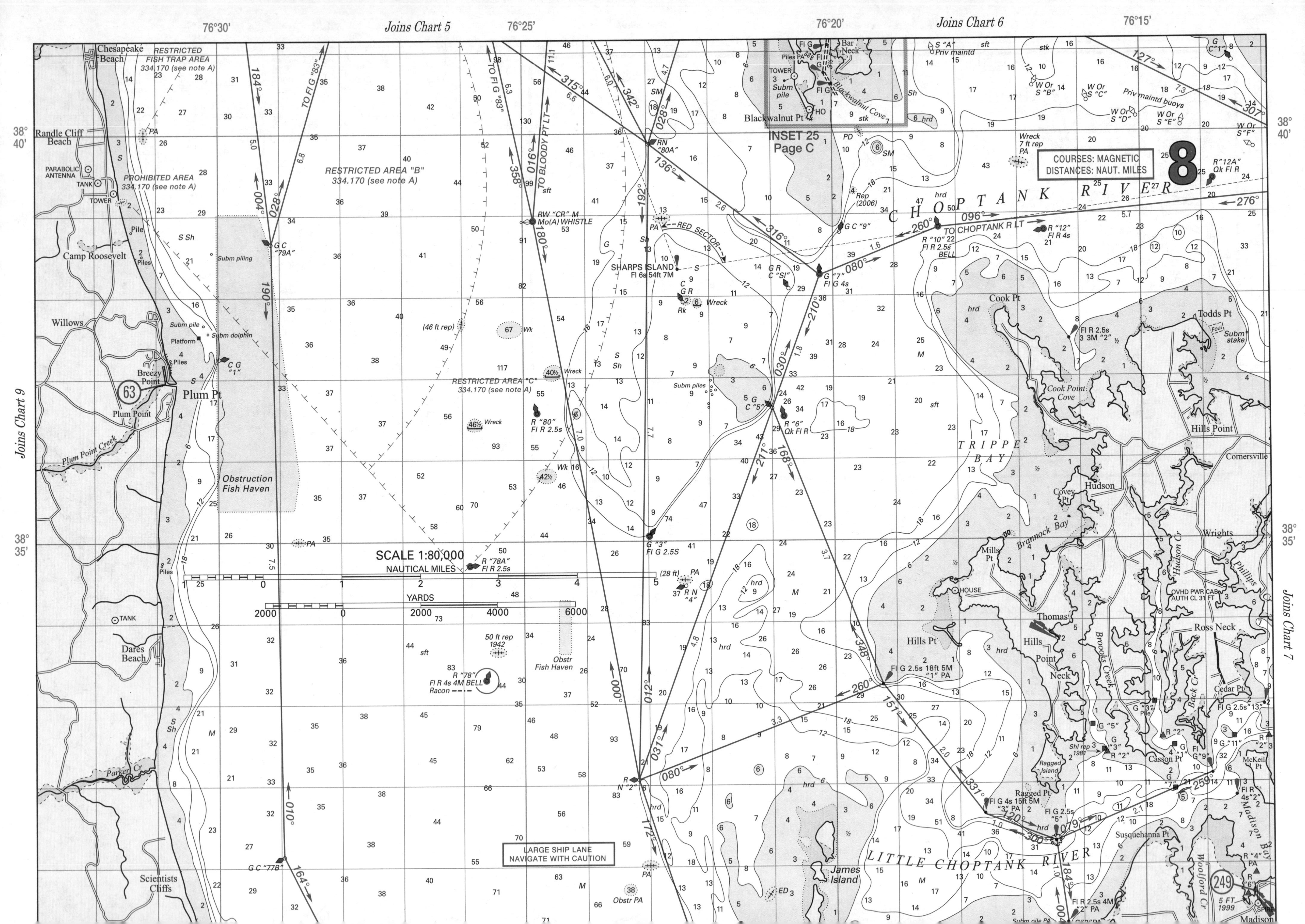

Joins Chart 5
Joins Chart 6
Joins Chart 7
Joins Chart 9
76°30'
76°25'
76°20'
76°15'
38° 40'
38° 35'
8
COURSES: MAGNETIC
DISTANCES: NAUT. MILES
CHOPTANK RIVER
LITTLE CHOPTANK RIVER
TRIPPE BAY
INSET 25
Page C
SCALE 1:80,000
NAUTICAL MILES
YARDS
LARGE SHIP LANE
NAVIGATE WITH CAUTION
RESTRICTED FISH TRAP AREA
334.170 (see note A)
PROHIBITED AREA
334.170 (see note A)
RESTRICTED AREA "B"
334.170 (see note A)
RESTRICTED AREA "C"
334.170 (see note A)
Obstruction
Fish Haven
Obstr
Fish Haven
SHARPS ISLAND
Fl 6s 54ft 7M
RW "CR" M
Mo(A) WHISTLE
R "78"
Fl R 4s 4M BELL
Racon
TO FL G "83"
TO BLOODY PT LT
TO CHOPTANK R LT
RED SECTOR
Chesapeake Beach
Randle Cliff Beach
PARABOLIC ANTENNA
TANK
TOWER
Camp Roosevelt
Willows
Breezy Point
Plum Pt
Plum Point
Plum Point Creek
Dares Beach
Parker Cr
Scientists Cliffs
Blackwalnut Pt
Blackwalnut Cove
Bar Neck
Cook Pt
Cook Point Cove
Todds Pt
Hills Point
Cornersville
Hudson
Covey Pt
Brannock Bay
Mills Pt
Wrights
Hudson Cr
Phillips
Thomas
Hills Point Neck
Hills Pt
Brooks Creek
Ross Neck
Back Cr
Cedar Pt
Casson Pt
McKeil Pt
Ragged Island
Ragged Pt
Susquehanna Pt
Madison Bay
Woolford Cr
Madison
James Island
OVHD PWR CAB
AUTH CL 31 FT

NOTE A
Navigation regulations are published in Chapter 2, U.S. Coast Pilot 3. Additions or revisions to Chapter 2 are Published in the Notice to Mariners. Information concerning the regulations may be obtained at the Office of the Commander, 5th Coast Guard District in Portsmouth, Virginia or at the Office of the District Engineer, Corps of Engineers in Norfolk, Virginia.
Refer to charted regulation section numbers.
NOTE C
Strong currents exist between buoys creating hazardous navigating conditions. USE EXTREME CAUTION.
Caution - Other lighted and unlighted buoys in this area
NOTE
TAR BAY channel has been relocated due to dredging. The aids have been moved to mark best water.
INSET 30 - Chart 9
INSET 31 Chart 9
INSET 32 - Page C
SAFETY ZONE 165.502
Numerous Research Buoys
BRIDGE OPEN 24 HRS
FIXED BRIDGE HOR CL 300 FT VERT CL 140 FT
FIXED BRIDGE HOR CL 30 FT VERT CL 10 FT
FIXED BRIDGE HOR CL 110 FT VERT CL 24 FT
OVHD PWR CAB AUTH CL 38 FT
OVHD PWR CAB AUTH CL 28 FT
USCG STATION
TAYLORS ISLAND
PATUXENT RIVER
TAR BAY
Honga River
Taylors Island
Smithville
Parsons Creek Neck
Hooper Neck
Robinson Neck
Meekins Neck
Golden Hill
Cove Pt
Cove Point Beach
Little Cove Pt
Calvert Beach
Long Beach
Power Plant
Camp Conoy
Lusby
Bertha
Wallville
Hoopers Neck
Coster
Point Patience
Solomons Island
Drum Pt
Sotterly Pt
Sotterly Wharf
Broomes Island
Clarks Wharf
Half Pone Pt
Rocky Pt
Opossum Island
TANK (SE OF FOUR)
VAR 11°00' W(2006) NO ANNUAL CHANGE
MAGNETIC
Joins Chart 9
Joins Chart 10
38° 25'
38° 20'
76°30'
76°25'
76°20'
76°15'

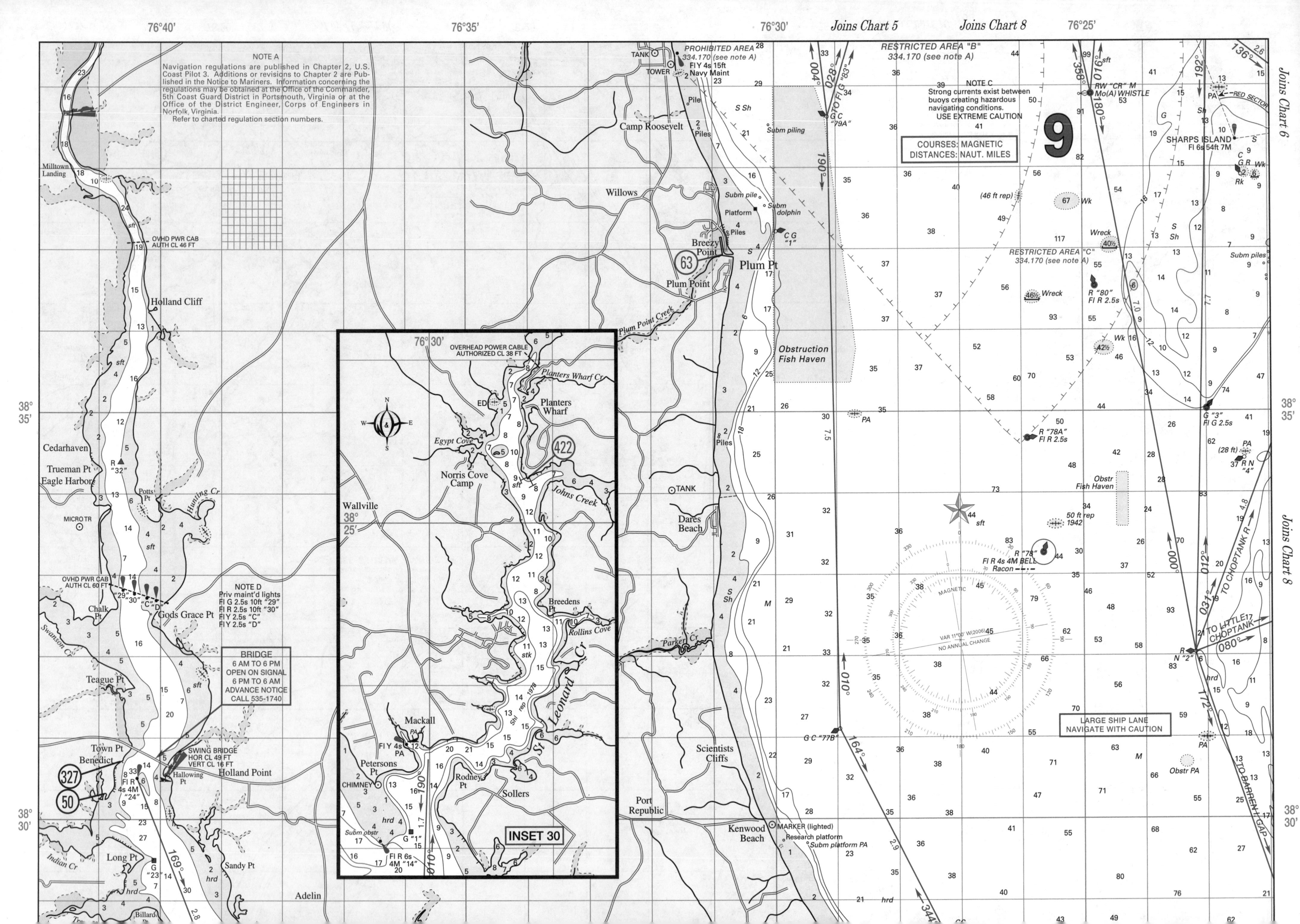Joins Chart 5
Joins Chart 8
Joins Chart 6
Joins Chart 8
9
NOTE A
Navigation regulations are published in Chapter 2, U.S. Coast Pilot 3. Additions or revisions to Chapter 2 are published in the Notice to Mariners. Information concerning the regulations may be obtained at the Office of the Commander, 5th Coast Guard District in Portsmouth, Virginia or at the Office of the District Engineer, Corps of Engineers in Norfolk, Virginia.
Refer to charted regulation section numbers.
NOTE C
Strong currents exist between buoys creating hazardous navigating conditions.
USE EXTREME CAUTION
COURSES: MAGNETIC
DISTANCES: NAUT. MILES
PROHIBITED AREA
334.170 (see note A)
RESTRICTED AREA "B"
334.170 (see note A)
RESTRICTED AREA "C"
334.170 (see note A)
NOTE D
Priv maint'd lights
Fl G 2.5s 10ft "29"
Fl R 2.5s 10ft "30"
Fl Y 2.5s "C"
Fl Y 2.5s "D"
BRIDGE
6 AM TO 6 PM
OPEN ON SIGNAL
6 PM TO 6 AM
ADVANCE NOTICE
CALL 535-1740
SWING BRIDGE
HOR CL 49 FT
VERT CL 16 FT
OVHD PWR CAB
AUTH CL 46 FT
OVHD PWR CAB
AUTH CL 60 FT
LARGE SHIP LANE
NAVIGATE WITH CAUTION
SHARPS ISLAND
Fl 6s 54ft 7M
RW "CR" M
Mo(A) WHISTLE
R "78"
Fl R 4s 4M BELL
Racon
VAR 11°00' W(2006)
NO ANNUAL CHANGE
TO CHOPTANK R
TO LITTLE CHOPTANK
TO BARREN I GAP
Obstruction
Fish Haven
Obstr
Fish Haven
50 ft rep
1942
Camp Roosevelt
Willows
Breezy Point
Plum Pt
Plum Point
Plum Point Creek
Dares Beach
Parker Cr
Scientists Cliffs
Port Republic
Kenwood Beach
MARKER (lighted)
Research platform
Subm platform PA
Holland Cliff
Milltown Landing
Cedarhaven
Trueman Pt
Eagle Harbor
Potts Pt
Hunting Cr
Chalk Pt
Gods Grace Pt
Swanson Cr
Teague Pt
Town Pt
Benedict
Hallowing Pt
Holland Point
Long Pt
Indian Cr
Sandy Pt
Adelin
Billards
INSET 30
OVERHEAD POWER CABLE
AUTHORIZED CL 38 FT
Planters Wharf Cr
Planters Wharf
Egypt Cove
Norris Cove Camp
Johns Creek
Wallville
Breedens Pt
Rollins Cove
St Leonard Cr
Mackall
Petersons Pt
CHIMNEY
Rodney Pt
Sollers
Subm obstr
Fl R 6s 4M "14"
76°40'
76°35'
76°30'
76°25'
38° 35'
38° 30'
38° 25'

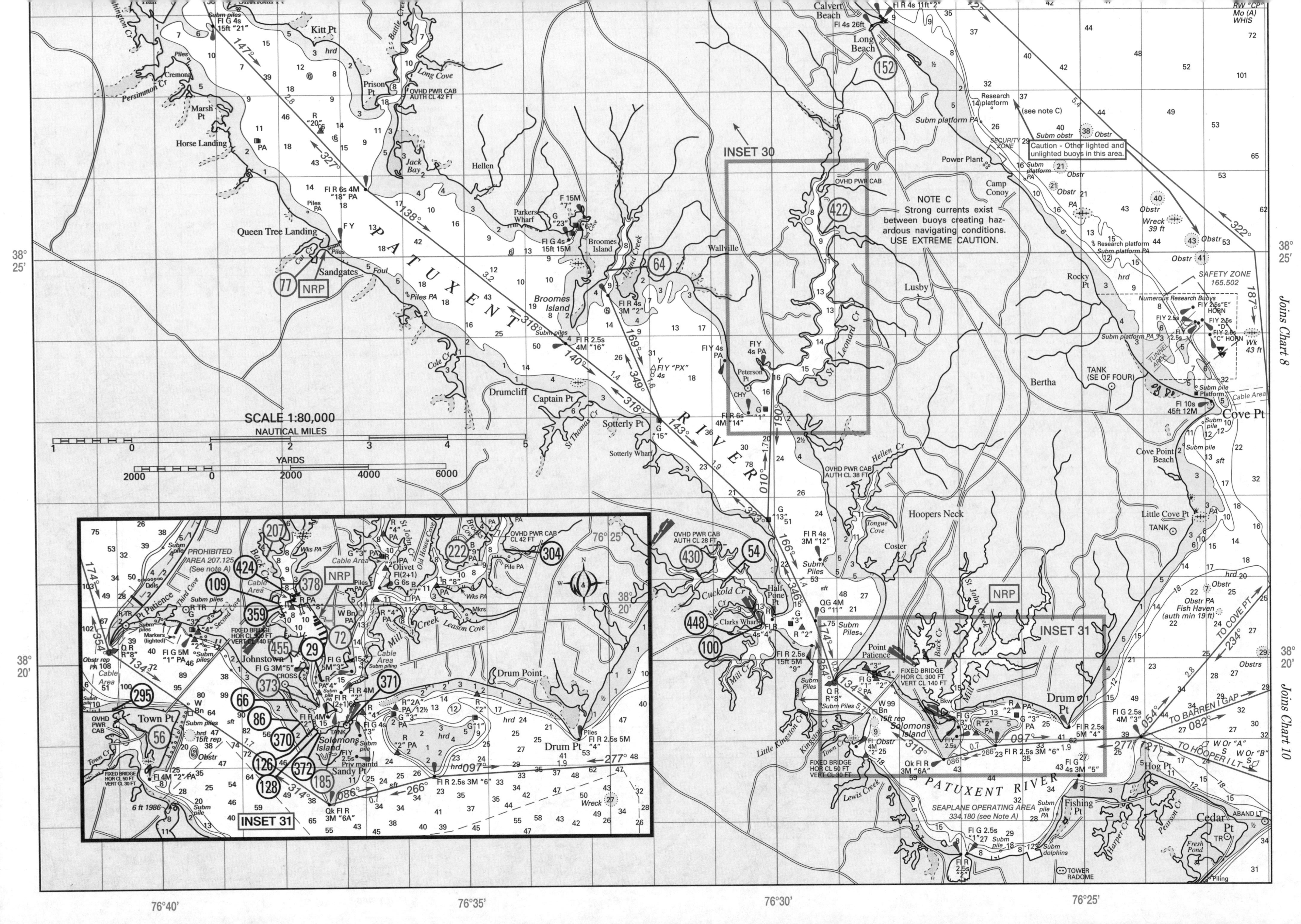

Joins Chart 8
Joins Chart 10
PATUXENT RIVER
INSET 30
INSET 31
SCALE 1:80,000
NAUTICAL MILES
YARDS
NOTE C
Strong currents exist between buoys creating hazardous navigating conditions. USE EXTREME CAUTION.
Caution - Other lighted and unlighted buoys in this area.
SAFETY ZONE 165.502
SEAPLANE OPERATING AREA 334.180 (see Note A)
PROHIBITED AREA 207.125 (See note A)
Cove Pt
Cove Point Beach
Little Cove Pt
Calvert Beach
Long Beach
Lusby
Hoopers Neck
Drum Pt
Solomons Island
Point Patience
Cedar Pt
Hog Pt
Fishing Pt
St John Creek
Mill Cr
Back Cr
Town Cr
Kingston Cr
Little Kingston Cr
Lewis Creek
Cuckold Cr
Clarks Wharf
Half Pone Pt
Peterson Pt
Wallville
Broomes Island
Parkers Wharf
Hellen
Jack Bay
Long Cove
Prison Pt
Kitt Pt
Marsh Pt
Horse Landing
Queen Tree Landing
Sandgates
Drumcliff
Captain Pt
Sotterly Pt
Sotterly Wharf
St Thomas Cr
Cole Cr
Persimmon Cr
Camp Conoy
Power Plant
Bertha
Rocky Pt
Johnstown
Town Pt
Sandy Pt
Drum Point
Leason Cove
Olivet
Hellen Cr
St Leonard Cr
Coster
Tongue Cove

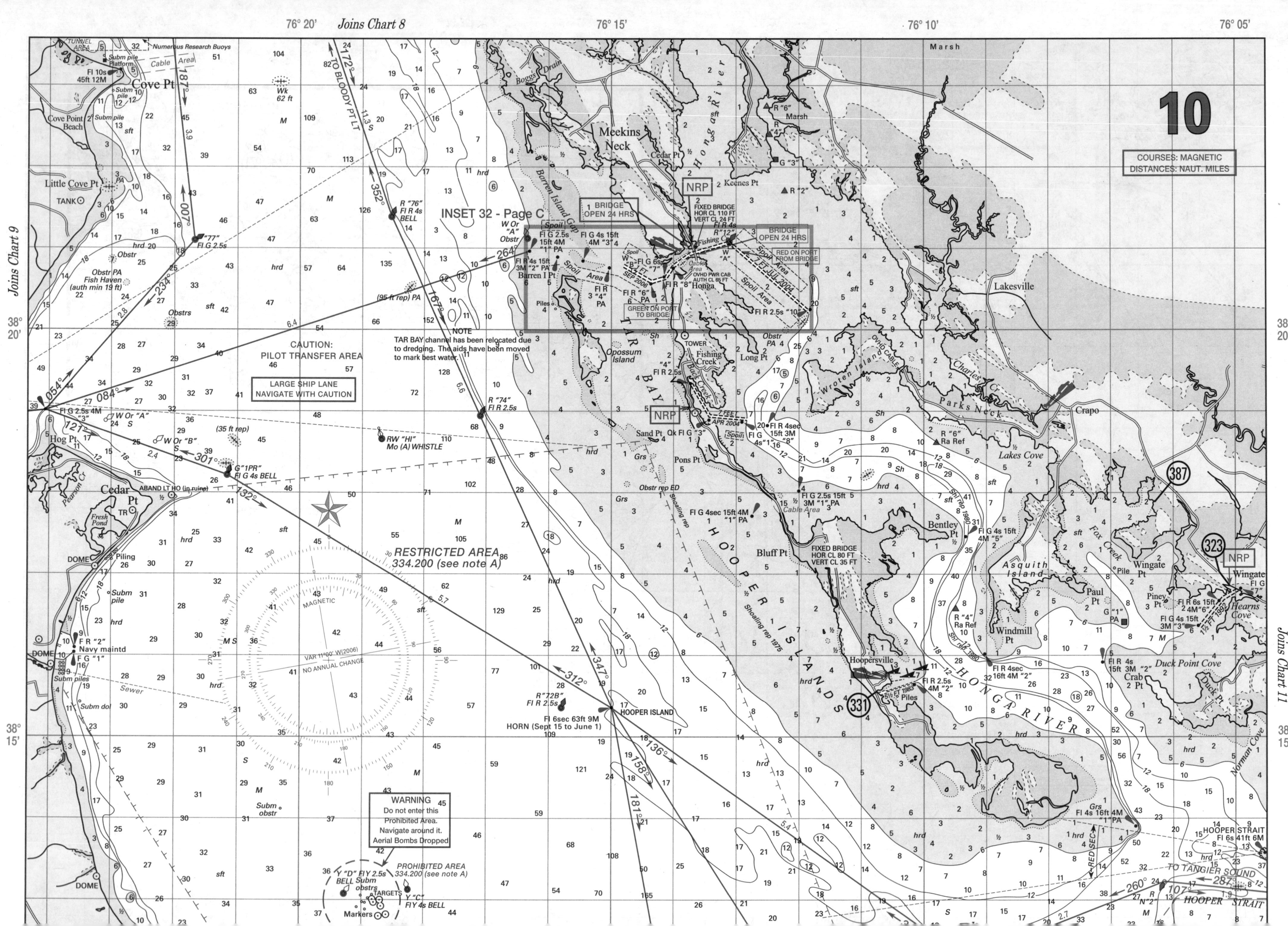

10
COURSES: MAGNETIC
DISTANCES: NAUT. MILES
Joins Chart 8
Joins Chart 9
Joins Chart 11
76° 20'
76° 15'
76° 10'
76° 05'
38° 20'
38° 15'
INSET 32 - Page C
BRIDGE OPEN 24 HRS
FIXED BRIDGE HOR CL 110 FT VERT CL 24 FT
RED ON PORT FROM BRIDGE
GREEN ON PORT TO BRIDGE
FIXED BRIDGE HOR CL 80 FT VERT CL 35 FT
NRP
CAUTION: PILOT TRANSFER AREA
LARGE SHIP LANE NAVIGATE WITH CAUTION
NOTE
TAR BAY channel has been relocated due to dredging. The aids have been moved to mark best water.
RESTRICTED AREA 334.200 (see note A)
PROHIBITED AREA 334.200 (see note A)
WARNING
Do not enter this Prohibited Area. Navigate around it. Aerial Bombs Dropped
VAR 11°00' W(2006) NO ANNUAL CHANGE
MAGNETIC
HOOPER ISLAND
Fl 6sec 63ft 9M HORN (Sept 15 to June 1)
TO BLOODY PT LT
TO TANGIER SOUND
HOOPER STRAIT
Fl 6s 41ft 6M
Cove Pt
Fl 10s 45ft 12M
Little Cove Pt
Cove Point Beach
Obstr PA Fish Haven (auth min 19 ft)
Numerous Research Buoys
Cable Area
Hog Pt
Cedar Pt
ABAND LT HO (in ruins)
Fresh Pond
Pearson Cr
Navy maintd
Sewer
Meekins Neck
Cedar Pt
Keenes Pt
Honga River
Barren Island Gap
Barren I Pt
Boggs Drain
Opossum Island
TAR BAY
Fishing Creek
Back Creek
Long Pt
Sand Pt
Pons Pt
Bluff Pt
HOOPER ISLANDS
Shoaling rep 1975
Hoopersville
HONGA RIVER
Bentley Pt
Wroten Island
Parks Neck
Charles Cr
Lakesville
Crapo
Lakes Cove
Asquith Island
Windmill Pt
Fox Creek
Paul Pt
Wingate Pt
Wingate
Piney Pt
Hearns Cove
Duck Point Cove
Crab Pt
Duck Pt
Norman Cove
Marsh
RW "HI" Mo (A) WHISTLE
G "1PR" Fl G 4s BELL
R "76" Fl R 4s BELL
R "74" Fl R 2.5s
R "72B" Fl R 2.5s
"77" Fl G 2.5s

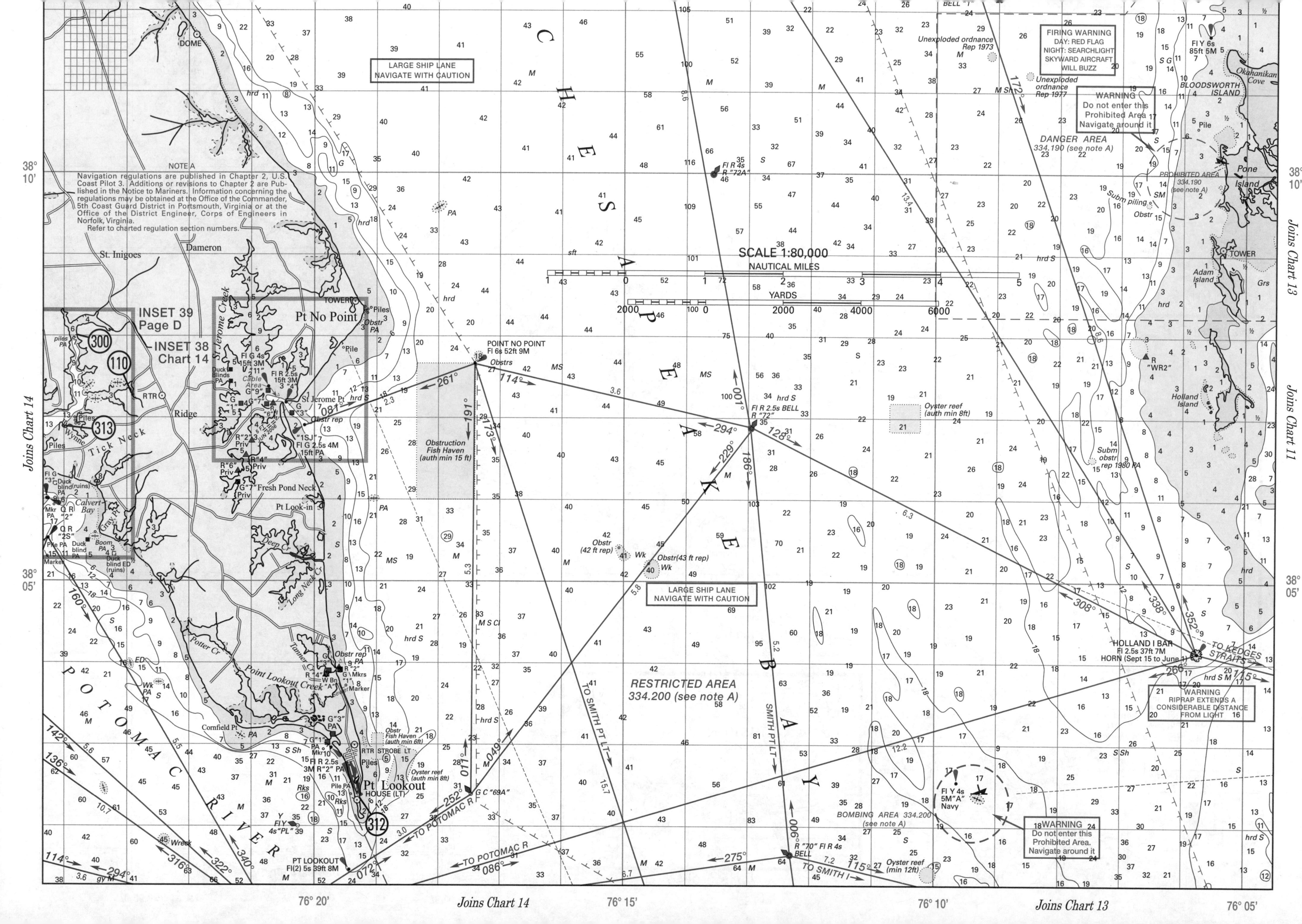

CHESAPEAKE BAY
POTOMAC RIVER
SCALE 1:80,000
NAUTICAL MILES
YARDS
LARGE SHIP LANE NAVIGATE WITH CAUTION
RESTRICTED AREA 334.200 (see note A)
DANGER AREA 334.190 (see note A)
BOMBING AREA 334.200 (see note A)
PROHIBITED AREA 334.190 (see note A)
FIRING WARNING DAY: RED FLAG NIGHT: SEARCHLIGHT SKYWARD AIRCRAFT WILL BUZZ
WARNING Do not enter this Prohibited Area. Navigate around it
WARNING RIPRAP EXTENDS A CONSIDERABLE DISTANCE FROM LIGHT
HOLLAND I BAR Fl 2.5s 37ft 7M HORN (Sept 15 to June 1)
POINT NO POINT Fl 6s 52ft 9M
PT LOOKOUT Fl(2) 5s 39ft 8M
BLOODSWORTH ISLAND
Okahanikan Cove
Pone Island
Adam Island
Holland Island
Pt No Point
Pt Lookout
St Jerome Creek
Point Lookout Creek
Tanner Cr
Long Neck Cr
Deep Cr
Potter Cr
Cornfield Pt
Calvert Bay
Gray Pt
Tick Neck
Wynne
St. Inigoes
Dameron
Ridge
Fresh Pond Neck
Pt Look-in
TO SMITH PT LT
TO POTOMAC R
TO SMITH I
TO KEDGES STRAITS
Obstruction Fish Haven (auth min 15 ft)
Oyster reef (auth min 8ft)
Oyster reef (min 12ft)
Unexploded ordnance Rep 1973
Unexploded ordnance Rep 1977
INSET 38 Chart 14
INSET 39 Page D
NOTE A
Navigation regulations are published in Chapter 2, U.S. Coast Pilot 3. Additions or revisions to Chapter 2 are published in the Notice to Mariners. Information concerning the regulations may be obtained at the Office of the Commander, 5th Coast Guard District in Portsmouth, Virginia or at the Office of the District Engineer, Corps of Engineers in Norfolk, Virginia.
Refer to charted regulation section numbers.
Joins Chart 14
Joins Chart 13
Joins Chart 11

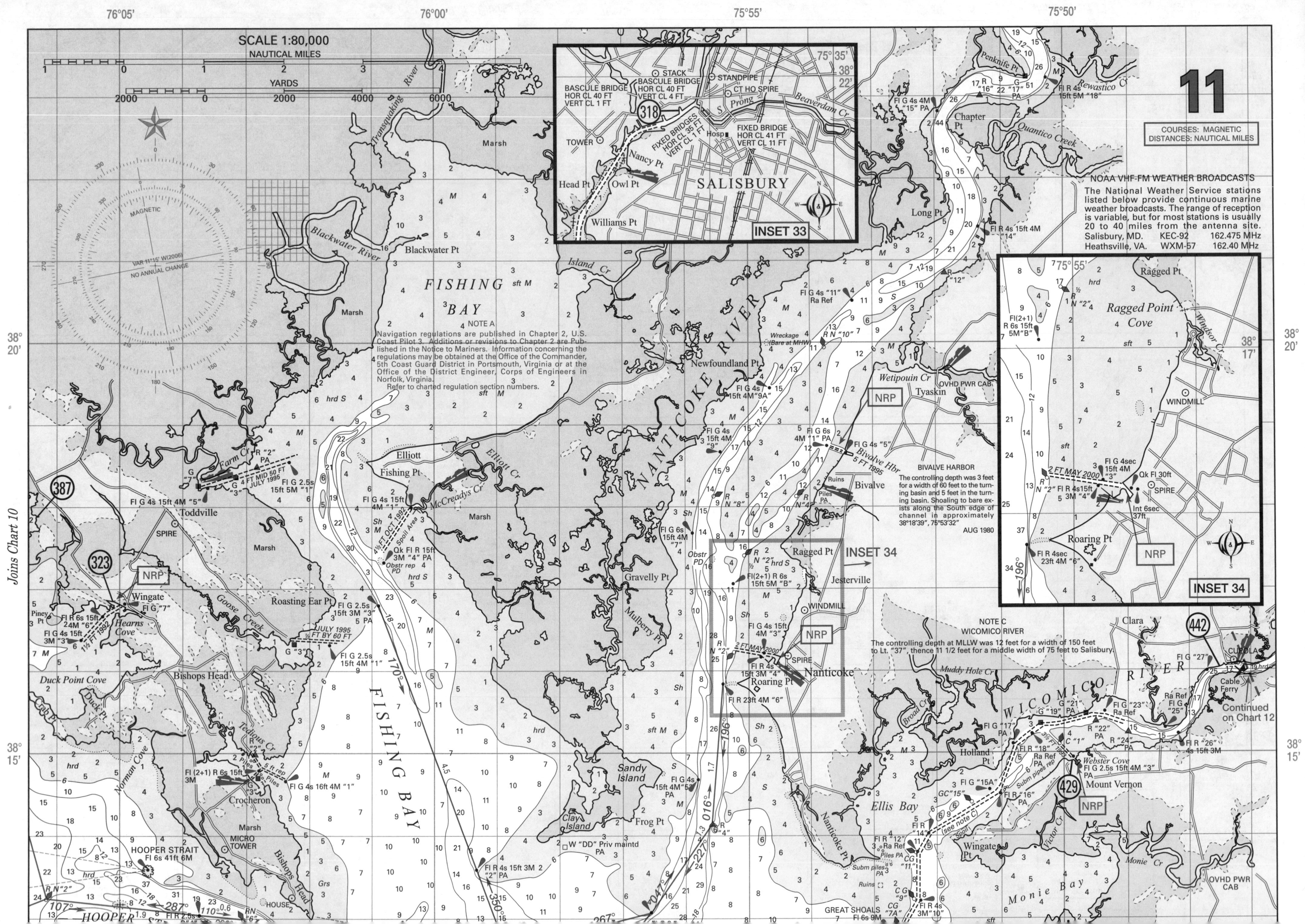
11
SCALE 1:80,000
NAUTICAL MILES
YARDS
COURSES: MAGNETIC
DISTANCES: NAUTICAL MILES
NOAA VHF-FM WEATHER BROADCASTS
The National Weather Service stations listed below provide continuous marine weather broadcasts. The range of reception is variable, but for most stations is usually 20 to 40 miles from the antenna site.
Salisbury, MD. KEC-92 162.475 MHz
Heathsville, VA. WXM-57 162.40 MHz
NOTE A
Navigation regulations are published in Chapter 2, U.S. Coast Pilot 3. Additions or revisions to Chapter 2 are Published in the Notice to Mariners. Information concerning the regulations may be obtained at the Office of the Commander, 5th Coast Guard District in Portsmouth, Virginia or at the Office of the District Engineer, Corps of Engineers in Norfolk, Virginia.
Refer to charted regulation section numbers.
BIVALVE HARBOR
The controlling depth was 3 feet for a width of 60 feet to the turning basin and 5 feet in the turning basin. Shoaling to bare exists along the South edge of channel in approximately 38°18'39", 75°53'32"
AUG 1980
NOTE C
WICOMICO RIVER
The controlling depth at MLLW was 12 feet for a width of 150 feet to Lt. "37", thence 11 1/2 feet for a middle width of 75 feet to Salisbury.
INSET 33
SALISBURY
BASCULE BRIDGE HOR CL 40 FT VERT CL 1 FT
BASCULE BRIDGE HOR CL 40 FT VERT CL 4 FT
FIXED BRIDGES HOR CL 35 FT VERT CL 1 FT
FIXED BRIDGE HOR CL 41 FT VERT CL 11 FT
INSET 34
Ragged Point Cove
Roaring Pt
FISHING BAY
NANTICOKE RIVER
WICOMICO RIVER
Continued on Chart 12
HOOPER STRAIT
Fl 6s 41ft 6M
VAR 11°15' W(2006)
NO ANNUAL CHANGE
MAGNETIC
Joins Chart 10

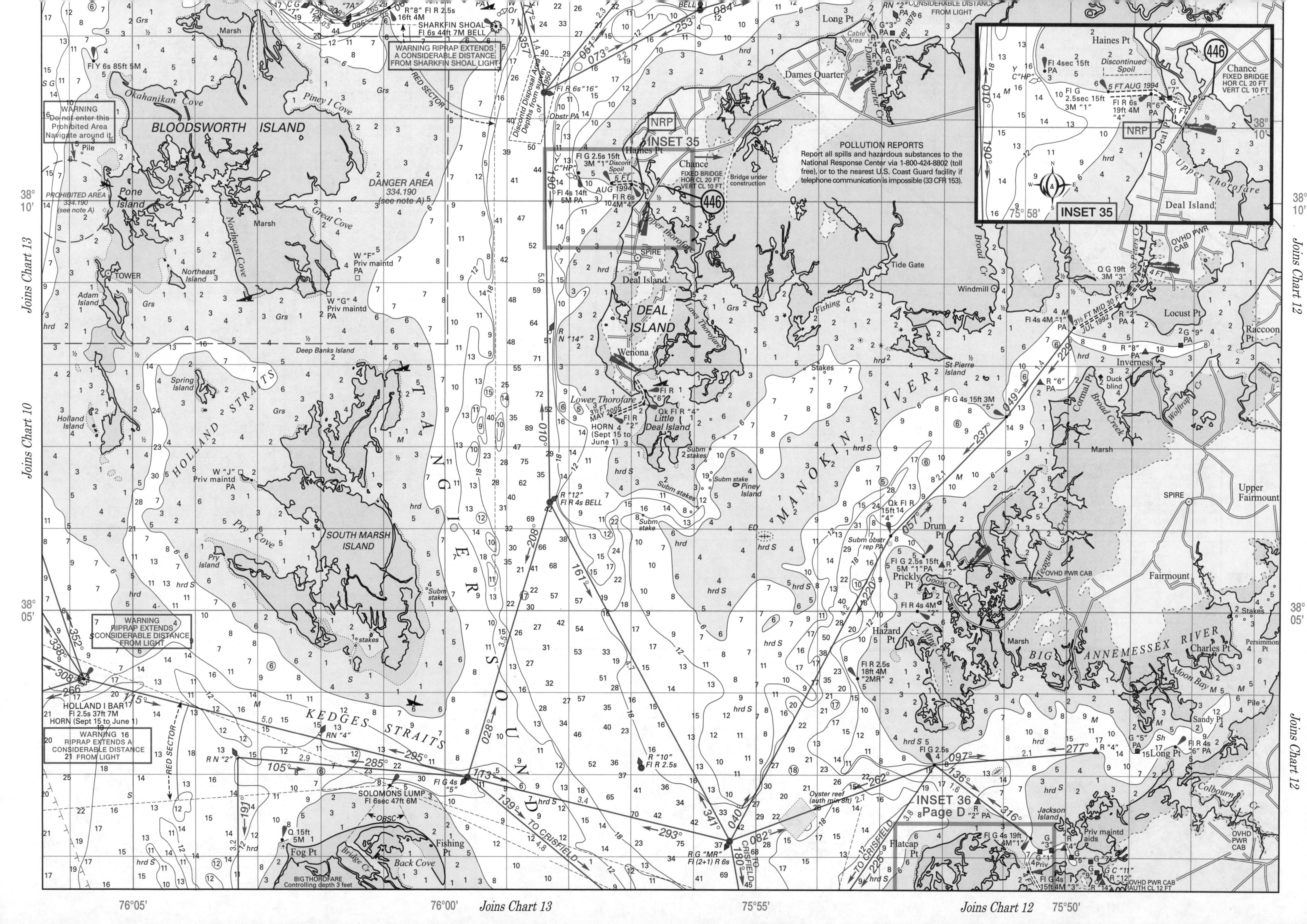
Joins Chart 13
Joins Chart 10
Joins Chart 12
Joins Chart 12
Joins Chart 13
Joins Chart 12
TANGIER SOUND
BLOODSWORTH ISLAND
SOUTH MARSH ISLAND
DEAL ISLAND
MANOKIN RIVER
BIG ANNEMESSEX RIVER
KEDGES STRAITS
HOLLAND STRAITS
INSET 35
INSET 36 Page D
POLLUTION REPORTS
Report all spills and hazardous substances to the National Response Center via 1-800-424-8802 (toll free), or to the nearest U.S. Coast Guard facility if telephone communication is impossible (33 CFR 153).
WARNING Do not enter this Prohibited Area Navigate around it
WARNING RIPRAP EXTENDS A CONSIDERABLE DISTANCE FROM SHARKFIN SHOAL LIGHT
WARNING RIPRAP EXTENDS A CONSIDERABLE DISTANCE FROM LIGHT
WARNING RIPRAP EXTENDS A CONSIDERABLE DISTANCE FROM LIGHT
DANGER AREA 334.190 (see note A)
PROHIBITED AREA 334.190 (see note A)
Chance FIXED BRIDGE HOR CL 20 FT VERT CL 10 FT
BIG THOROFARE Controlling depth 3 feet
TO CRISFIELD

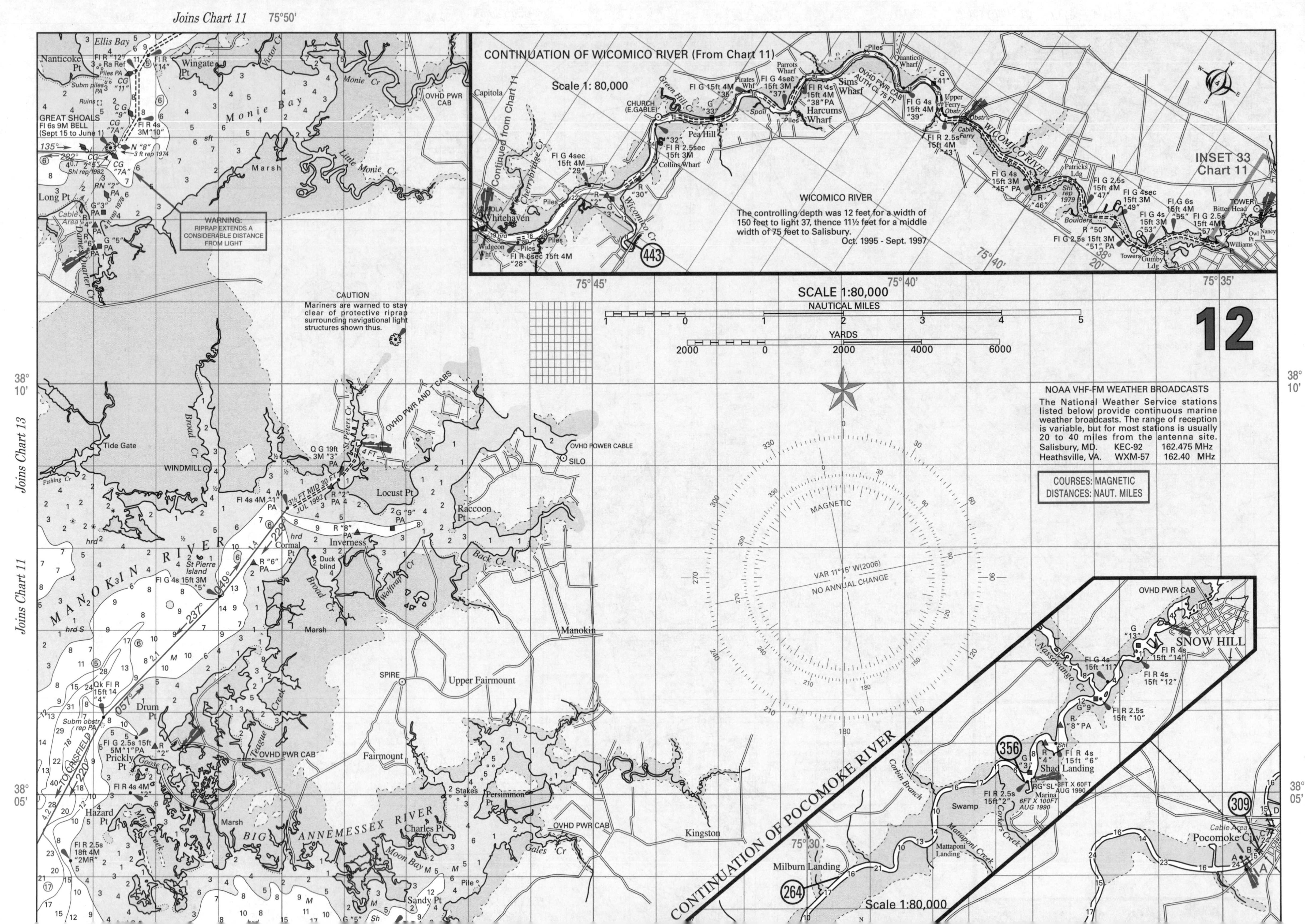

Joins Chart 11
75°50'
12
CONTINUATION OF WICOMICO RIVER (From Chart 11)
Scale 1: 80,000
Continued from Chart 11
INSET 33
Chart 11
WICOMICO RIVER
The controlling depth was 12 feet for a width of 150 feet to light 37, thence 11½ feet for a middle width of 75 feet to Salisbury.
Oct. 1995 - Sept. 1997
CAUTION
Mariners are warned to stay clear of protective riprap surrounding navigational light structures shown thus.
WARNING:
RIPRAP EXTENDS A CONSIDERABLE DISTANCE FROM LIGHT
SCALE 1:80,000
NAUTICAL MILES
YARDS
NOAA VHF-FM WEATHER BROADCASTS
The National Weather Service stations listed below provide continuous marine weather broadcasts. The range of reception is variable, but for most stations is usually 20 to 40 miles from the antenna site.
Salisbury, MD. KEC-92 162.475 MHz
Heathsville, VA. WXM-57 162.40 MHz
COURSES: MAGNETIC
DISTANCES: NAUT. MILES
MAGNETIC
VAR 11°15' W(2006)
NO ANNUAL CHANGE
CONTINUATION OF POCOMOKE RIVER
Scale 1:80,000
Joins Chart 13
Joins Chart 11
GREAT SHOALS
Fl 6s 9M BELL
(Sept 15 to June 1)
MANOKIN RIVER
BIG ANNEMESSEX RIVER
Monie Bay
Little Monie Cr
Nanticoke Pt
Wingate Pt
Long Pt
Dames Quarter Cr
Tide Gate
Broad Cr
St Peters Cr
Locust Pt
Raccoon Pt
Inverness
Back Cr
Manokin
Upper Fairmount
Fairmount
Drum Pt
Prickly Pt
Hazard Pt
Kingston
Persimmon Pt
Charles Pt
Sandy Pt
Gales Cr
SNOW HILL
Shad Landing
Milburn Landing
Pocomoke City
Whitehaven
Sims Wharf
Harcums Wharf
Pea Hill
Patricks Ldg
Quantico Wharf

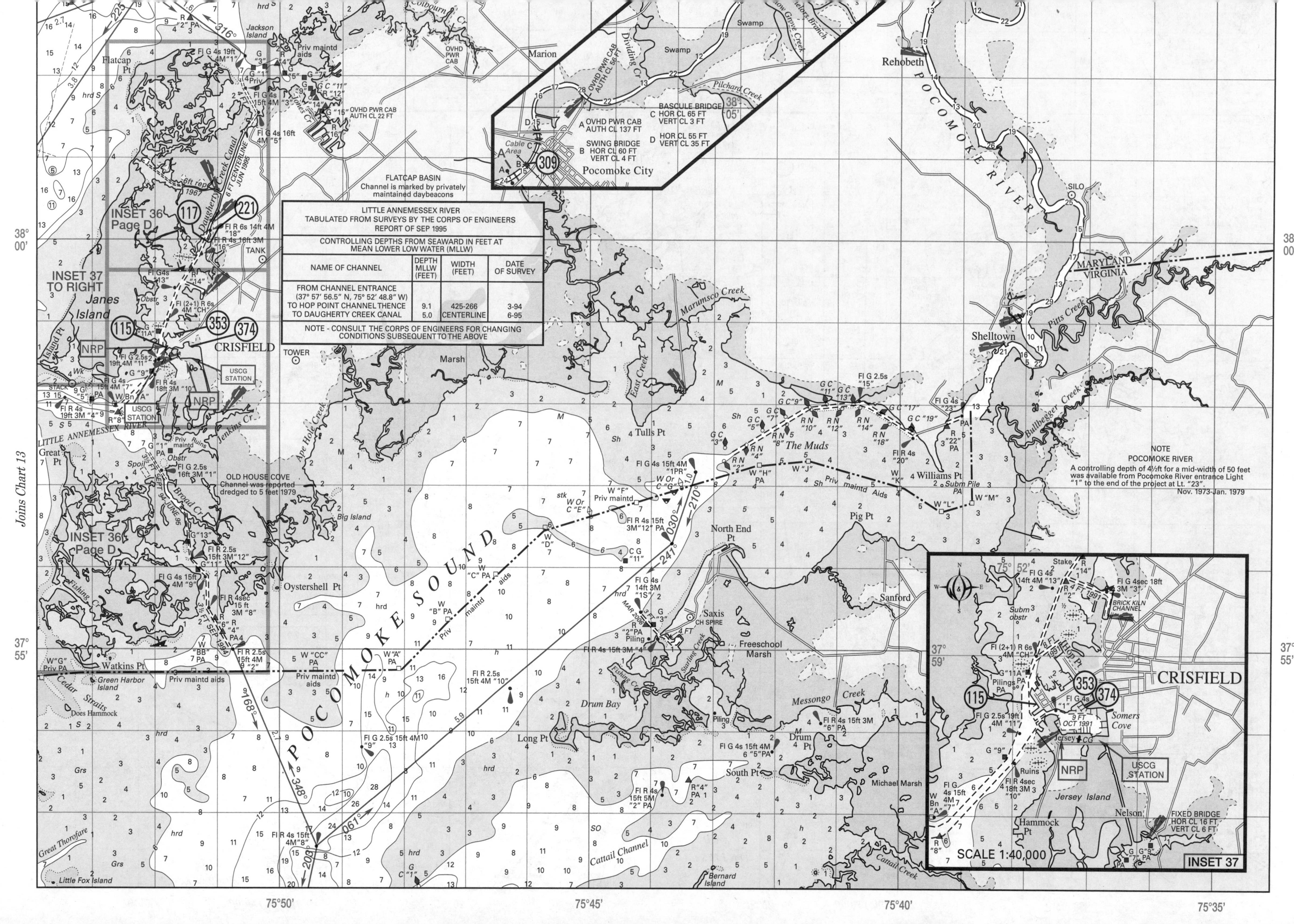


LITTLE ANNEMESSEX RIVER
TABULATED FROM SURVEYS BY THE CORPS OF ENGINEERS
REPORT OF SEP 1995

CONTROLLING DEPTHS FROM SEAWARD IN FEET AT MEAN LOWER LOW WATER (MLLW)

| NAME OF CHANNEL | DEPTH MLLW (FEET) | WIDTH (FEET) | DATE OF SURVEY |
|---|---|---|---|
| FROM CHANNEL ENTRANCE (37° 57′ 56.5″ N, 75° 52′ 48.8″ W) TO HOP POINT CHANNEL THENCE TO DAUGHERTY CREEK CANAL | 9.1<br>5.0 | 425-266<br>CENTERLINE | 3-94<br>6-95 |

NOTE - CONSULT THE CORPS OF ENGINEERS FOR CHANGING CONDITIONS SUBSEQUENT TO THE ABOVE

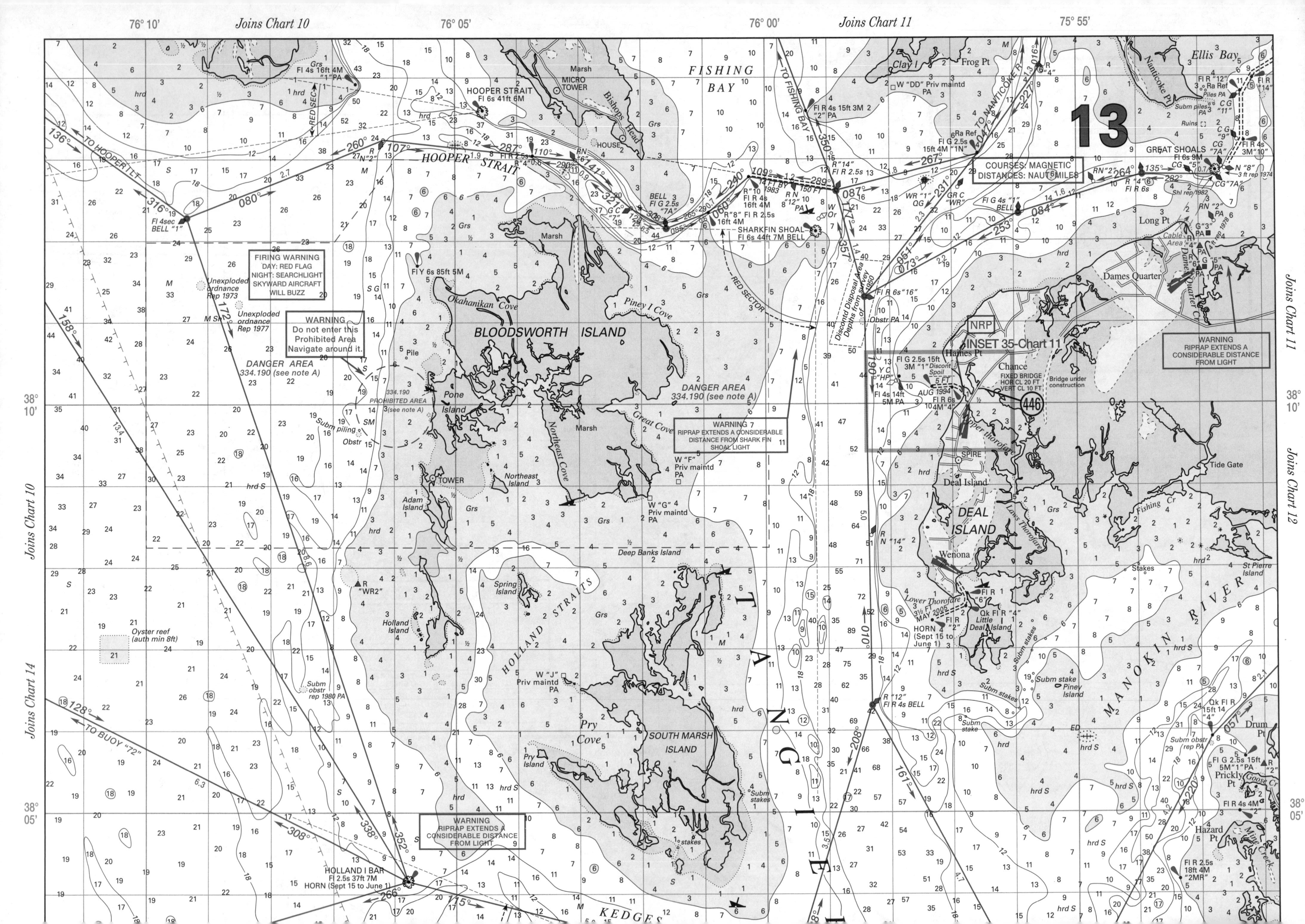

Joins Chart 10
Joins Chart 11
Joins Chart 12
Joins Chart 14
76° 10'
76° 05'
76° 00'
75° 55'
38° 10'
38° 05'
13
COURSES: MAGNETIC
DISTANCES: NAUTICAL MILES
FISHING BAY
HOOPER STRAIT
HOOPER STRAIT
Fl 6s 41ft 6M
MICRO TOWER
Bishops Head
HOUSE
Marsh
GREAT SHOALS
Fl 6s 9M
SHARKFIN SHOAL
Fl 6s 44ft 7M BELL
RED SECTOR
FIRING WARNING
DAY: RED FLAG
NIGHT: SEARCHLIGHT
SKYWARD AIRCRAFT
WILL BUZZ
WARNING
Do not enter this
Prohibited Area
Navigate around it.
DANGER AREA
334.190 (see note A)
PROHIBITED AREA
Unexploded ordnance Rep 1973
Unexploded ordnance Rep 1977
BLOODSWORTH ISLAND
Okahanikan Cove
Piney I Cove
Great Cove
Northeast Cove
Northeast Island
Pone Island
Adam Island
TOWER
WARNING
RIPRAP EXTENDS A CONSIDERABLE DISTANCE FROM SHARK FIN SHOAL LIGHT
Deep Banks Island
Spring Island
HOLLAND STRAITS
Holland Island
Pry Cove
Pry Island
SOUTH MARSH ISLAND
TANGIER
KEDGES
WARNING
RIPRAP EXTENDS A CONSIDERABLE DISTANCE FROM LIGHT
HOLLAND I BAR
Fl 2.5s 37ft 7M
HORN (Sept 15 to June 1)
Oyster reef (auth min 8ft)
TO HOOPER I LT
TO FISHING BAY
TO NANTICOKE R
TO BUOY "72"
Clay I
Frog Pt
Nanticoke Pt
Ellis Bay
Long Pt
Dames Quarter
Dames Quarter Cr
WARNING
RIPRAP EXTENDS A CONSIDERABLE DISTANCE FROM LIGHT
NRP
INSET 35-Chart 11
Haines Pt
Chance
FIXED BRIDGE
HOR CL 20 FT
VERT CL 10 FT
Bridge under construction
Upper thorofare
SPIRE
Deal Island
DEAL ISLAND
Laws Thorofare
Wenona
Lower Thorofare
Little Deal Island
Tide Gate
Fishing Cr
St Pierre Island
MANOKIN RIVER
Piney Island
Drum Pt
Prickly Pt
Goose Cr
Hazard Pt
Mine Creek

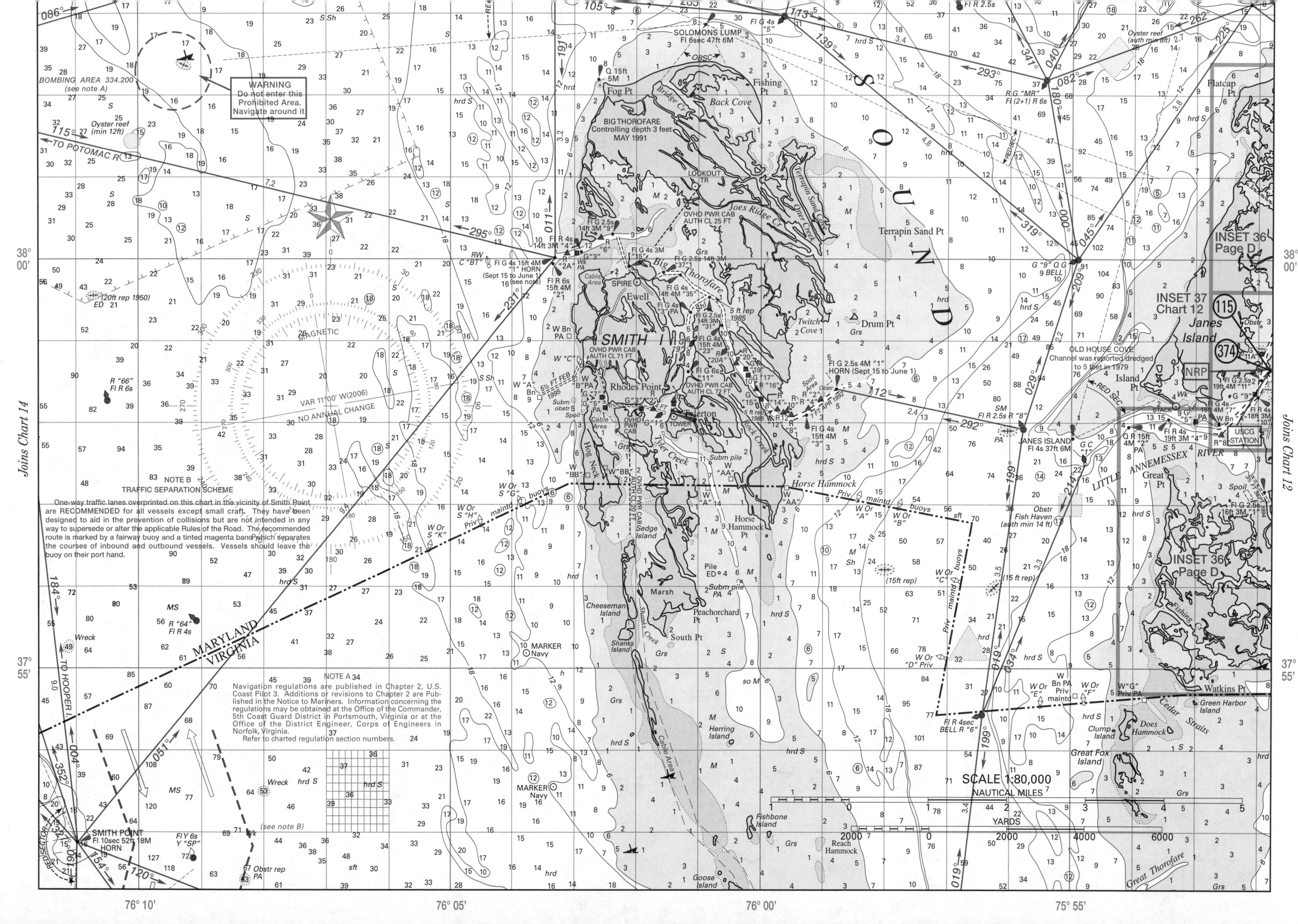
SOUND
SMITH I
Janes Island
INSET 37 Chart 12
INSET 36 Page D
Terrapin Sand Pt
Drum Pt
Fog Pt
Fishing Pt
Back Cove
Bridge Cr
Joes Ridge Cr
Otter Creek
Terrapin Sand Cove
Big Thorofare
Ewell
Rhodes Point
Tylerton
Tyler Creek
Rock Creek
Hog Neck
Horse Hammock
Horse Hammock Pt
Peachorchard Pt
South Pt
Marsh
Shanks Creek
Shanks Island
Cheeseman Island
Sedge Island
Herring Island
Goose Island
Fishbone Island
Reach Hammock
Great Fox Island
Clump Island
Does Hammock
Cedar Straits
Green Harbor Island
Watkins Pt
Great Thorofare
Island Pt
Great Pt
Flatcap Pt
Fishing Cr
LITTLE ANNEMESSEX RIVER
SOLOMONS LUMP Fl 6sec 47ft 6M
BIG THOROFARE Controlling depth 3 feet MAY 1991
OLD HOUSE COVE Channel was reported dredged to 5 feet in 1979
JANES ISLAND Fl 4s 37ft 6M
USCG STATION
Obstr Fish Haven (auth min 14 ft)
MARYLAND
VIRGINIA
TO HOOPER I.
TO POTOMAC R
BOMBING AREA 334.200 (see note A)
Oyster reef (min 12ft)
SMITH POINT Fl 10sec 52ft 18M HORN
MARKER Navy
SCALE 1:80,000
NAUTICAL MILES
YARDS
VAR 11°00'W(2006) NO ANNUAL CHANGE
MAGNETIC
WARNING
Do not enter this Prohibited Area. Navigate around it
NOTE A
Navigation regulations are published in Chapter 2, U.S. Coast Pilot 3. Additions or revisions to Chapter 2 are Published in the Notice to Mariners. Information concerning the regulations may be obtained at the Office of the Commander, 5th Coast Guard District in Portsmouth, Virginia or at the Office of the District Engineer, Corps of Engineers in Norfolk, Virginia.
Refer to charted regulation section numbers.
NOTE B
TRAFFIC SEPARATION SCHEME
One-way traffic lanes overprinted on this chart in the vicinity of Smith Point are RECOMMENDED for all vessels except small craft. They have been designed to aid in the prevention of collisions but are not intended in any way to supersede or alter the applicable Rules of the Road. The recommended route is marked by a fairway buoy and a tinted magenta band which separates the courses of inbound and outbound vessels. Vessels should leave the buoy on their port hand.
38° 00'
37° 55'
76° 10'
76° 05'
76° 00'
75° 55'

14
CHESAPEAKE
COURSES: MAGNETIC
DISTANCES: NAUT. MILES
TO HOOPER I LT
TO HOOPER I. LT
TO HOLLAND I BAR LT
RW "HS"
52 Mo(A) WHISTLE
PROHIBITED AREA
334.200 (see note A)
WARNING
Do not enter this
Prohibited Area.
Navigate around it.
Aerial Bombs Dropped
POINT NO POINT
Fl 6sec 52ft 9M
Obstrs
Obstruction
Fish Haven
(auth min 15 ft)
LARGE SHIP LANE
NAVIGATE WITH CAUTION
RESTRICTED AREA
334.200 (see note A)
Oyster reef
(auth min 8ft)
NOTE A
Navigation regulations are published in Chapter 2, U.S. Coast Pilot 3. Additions or revisions to Chapter 2 are published in the Notice to Mariners. Information concerning the regulations may be obtained at the Office of the Commander, 5th Coast Guard District in Portsmouth, Virginia or at the Office of the District Engineer, Corps of Engineers in Norfolk, Virginia.
Refer to charted regulation section numbers.
OVHD PWR CAB
CL 30 FT
OVHD PWR
CAB REPORTED
Approx 15 ft 1983
INSET 40
BELOW
INSET 39
Page D
INSET 38
BELOW
Pt No Point
St Jerome Creek
St Jerome Pt
Fresh Pond Neck
Pt Look-in
Dameron
Ridge
St. Inigoes
St Inigoes Creek
St Marys City
West St Marys
Pagan Pt
Horseshoe Pt
Short Pt
USCG
STATION
Chancellor Pt
Rose Croft Pt
Priests Pt
Fort Pt
Targets
Smith Creek
Tick Neck
Kitts Pt
Calvert Bay
Gray Pt
Long Neck Cr
Deep Cr
Potter Cr
Tanner Cr
Point Lookout Creek
Park Hall
Martin Cove
Martin
Long Pt
Portobello Pt
Coopers Cr
Windmill Pt
Walnut Pt
Buzzard Pt
Dennis Pt
Josh Pt
Coade Pt
Edmund Pt
Cherryfield Pt
Price Cove
Goose Pt
Russel Pt
Ball Pt
Indigo Pt
Island Cr
ST GEORGE ISLAND
Deep Pt
St George Bar
Drayden
Tippity Wichity Island
Wreck
DOME
TANK
TOWER
NRP
ST MARYS RIVER
ST. MARYS RIVER
76° 25'
76° 20'
76° 15'
76° 10'
38° 10'
38° 05'

Joins Chart 15
Joins Chart 13

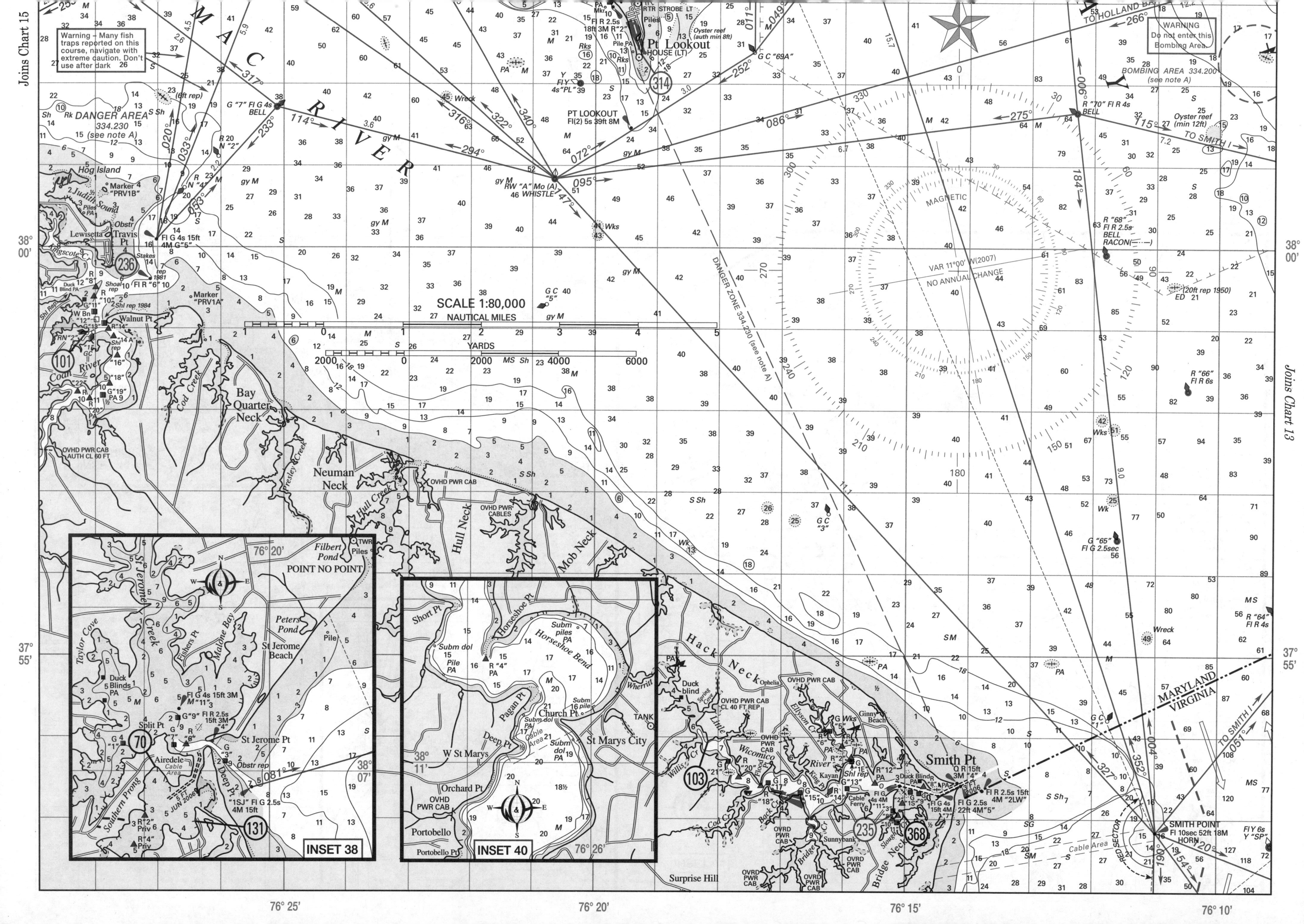

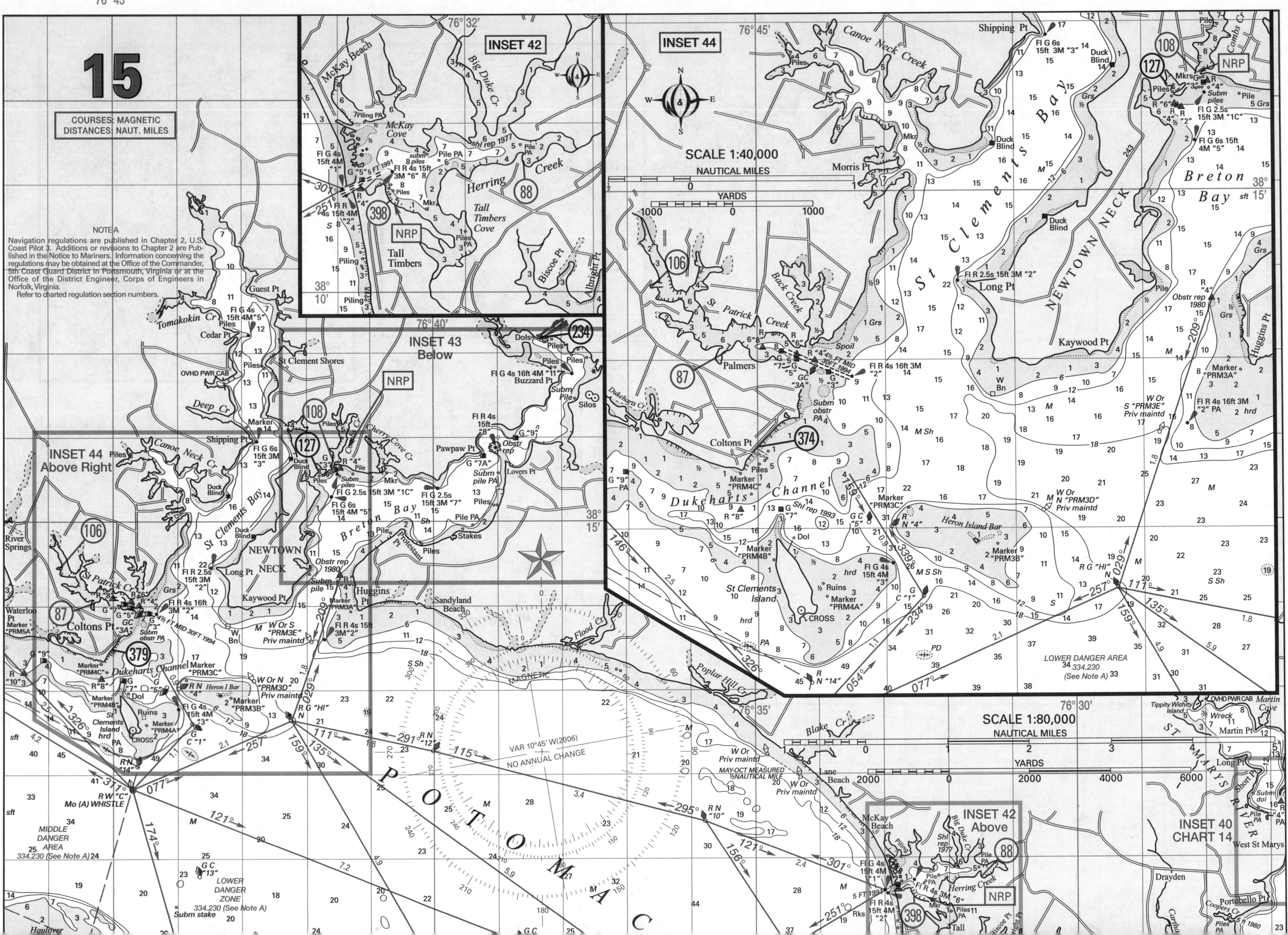
15
COURSES: MAGNETIC
DISTANCES: NAUT. MILES
NOTE A
Navigation regulations are published in Chapter 2, U.S. Coast Pilot 3. Additions or revisions to Chapter 2 are published in the Notice to Mariners. Information concerning the regulations may be obtained at the Office of the Commander, 5th Coast Guard District in Portsmouth, Virginia or at the Office of the District Engineer, Corps of Engineers in Norfolk, Virginia.
Refer to charted regulation section numbers.
Joins Chart 16
Joins Chart 14
INSET 42
INSET 43
Below
INSET 44
INSET 44
Above Right
INSET 42
Above
INSET 40
CHART 14
SCALE 1:40,000
NAUTICAL MILES
YARDS
SCALE 1:80,000
NAUTICAL MILES
YARDS
VAR 10°45' W(2006)
NO ANNUAL CHANGE
MAGNETIC
P O T O M A C
St Clements Bay
Breton Bay
NEWTOWN NECK
Dukeharts Channel
St Clements Island
Heron Island Bar
St Patrick Creek
Canoe Neck Creek
Herring Creek
Big Duke Cr
Tall Timbers Cove
Tall Timbers
McKay Beach
McKay Cove
Biscoe Pt
Albright Pt
Tomakokin Cr
Cedar Pt
Guest Pt
St Clement Shores
Deep Cr
Shipping Pt
Long Pt
Kaywood Pt
Coltons Pt
Morris Pt
Palmers
Back Creek
Dukeharts Cr
Huggins Pt
Protestant Pt
Pawpaw Pt
Lovers Pt
Buzzard Pt
Dols
Silos
Sandyland Beach
Flood Cr
Poplar Hill Cr
Blake Cr
Lane Beach
Waterloo Pt
River Springs
Haulover
ST MARYS RIVER
Martin Pt
Martin Cove
Tippity Wichity Island
Wreck
Short Pt
West St Marys
Drayden
Portobello Pt
Coopers Cr
LOWER DANGER AREA
334.230 (See Note A)
MIDDLE DANGER AREA
334.230 (See Note A)
LOWER DANGER ZONE
334.230 (See Note A)
Mo (A) WHISTLE
MAY-OCT MEASURED ½ NAUTICAL MILE
OVHD PWR CAB
NRP

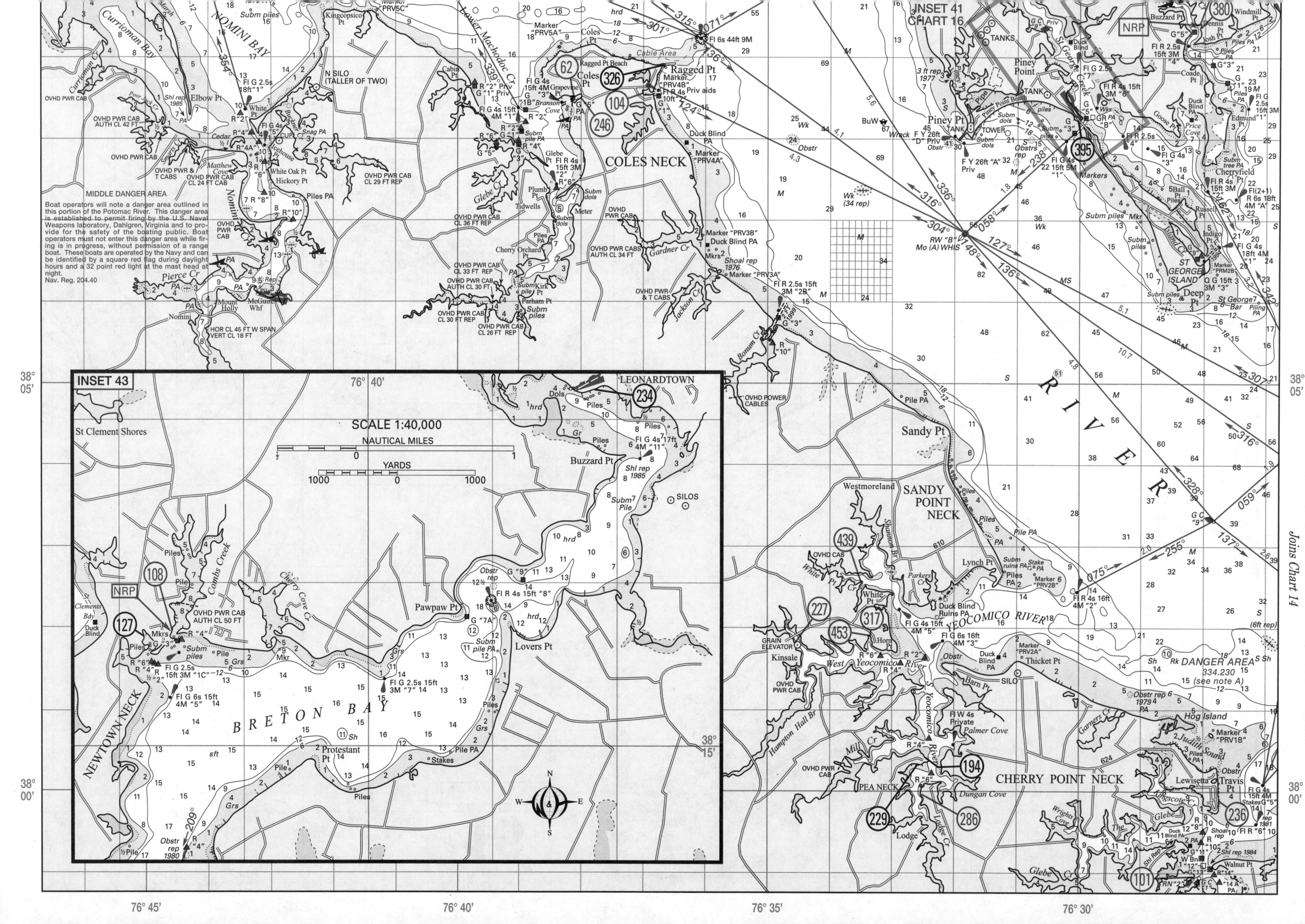

Joins Chart 14
INSET 41 CHART 16
INSET 43
SCALE 1:40,000
NAUTICAL MILES
YARDS
MIDDLE DANGER AREA
Boat operators will note a danger area outlined in this portion of the Potomac River. This danger area is established to permit firing by the U.S. Naval Weapons laboratory, Dahlgren, Virginia and to provide for the safety of the boating public. Boat operators must not enter this danger area while firing is in progress, without permission of a range boat. These boats are operated by the Navy and can be identified by a square red flag during daylight hours and a 32 point red light at the mast head at night.
Nav. Reg. 204.40
RIVER
NOMINI BAY
Curritoman Bay
Elbow Pt
White Pt
Kingcopsico Pt
N SILO (TALLER OF TWO)
Lower Machodoc Cr
Cabin Pt
Coles Pt
Ragged Pt Beach
Ragged Pt
COLES NECK
Glebe Cr
Cherry Orchard Pt
Tidwells
Plumb Pt
Meter
Gardner Cr
Jackson Cr
Bonum Cr
Nomini Cr
Pierce Cr
Mount Holly
McGuires Whf
Nomini
Hickory Pt
White Oak Pt
Matthew Cove
Cedar Pt
Piney Point
Piney Pt
TANKS
TOWER
St George Creek
ST GEORGE ISLAND
Deep Pt
St George Bar
Cherryfield Pt
Russell Pt
Indigo Pt
Price Cove
Goose Pt
Coade Pt
Dennis Pt
Josh Pt
Buzzard Pt
Windmill Pt
Sandy Pt
SANDY POINT NECK
Westmoreland
Shannon Br
Parkers Cr
White Pt Cr
White Pt
Lynch Pt
YEOCOMICO RIVER
West Yeocomico River
S Yeocomico River
Horn Pt
Kinsale
GRAIN ELEVATOR
Hampton Hall Br
Mill Cr
PEA NECK
Lodge
Lodge Cr
Dungan Cove
Palmer Cove
Barn Pt
Thicket Pt
SILO
CHERRY POINT NECK
Garners Cr
Hog Island
Judith Sound
Lewisetta
Travis Pt
Kingscote Cr
Glebe
Wrights Cove
Glebe Cr
Walnut Pt
DANGER AREA 334.230 (see note A)
LEONARDTOWN
Buzzard Pt
SILOS
Lovers Pt
Pawpaw Pt
Cherry Cove Cr
Combs Creek
St Clement Shores
St Clements Bay
NEWTOWN NECK
BRETON BAY
Protestant Pt
Stakes
76° 45'
76° 40'
76° 35'
76° 30'
38° 05'
38° 00'
38° 15'

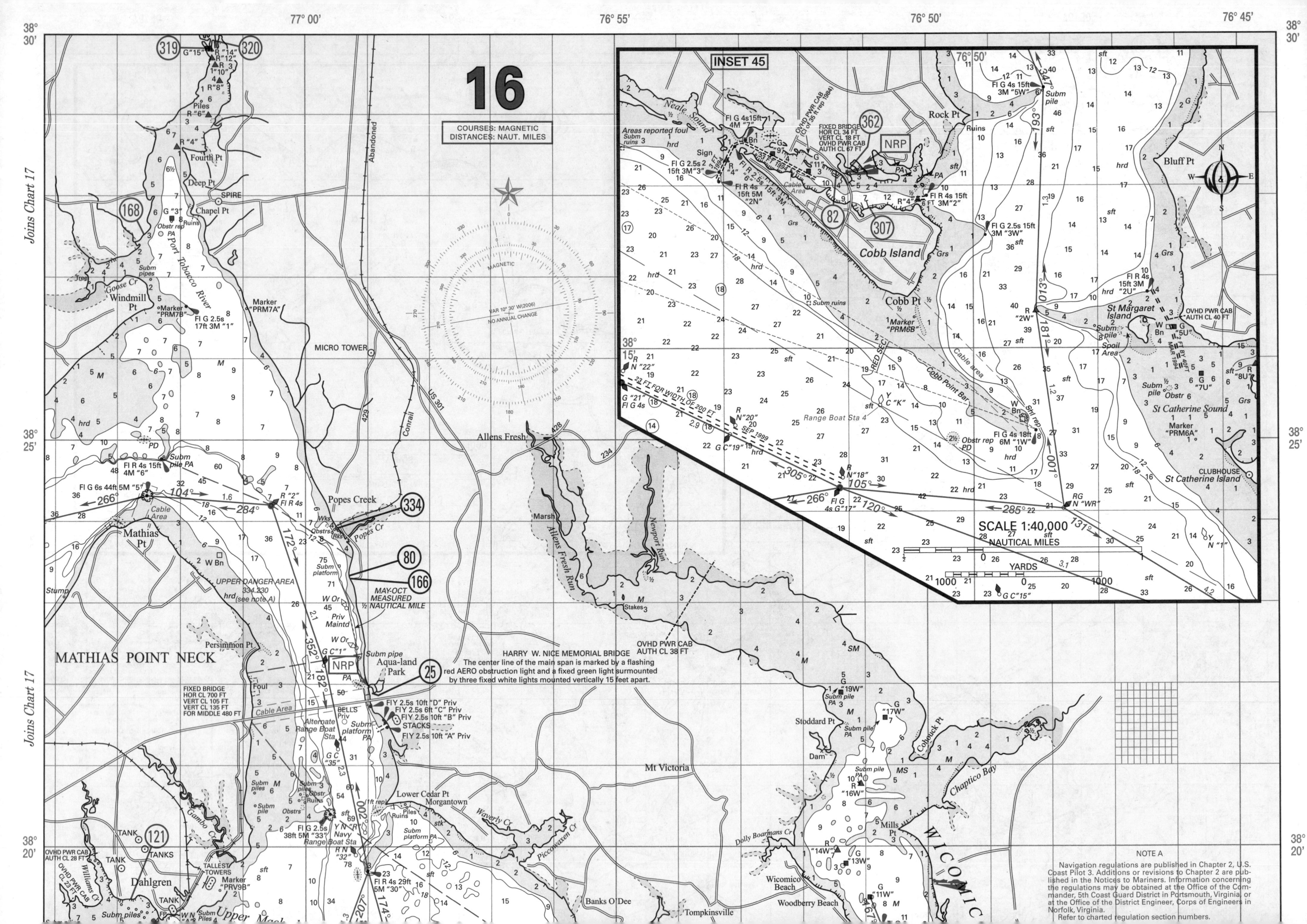

16
COURSES: MAGNETIC
DISTANCES: NAUT. MILES
INSET 45
SCALE 1:40,000
NAUTICAL MILES
YARDS
Joins Chart 17
Joins Chart 17
77° 00'
76° 55'
76° 50'
76° 45'
Port Tobacco River
Chapel Pt
Deep Pt
Fourth Pt
Windmill Pt
Goose Cr
Mathias Pt
MATHIAS POINT NECK
Persimmon Pt
Popes Creek
Popes Cr
Allens Fresh
Allens Fresh Run
Newport Run
MICRO TOWER
SPIRE
Marsh
US 301
Conrail
Abandoned
Aqua-land Park
Dahlgren
Gambo Cr
Williams Cr
Upper Machodoc
Mt Victoria
Lower Cedar Pt
Morgantown
Waverly Cr
Piccowaxen Cr
Banks O'Dee
Tompkinsville
Stoddard Pt
Cobrook Pt
Chaptico Bay
Mills Pt
Wicomico Beach
Woodberry Beach
Dolly Boarmans Cr
WICOMIC
Neale Sound
Cobb Island
Cobb Pt
Cobb Point Bar
Rock Pt
Bluff Pt
St Margaret Island
St Catherine Sound
St Catherine Island
CLUBHOUSE
Range Boat Sta 4
Areas reported foul
UPPER DANGER AREA 334.230
MAY-OCT MEASURED ½ NAUTICAL MILE
FIXED BRIDGE HOR CL 700 FT VERT CL 105 FT VERT CL 135 FT FOR MIDDLE 480 FT
FIXED BRIDGE HOR CL 34 FT VERT CL 18 FT OVHD PWR CAB AUTH CL 67 FT
OVHD PWR CAB AUTH CL 38 FT
OVHD PWR CAB AUTH CL 40 FT
HARRY W. NICE MEMORIAL BRIDGE
The center line of the main span is marked by a flashing red AERO obstruction light and a fixed green light surmounted by three fixed white lights mounted vertically 15 feet apart.
VAR 10° 30' W(2006)
NO ANNUAL CHANGE
NOTE A
Navigation regulations are published in Chapter 2, U.S. Coast Pilot 3. Additions or revisions to Chapter 2 are published in the Notices to Mariners. Information concerning the regulations may be obtained at the Office of the Commander, 5th Coast Guard District in Portsmouth, Virginia, or at the Office of the District Engineer, Corps of Engineers in Norfolk, Virginia.
Refer to charted regulation section numbers.

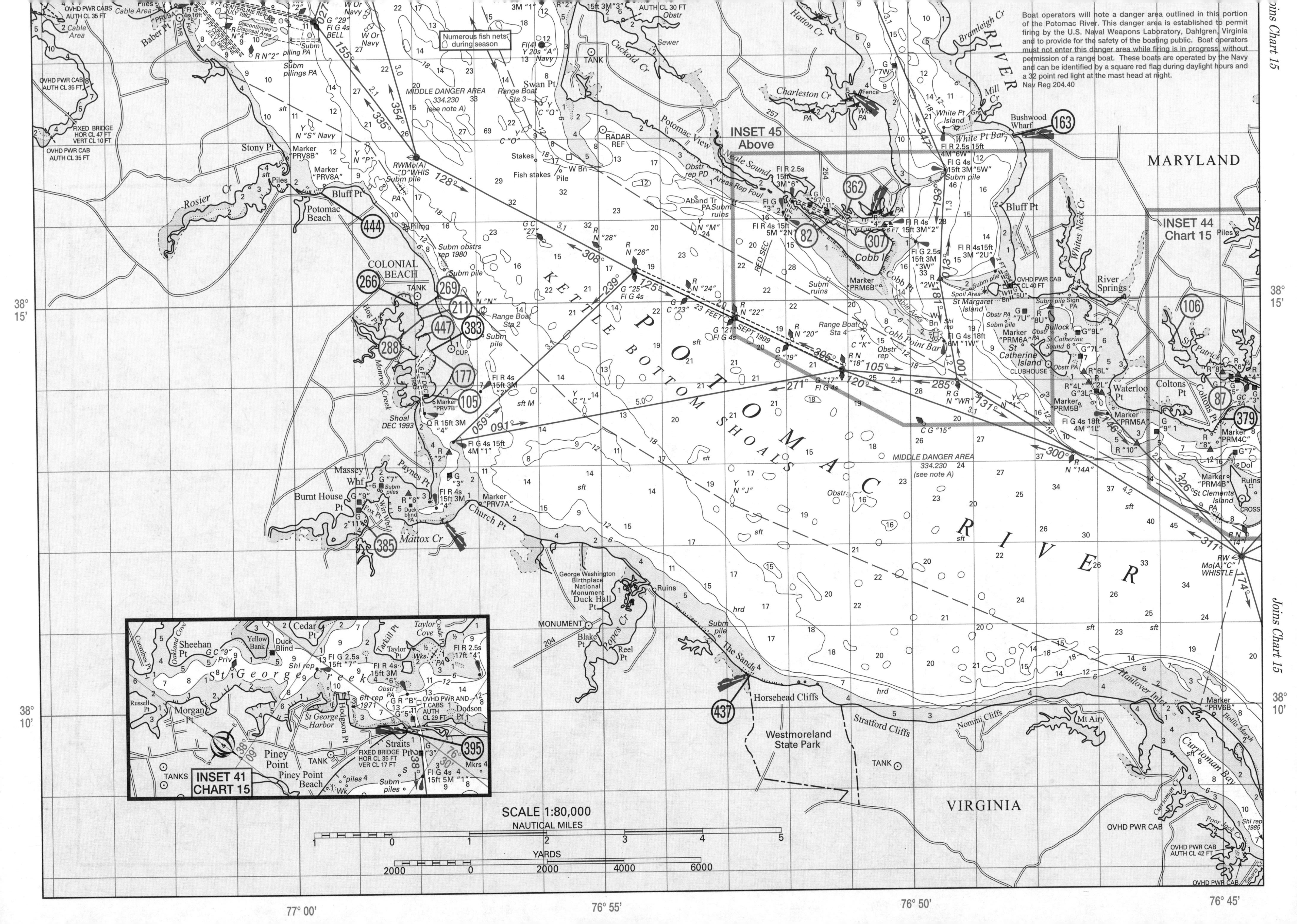

Joins Chart 15
Boat operators will note a danger area outlined in this portion of the Potomac River. This danger area is established to permit firing by the U.S. Naval Weapons Laboratory, Dahlgren, Virginia and to provide for the safety of the boating public. Boat operators must not enter this danger area while firing is in progress without permission of a range boat. These boats are operated by the Navy and can be identified by a square red flag during daylight hours and a 32 point red light at the mast head at night.
Nav Reg 204.40
MARYLAND
VIRGINIA
POTOMAC RIVER
KETTLE BOTTOM SHOALS
INSET 45
Above
INSET 44
Chart 15
INSET 41
CHART 15
MIDDLE DANGER AREA
334.230
(see note A)
Numerous fish nets during season
Stony Pt
Rosier Cr
Bluff Pt
Potomac Beach
COLONIAL BEACH
Monroe Creek
Swan Pt
Cuckold Cr
Potomac View
Neale Sound
Cobb I
Cobb Pt
Cobb Point Bar
Charleston Cr
Hatton Cr
White Pt Island
White Pt Bar
Bushwood Wharf
Bramleigh Cr
Mill Cr
Whites Neck Cr
River Springs
St Margaret Island
St Catherine Island
St Catherine Sound
Bullock I
Waterloo Pt
Coltons Pt
St Clements Island
St Patrick Cr
Massey Whf
Burnt House Pt
Paynes Pt
Church Pt
Mattox Cr
George Washington Birthplace National Monument
Duck Hall Pt
Blake Pt
Popes Cr
Reel Pt
The Sands
Horsehead Cliffs
Westmoreland State Park
Stratford Cliffs
Nomini Cliffs
Mt Airy
Haulover Inlet
Currioman Bay
Currioman Cr
Poor Jack Cr
Hollis Marsh
St George Creek
Sheehan Pt
Oakland Cove
Yellow Bank
Duck Blind
Cedar Pt
Tarkill Pt
Taylor Pt
Taylor Cove
Coade Pt
Morgan Pt
Russell Pt
Coombes Pt
St George Harbor
Hodgson Pt
Dodson Pt
Straits Pt
Piney Point
Piney Point Beach
FIXED BRIDGE HOR CL 47 FT VERT CL 10 FT
FIXED BRIDGE HOR CL 35 FT VER CL 17 FT
OVHD PWR CAB AUTH CL 35 FT
OVHD PWR CAB AUTH CL 42 FT
OVHD PWR CAB CL 40 FT
SCALE 1:80,000
NAUTICAL MILES
YARDS
38° 15'
38° 10'
77° 00'
76° 55'
76° 50'
76° 45'

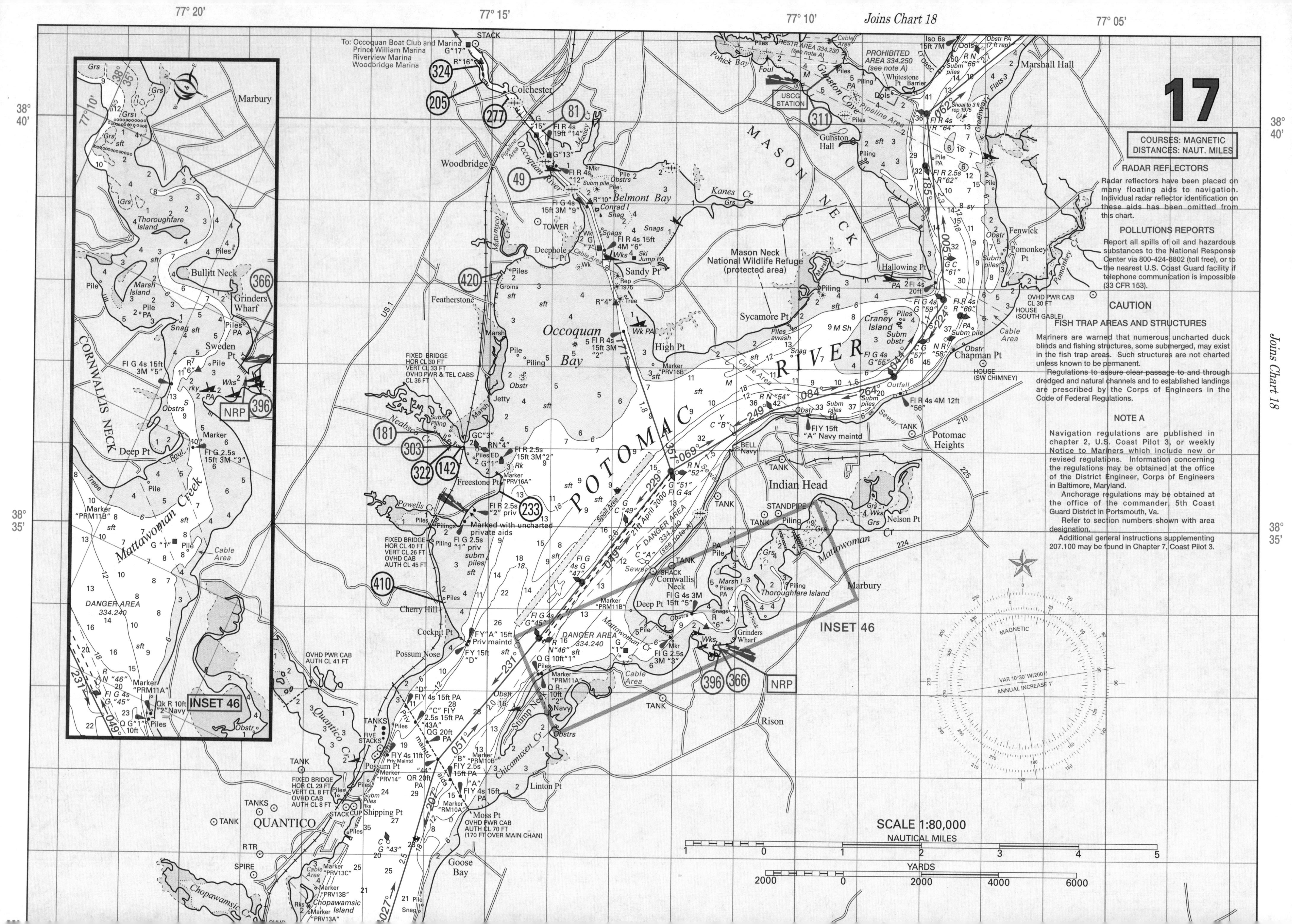

17
Joins Chart 18
COURSES: MAGNETIC
DISTANCES: NAUT. MILES
RADAR REFLECTORS
Radar reflectors have been placed on many floating aids to navigation. Individual radar reflector identification on these aids has been omitted from this chart.
POLLUTIONS REPORTS
Report all spills of oil and hazardous substances to the National Response Center via 800-424-8802 (toll free), or to the nearest U.S. Coast Guard facility if telephone communication is impossible (33 CFR 153).
CAUTION
FISH TRAP AREAS AND STRUCTURES
Mariners are warned that numerous uncharted duck blinds and fishing structures, some submerged, may exist in the fish trap areas. Such structures are not charted unless known to be permanent.
Regulations to assure clear passage to and through dredged and natural channels and to established landings are prescribed by the Corps of Engineers in the Code of Federal Regulations.
NOTE A
Navigation regulations are published in chapter 2, U.S. Coast Pilot 3, or weekly Notice to Mariners which include new or revised regulations. Information concerning the regulations may be obtained at the office of the District Engineer, Corps of Engineers in Baltimore, Maryland.
Anchorage regulations may be obtained at the office of the commander, 5th Coast Guard District in Portsmouth, Va.
Refer to section numbers shown with area designation.
Additional general instructions supplementing 207.100 may be found in Chapter 7, Coast Pilot 3.
To: Occoquan Boat Club and Marina
Prince William Marina
Riverview Marina
Woodbridge Marina
POTOMAC RIVER
MASON NECK
Mason Neck
National Wildlife Refuge
(protected area)
Occoquan Bay
Belmont Bay
Gunston Cove
Marshall Hall
Indian Head
Mattawoman Cr
Quantico
INSET 46
SCALE 1:80,000
NAUTICAL MILES
YARDS

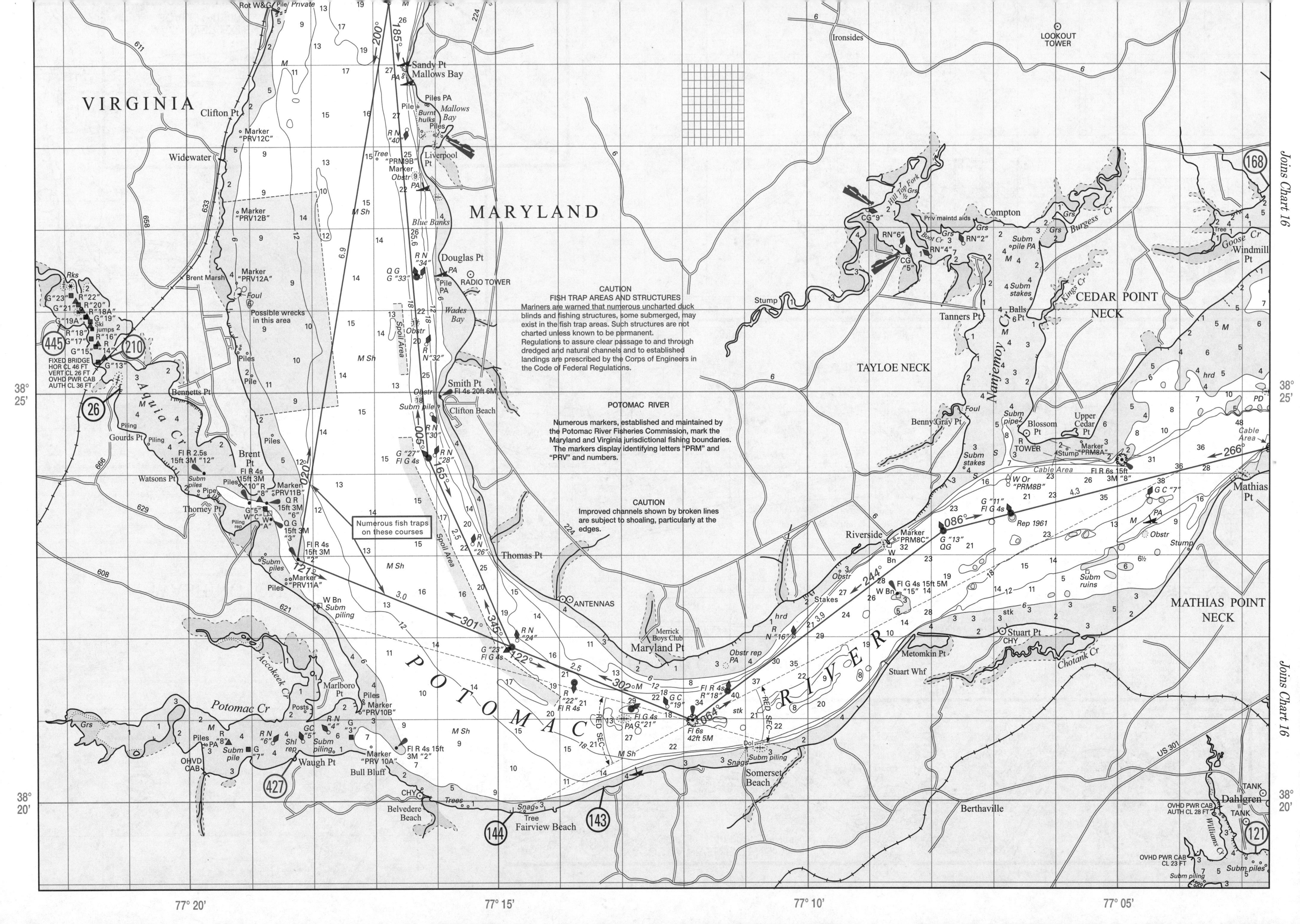

Joins Chart 16
Joins Chart 16
VIRGINIA
MARYLAND
POTOMAC RIVER
CAUTION
FISH TRAP AREAS AND STRUCTURES
Mariners are warned that numerous uncharted duck blinds and fishing structures, some submerged, may exist in the fish trap areas. Such structures are not charted unless known to be permanent.
Regulations to assure clear passage to and through dredged and natural channels and to established landings are prescribed by the Corps of Engineers in the Code of Federal Regulations.
POTOMAC RIVER
Numerous markers, established and maintained by the Potomac River Fisheries Commission, mark the Maryland and Virginia jurisdictional fishing boundaries. The markers display identifying letters "PRM" and "PRV" and numbers.
CAUTION
Improved channels shown by broken lines are subject to shoaling, particularly at the edges.
Numerous fish traps on these courses
FIXED BRIDGE HOR CL 46 FT VERT CL 26 FT OVHD PWR CAB AUTH CL 36 FT
OVHD PWR CAB AUTH CL 28 FT
OVHD PWR CAB CL 23 FT
Possible wrecks in this area
Spoil Area
Cable Area
RED SEC
Clifton Pt
Widewater
Brent Marsh
Aquia Cr
Bennetts Pt
Gourds Pt
Watsons Pt
Thorney Pt
Brent Pt
Accokeek Cr
Potomac Cr
Marlboro Pt
Waugh Pt
Bull Bluff
Belvedere Beach
Fairview Beach
Somerset Beach
Berthaville
Stuart Whf
Metomkin Pt
Stuart Pt
Chotank Cr
MATHIAS POINT NECK
Mathias Pt
Dahlgren
Williams Cr
Sandy Pt
Mallows Bay
Liverpool Pt
Blue Banks
Douglas Pt
RADIO TOWER
Wades Bay
Smith Pt
Clifton Beach
Thomas Pt
ANTENNAS
Maryland Pt
Merrick Boys Club
Riverside
Benny Gray Pt
Tanners Pt
Nanjemoy Cr
TAYLOE NECK
CEDAR POINT NECK
Blossom Pt
Upper Cedar Pt
Balls Pt
Kings Cr
Compton
Burgess Cr
Goose Cr
Windmill Pt
Hill Top Fork
Boot Cr
Priv maintd aids
Ironsides
LOOKOUT TOWER
Stump
Rep 1961
US 301
38° 25'
38° 20'
77° 20'
77° 15'
77° 10'
77° 05'

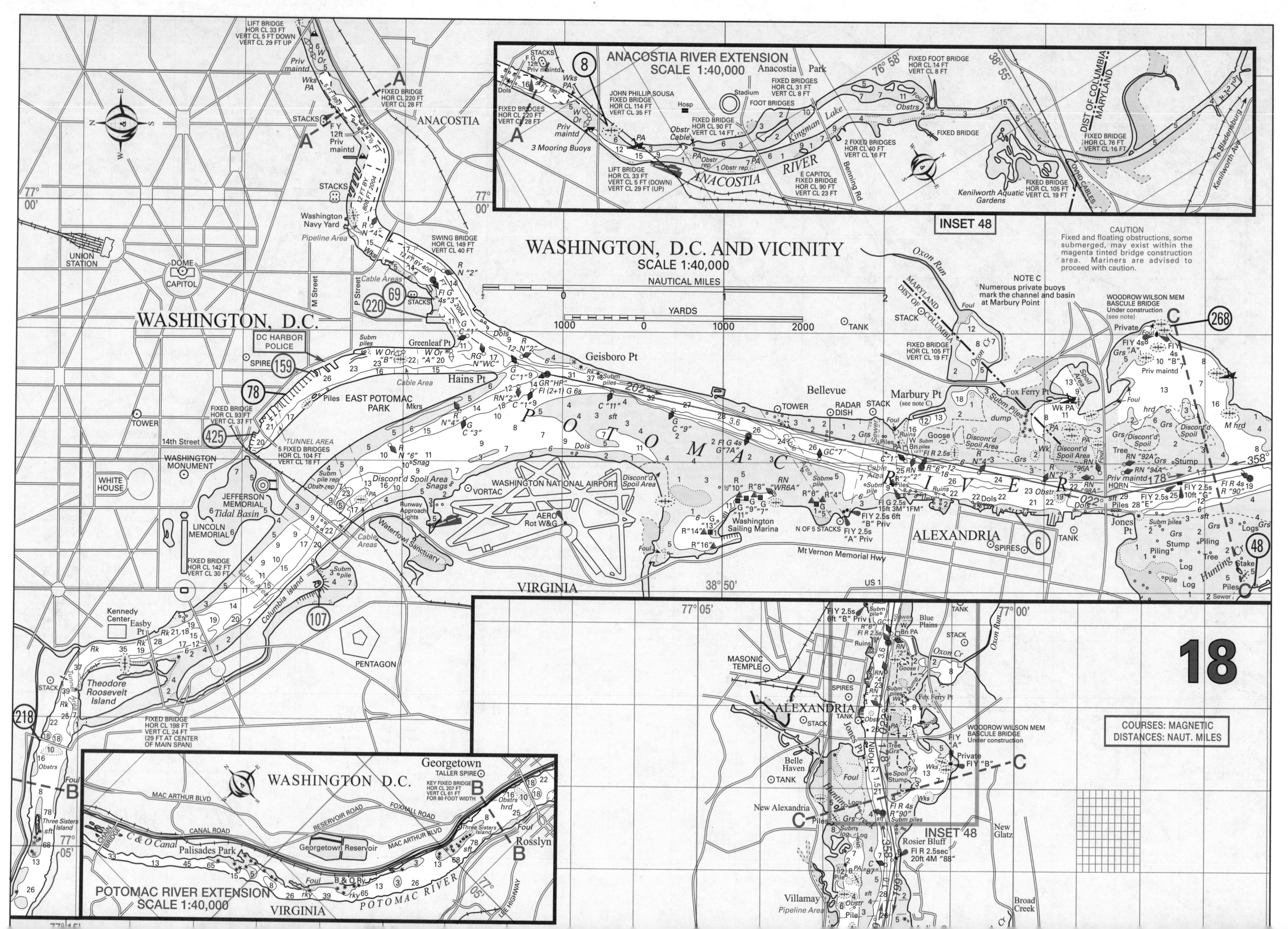

18
WASHINGTON, D.C. AND VICINITY
SCALE 1:40,000
NAUTICAL MILES
YARDS
ANACOSTIA RIVER EXTENSION
SCALE 1:40,000
INSET 48
POTOMAC RIVER EXTENSION
SCALE 1:40,000
COURSES: MAGNETIC
DISTANCES: NAUT. MILES
CAUTION
Fixed and floating obstructions, some submerged, may exist within the magenta tinted bridge construction area. Mariners are advised to proceed with caution.
NOTE C
Numerous private buoys mark the channel and basin at Marbury Point
WOODROW WILSON MEM BASCULE BRIDGE Under construction (see note)
WASHINGTON, D.C.
ALEXANDRIA
VIRGINIA
POTOMAC RIVER
ANACOSTIA
WASHINGTON NATIONAL AIRPORT
DC HARBOR POLICE
EAST POTOMAC PARK
JEFFERSON MEMORIAL
LINCOLN MEMORIAL
WASHINGTON MONUMENT
WHITE HOUSE
CAPITOL
UNION STATION
PENTAGON
Theodore Roosevelt Island
Georgetown
Rosslyn
Geisboro Pt
Hains Pt
Marbury Pt
Jones Pt
Bellevue
Washington Navy Yard
Washington Sailing Marina
Kenilworth Aquatic Gardens
DIST OF COLUMBIA
MARYLAND

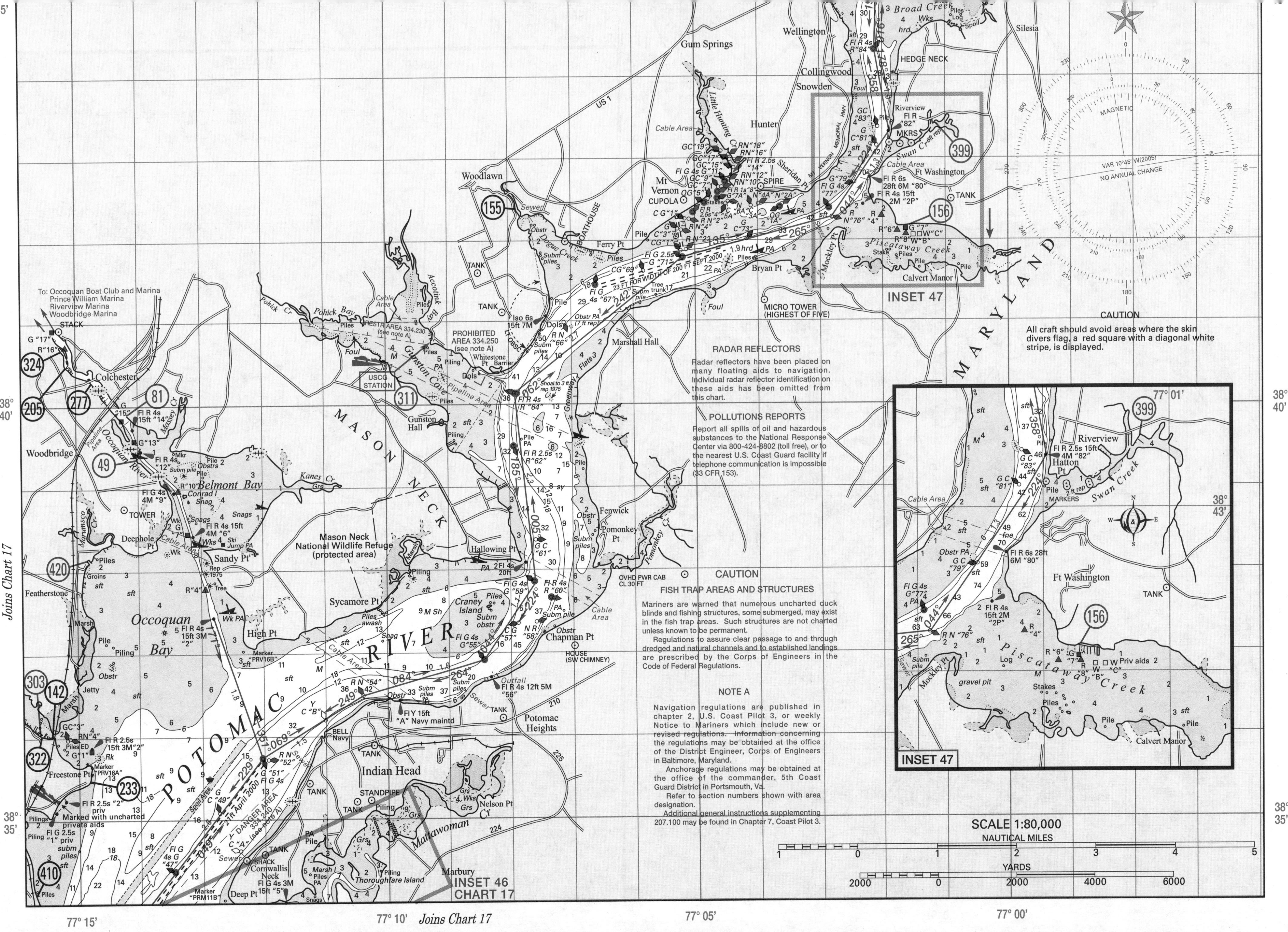
CAUTION
All craft should avoid areas where the skin divers flag, a red square with a diagonal white stripe, is displayed.
RADAR REFLECTORS
Radar reflectors have been placed on many floating aids to navigation. Individual radar reflector identification on these aids has been omitted from this chart.
POLLUTIONS REPORTS
Report all spills of oil and hazardous substances to the National Response Center via 800-424-8802 (toll free), or to the nearest U.S. Coast Guard facility if telephone communication is impossible (33 CFR 153).
CAUTION
FISH TRAP AREAS AND STRUCTURES
Mariners are warned that numerous uncharted duck blinds and fishing structures, some submerged, may exist in the fish trap areas. Such structures are not charted unless known to be permanent.
Regulations to assure clear passage to and through dredged and natural channels and to established landings are prescribed by the Corps of Engineers in the Code of Federal Regulations.
NOTE A
Navigation regulations are published in chapter 2, U.S. Coast Pilot 3, or weekly Notice to Mariners which include new or revised regulations. Information concerning the regulations may be obtained at the office of the District Engineer, Corps of Engineers in Baltimore, Maryland.
Anchorage regulations may be obtained at the office of the commander, 5th Coast Guard District in Portsmouth, Va.
Refer to section numbers shown with area designation.
Additional general instructions supplementing 207.100 may be found in Chapter 7, Coast Pilot 3.
SCALE 1:80,000
NAUTICAL MILES
YARDS
INSET 47
INSET 46
CHART 17
Joins Chart 17
MARYLAND
POTOMAC RIVER
MASON NECK
Mason Neck National Wildlife Refuge (protected area)
To: Occoquan Boat Club and Marina
Prince William Marina
Riverview Marina
Woodbridge Marina
PROHIBITED AREA 334.250 (see note A)
RESTR AREA 334.230 (see note A)
DANGER AREA 334.240 (see note A)
MICRO TOWER (HIGHEST OF FIVE)
OVHD PWR CAB CL 30 FT
VAR 10°45' W(2005)
NO ANNUAL CHANGE
MAGNETIC
USCG STATION
Occoquan Bay
Belmont Bay
Gunston Cove
Piscataway Creek
Mattawoman Cr
Indian Head
Potomac Heights
Mt Vernon
Ft Washington
Woodbridge
Colchester
Woodlawn
Gum Springs
Wellington
Collingwood
Snowden
Hunter
HEDGE NECK
Silesia
Calvert Manor
Riverview
Marshall Hall
Gunston Hall
Fenwick
Chapman Pt
Sandy Pt
High Pt
Sycamore Pt
Freestone Pt
Featherstone
Deephole Pt
Cornwallis Neck
Thoroughfare Island
Marbury
Nelson Pt
Bryan Pt
Ferry Pt
Mockley Pt
Sheridan Pt
Hallowing Pt
Whitestone Pt
Craney Island
Little Hunting Cr
Dogue Creek
Accotink Bay
Pohick Bay
Broad Creek
Swan Creek
US 1
77° 15'
77° 10'
77° 05'
77° 00'
77° 01'
38° 40'
38° 35'
38° 43'
45'

# 19

COURSES: MAGNETIC
DISTANCES: NAUT. MILES

Fenwick Island
DIRICKSON NECK
Bayville
Williamsville
Little Assawoman Bay
Maryland Beach
FIXED BRIDGE HOR CL 37 FT VERT CL 11 FT
Fl 4s 83ft 8M
Assawoman Bay
Horse Island
Devil Island
Swan Pt
Greys Creek
St Martin River
Isle of Wight
Poplar Pt
SILO
FIXED BRIDGES HOR CL 100 FT VERT CL 35 FT
Cedar Pt
Isle of Wight Bay
Reedy Island Spoil Area
Keyser Pt
Collier Island
Manklin Creek
Herring Creek
Turville Creek
Mallard Island
OCEAN CITY
Obstruction Fish Haven (auth min 18ft)
TO FENWICK SHOAL BUOY "1 FIS"
USCG STATION
NRP
Airport
Coffins Pt
Ocean City Inlet
INSET 49

NOTE
OCEAN CITY INLET
BUOYS OFTEN CHANGE
DUE TO CONDITIONS

## INSET 49

SCALE 1:20,000

NAUTICAL MILES

YARDS

FENWICK ISLAND
OCEAN CITY
ISLE OF WIGHT BAY
Horn Island
Pipeline Area
Cable Area
Shoaling 1983
6 FT BY 60 FT APR-SEPT 1972
BASCULE BRIDGE HOR CL 70 FT VERT CL 18 FT
WEST CHANNEL FIXED BRIDGE HOR CL 24 FT VERT CL 10 FT
West Ocean City
Commercial Fish Harbor
Ocean City Harbor
ASSATEAGUE ISLAND
Shoreline subject to change
SINEPUXENT BAY

WARNING:
STRONG CURRENT
EXERCISE EXTREME CAUTION
WHEN TRANSITING AREA

USE INLAND RULES OF THE ROAD
USE INTERNATIONAL RULES OF THE ROAD
COLREGS DEMARCATION LINE 80.505b (see note A)

MAGNETIC
VAR 11°45'W (2007)
NO ANNUAL CHANGE

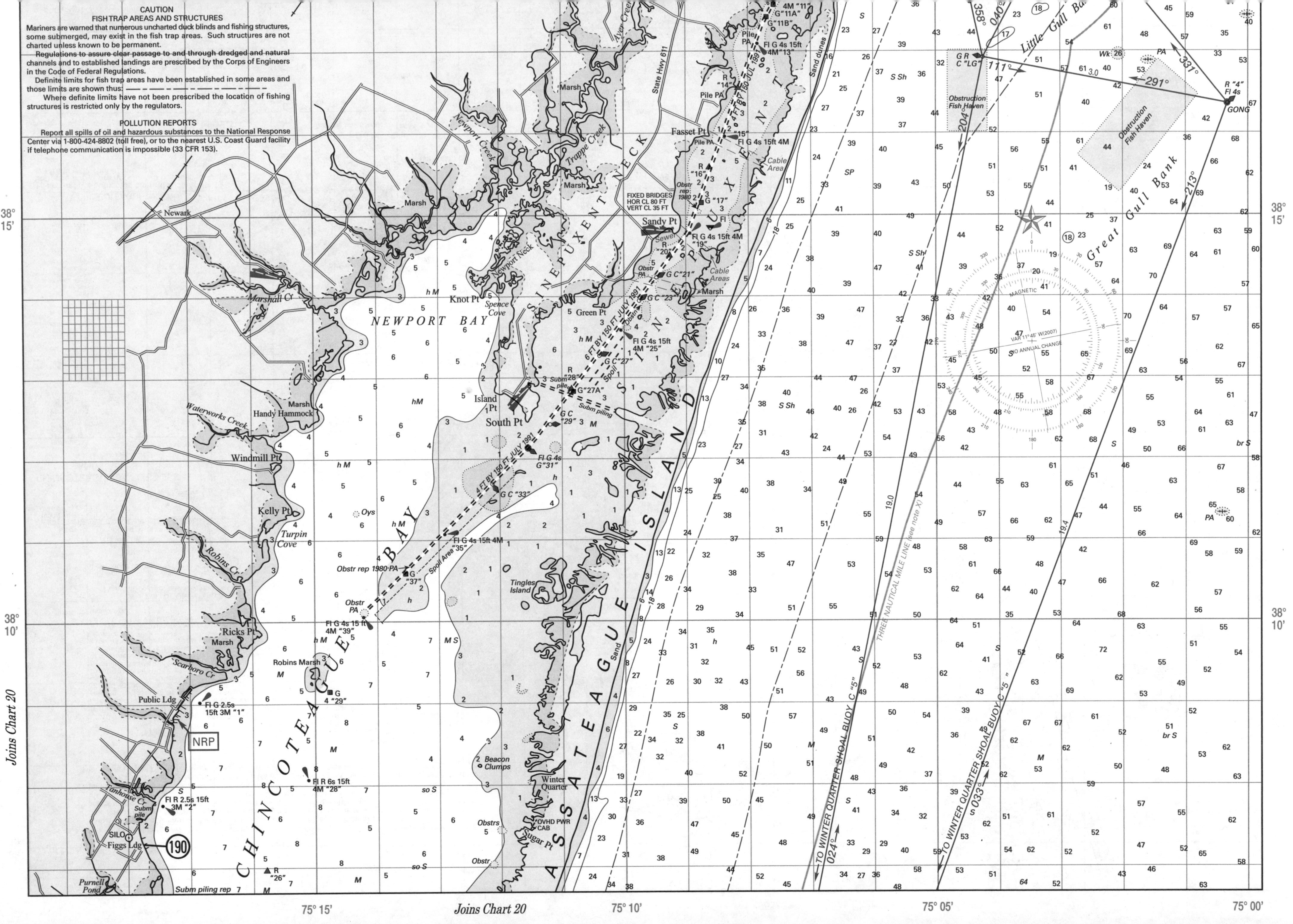
CAUTION
FISH TRAP AREAS AND STRUCTURES
Mariners are warned that numerous uncharted duck blinds and fishing structures, some submerged, may exist in the fish trap areas. Such structures are not charted unless known to be permanent.
Regulations to assure clear passage to and through dredged and natural channels and to established landings are prescribed by the Corps of Engineers in the Code of Federal Regulations.
Definite limits for fish trap areas have been established in some areas and those limits are shown thus:
Where definite limits have not been prescribed the location of fishing structures is restricted only by the regulators.
POLLUTION REPORTS
Report all spills of oil and hazardous substances to the National Response Center via 1-800-424-8802 (toll free), or to the nearest U.S. Coast Guard facility if telephone communication is impossible (33 CFR 153).
Newark
Newport Creek
Trappe Creek
Ayer Creek
State Hwy 611
Marsh
Marshall Cr
NEWPORT BAY
Knot Pt
Spence Cove
Newport Neck
SINEPUXENT NECK
SINEPUXENT BAY
Green Pt
Sandy Pt
Fasset Pt
FIXED BRIDGES HOR CL 80 FT VERT CL 35 FT
Cable Area
Cable Areas
Sand dunes
Island Pt
South Pt
Handy Hammock
Waterworks Creek
Windmill Pt
Kelly Pt
Turpin Cove
Robins Cr
Ricks Pt
Scarboro Cr
Public Ldg
NRP
Tanhouse Cr
SILO
Figgs Ldg
Purnell Pond
Robins Marsh
CHINCOTEAGUE BAY
Tingles Island
Beacon Clumps
Winter Quarter
Sugar Pt
OVHD PWR CAB
ASSATEAGUE ISLAND
Obstruction Fish Haven
Great Gull Bank
Little Gull Bank
GONG
MAGNETIC
VAR 11°45' W(2007)
NO ANNUAL CHANGE
THREE NAUTICAL MILE LINE (see note X)
TO WINTER QUARTER SHOAL BUOY C "5"
Subm piling rep
Spoil Area
Obstr rep 1980 PA
38° 15'
38° 10'
75° 15'
75° 10'
75° 05'
75° 00'
Joins Chart 20

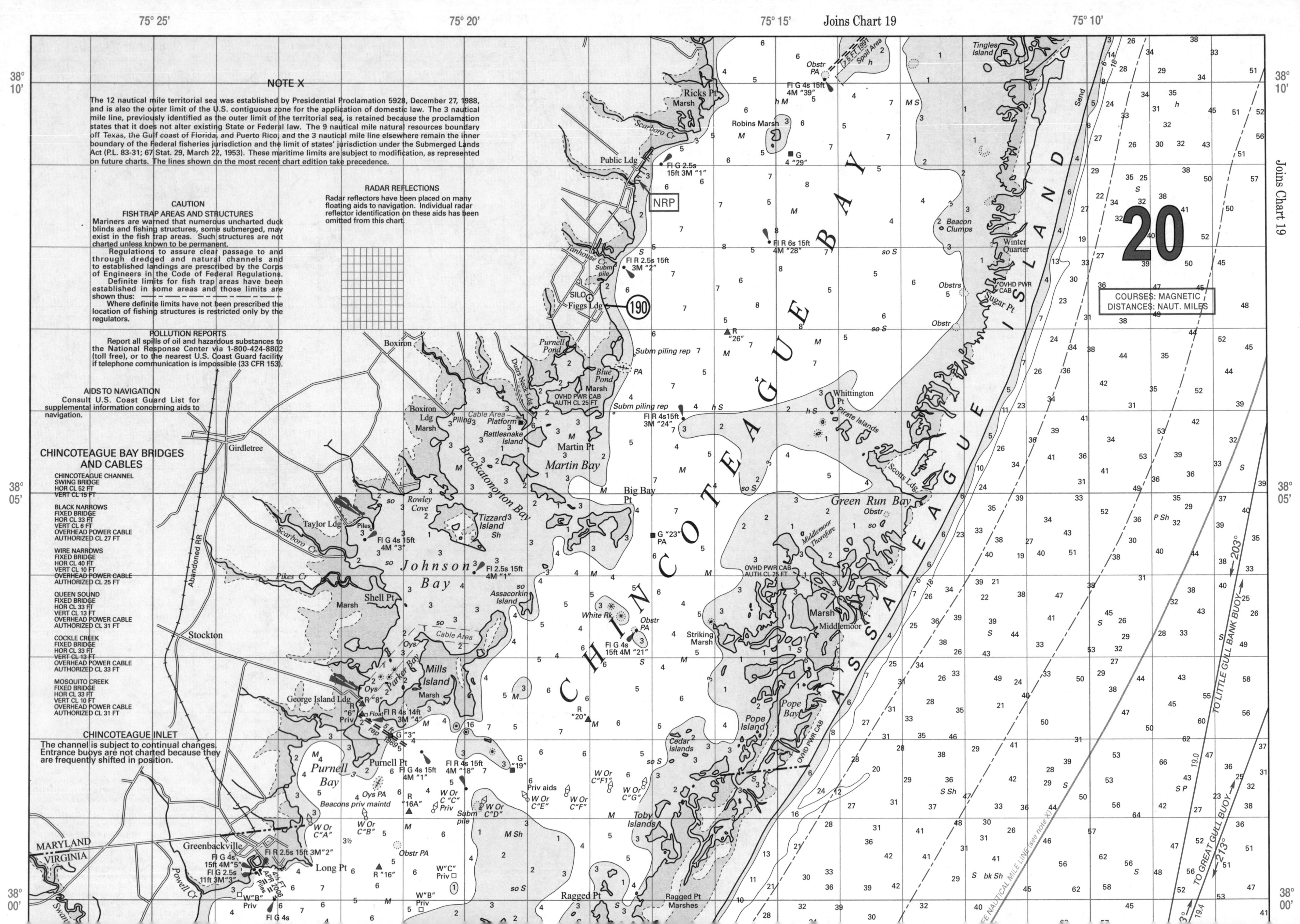

Joins Chart 19
75° 25'
75° 20'
75° 15'
75° 10'
38° 10'
38° 05'
38° 00'
20
COURSES: MAGNETIC
DISTANCES: NAUT. MILES
NOTE X
The 12 nautical mile territorial sea was established by Presidential Proclamation 5928, December 27, 1988, and is also the outer limit of the U.S. contiguous zone for the application of domestic law. The 3 nautical mile line, previously identified as the outer limit of the territorial sea, is retained because the proclamation states that it does not alter existing State or Federal law. The 9 nautical mile natural resources boundary off Texas, the Gulf coast of Florida, and Puerto Rico, and the 3 nautical mile line elsewhere remain the inner boundary of the Federal fisheries jurisdiction and the limit of states' jurisdiction under the Submerged Lands Act (P.L. 83-31; 67 Stat. 29, March 22, 1953). These maritime limits are subject to modification, as represented on future charts. The lines shown on the most recent chart edition take precedence.
RADAR REFLECTIONS
Radar reflectors have been placed on many floating aids to navigation. Individual radar reflector identification on these aids has been omitted from this chart.
CAUTION
FISHTRAP AREAS AND STRUCTURES
Mariners are warned that numerous uncharted duck blinds and fishing structures, some submerged, may exist in the fish trap areas. Such structures are not charted unless known to be permanent.
Regulations to assure clear passage to and through dredged and natural channels and to established landings are prescribed by the Corps of Engineers in the Code of Federal Regulations.
Definite limits for fish trap areas have been established in some areas and those limits are shown thus:
Where definite limits have not been prescribed the location of fishing structures is restricted only by the regulators.
POLLUTION REPORTS
Report all spills of oil and hazardous substances to the National Response Center via 1-800-424-8802 (toll free), or to the nearest U.S. Coast Guard facility if telephone communication is impossible (33 CFR 153).
AIDS TO NAVIGATION
Consult U.S. Coast Guard List for supplemental information concerning aids to navigation.
CHINCOTEAGUE BAY BRIDGES AND CABLES
CHINCOTEAGUE CHANNEL
SWING BRIDGE
HOR CL 52 FT
VERT CL 15 FT
BLACK NARROWS
FIXED BRIDGE
HOR CL 33 FT
VERT CL 6 FT
OVERHEAD POWER CABLE
AUTHORIZED CL 27 FT
WIRE NARROWS
FIXED BRIDGE
HOR CL 40 FT
VERT CL 10 FT
OVERHEAD POWER CABLE
AUTHORIZED CL 25 FT
QUEEN SOUND
FIXED BRIDGE
HOR CL 33 FT
VERT CL 13 FT
OVERHEAD POWER CABLE
AUTHORIZED CL 31 FT
COCKLE CREEK
FIXED BRIDGE
HOR CL 33 FT
VERT CL 13 FT
OVERHEAD POWER CABLE
AUTHORIZED CL 33 FT
MOSQUITO CREEK
FIXED BRIDGE
HOR CL 33 FT
VERT CL 10 FT
OVERHEAD POWER CABLE
AUTHORIZED CL 31 FT
CHINCOTEAGUE INLET
The channel is subject to continual changes. Entrance buoys are not charted because they are frequently shifted in position.
CHINCOTEAGUE BAY
ASSATEAGUE ISLAND
Tingles Island
Ricks Pt
Marsh
Scarboro Cr
Public Ldg
NRP
Robins Marsh
Beacon Clumps
Winter Quarter
Sugar Pt
OVHD PWR CAB
Obstrs
Obstr
Tanhouse Cr
Subm pile
SILO
Figgs Ldg
190
Purnell Pond
Blue Pond
Duers Neck Ldg
OVHD PWR CAB AUTH CL 25 FT
Subm piling rep
Whittington Pt
Pirate Islands
Scotts Ldg
Green Run Bay
Middlemoor Thorofare
Boxiron
Boxiron Ldg
Cable Area
Platform
Rattlesnake Island
Martin Pt
Martin Bay
Brockatonorton Bay
Big Bay Pt
Tizzard Island
Rowley Cove
Girdletree
Abandoned RR
Taylor Ldg
Piles
Johnson Bay
Assacorkin Island
Pikes Cr
Shell Pt
White Rk
Striking Marsh
Middlemoor
Stockton
Oys
Parker Bay
Mills Island
George Island Ldg
Pope Island
Pope Bay
Cedar Islands
Purnell Pt
Purnell Bay
Beacons priv maintd
Priv aids
Toby Islands
Ragged Pt
Ragged Pt Marshes
MARYLAND
VIRGINIA
Greenbackville
Long Pt
Powell Cr
Fl G 4s 15ft 4M "39"
Fl G 2.5s 15ft 3M "1"
Fl R 6s 15ft 4M "28"
Fl R 2.5s 15ft 3M "2"
Fl R 4s15ft 3M "24"
Fl G 4s 15ft 4M "3"
Fl 2.5s 15ft 4M "1"
Fl G 4s 15ft 4M "21"
Fl R 4s 14ft 3M "4"
Fl G 4s 15ft 4M "1"
Fl R 4s 15ft 4M "18"
Fl R 2.5s 15ft 3M "2"
Fl G 4s 15ft 4M "5"
Fl G 2.5s 11ft 3M "3"
TO LITTLE GULL BANK BUOY
TO GREAT GULL BUOY
203°
213°
19.0
19.4
3 NAUTICAL MILE LINE (see note X)
OVHD PWR CAB

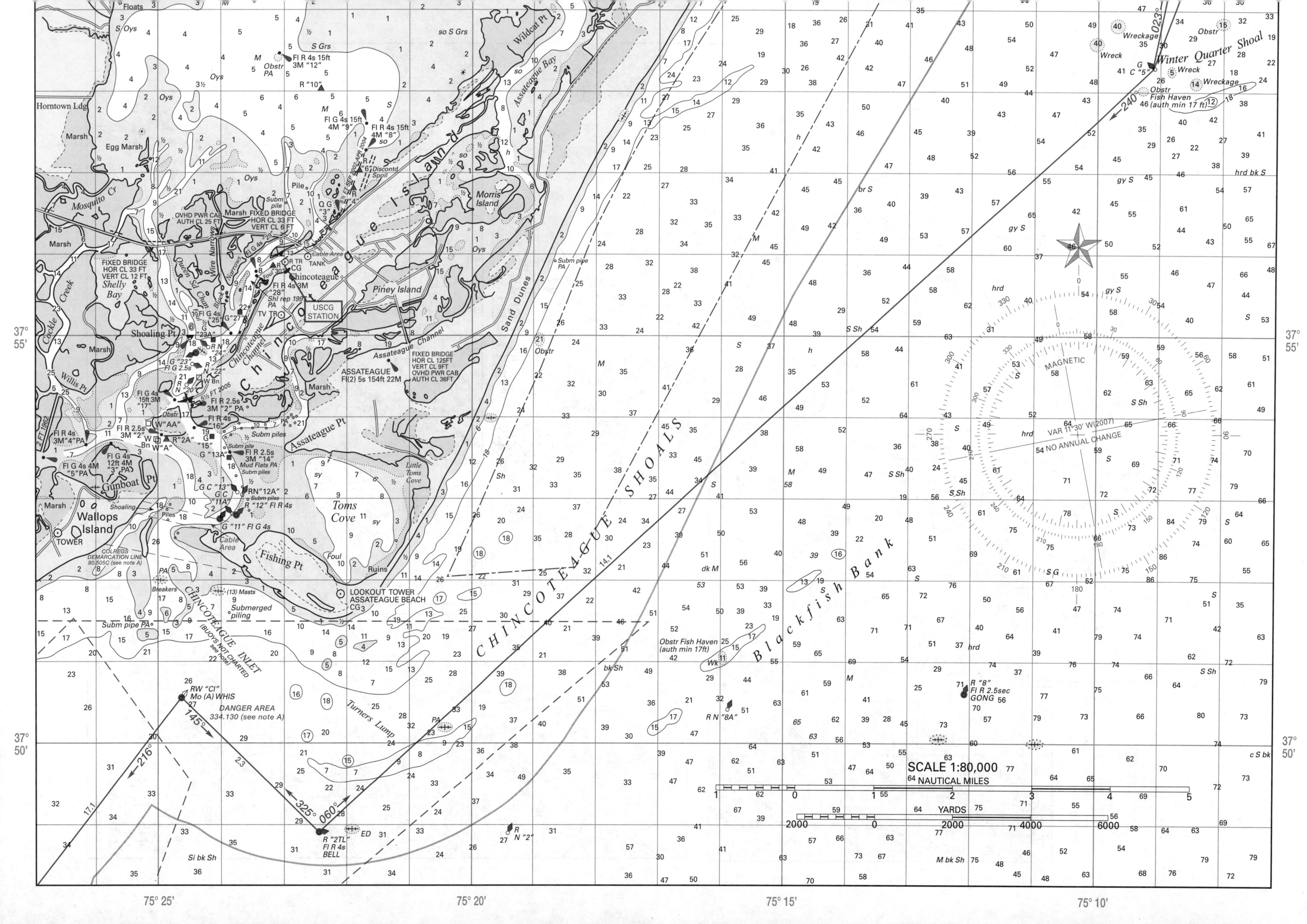

37° 55'
37° 50'
75° 25'
75° 20'
75° 15'
75° 10'
SCALE 1:80,000
NAUTICAL MILES
YARDS
MAGNETIC
VAR 11°30' W (2007)
NO ANNUAL CHANGE
Winter Quarter Shoal
Blackfish Bank
CHINCOTEAGUE SHOALS
Sand Dunes
Assateague Bay
Wildcat Pt
Morris Island
Piney Island
Chincoteague Island
Chincoteague Channel
Assateague Channel
USCG STATION
ASSATEAGUE Fl(2) 5s 154ft 22M
Assateague Pt
Little Toms Cove
Toms Cove
Fishing Pt
LOOKOUT TOWER ASSATEAGUE BEACH
CHINCOTEAGUE INLET
(BUOYS NOT CHARTED see note)
DANGER AREA 334.130 (see note A)
Turners Lump
Queen Sd Chan
Shoaling Pt
Shelly Bay
Wallops Island
Gunboat Pt
Mosquito Cr
Cockle Creek
Willis Pt
Egg Marsh
Horntown Ldg
FIXED BRIDGE HOR CL 33 FT VERT CL 12 FT
COLREGS DEMARCATION LINE 80.505C (see note A)

# PAGE A OF INSETS

Note H
WARNING

Small-craft operators in Frog Mortar Creek are advised to use extreme caution in the vicinity of Martin State Airport Runway 33. Small-craft with masts exceeding 37 feet in height above the waterline create an obstruction to aircraft using the airport. Operators of such craft transiting this area should contact the Martin State Airport Control Tower on channel 16 so the tower can warn approaching aircraft of a possible obstruction. Tower operations are from 6:15 a.m. to 9:45 p.m. daily.

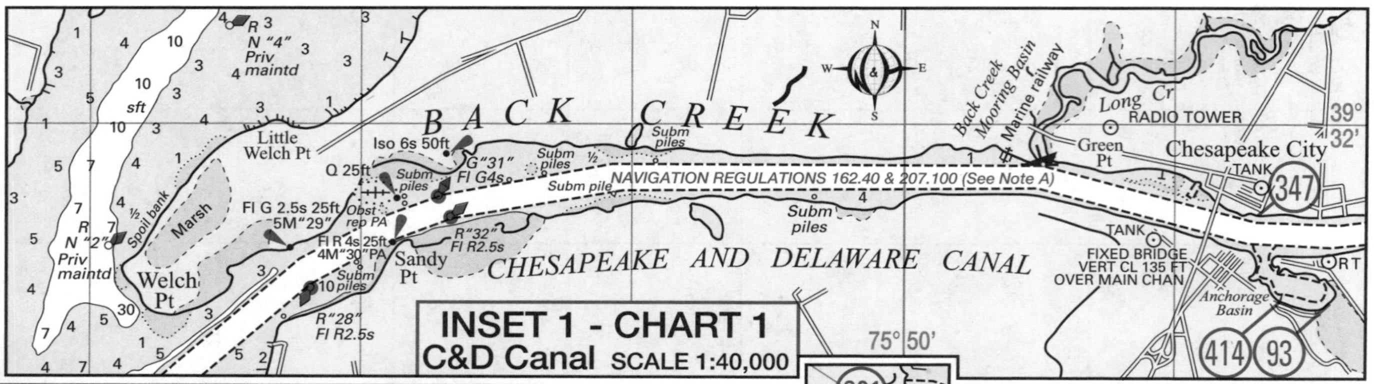

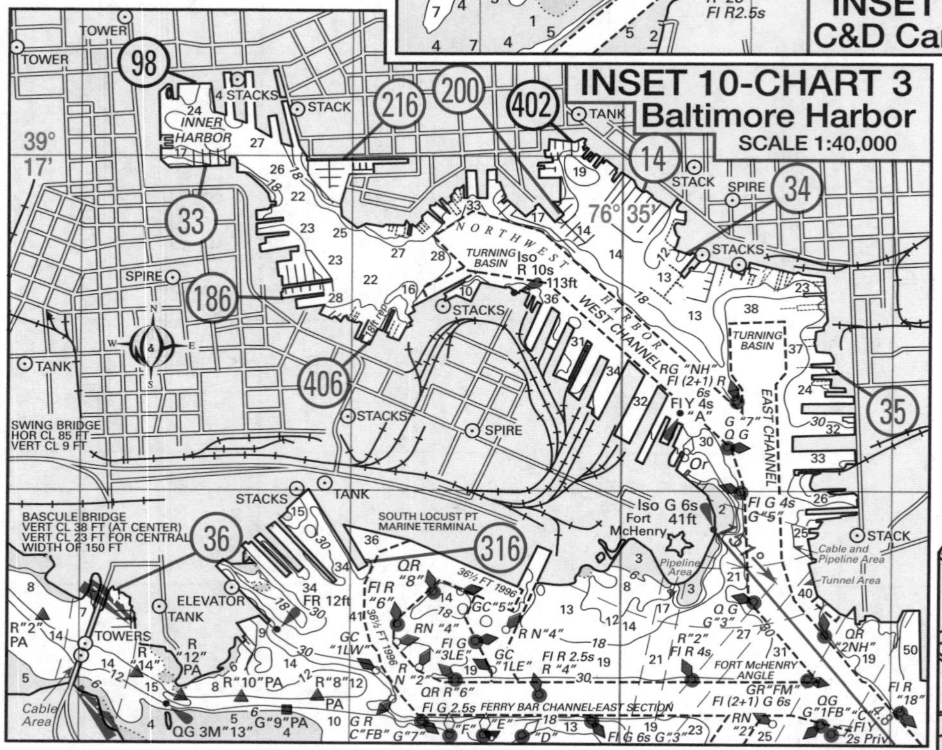

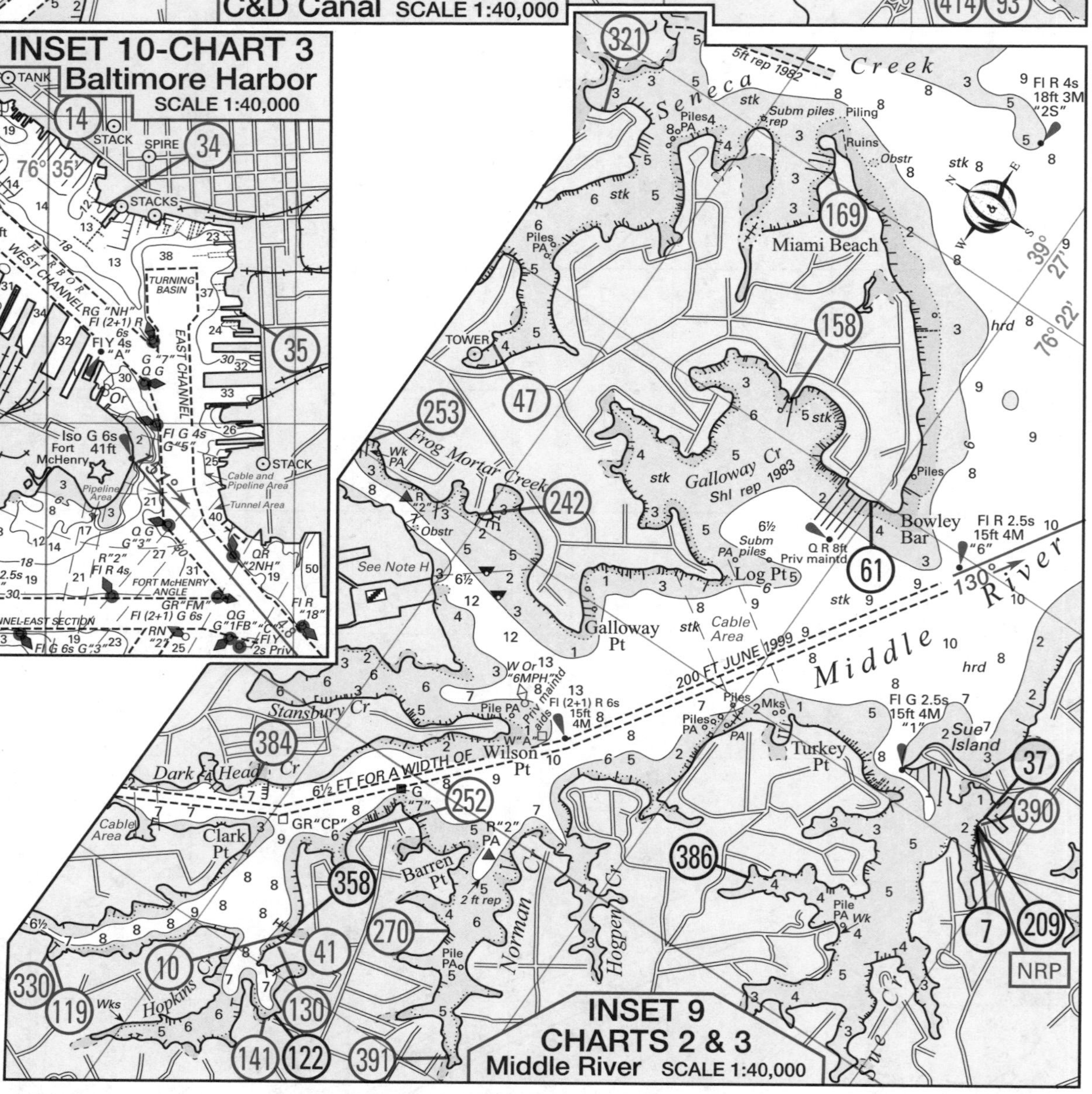

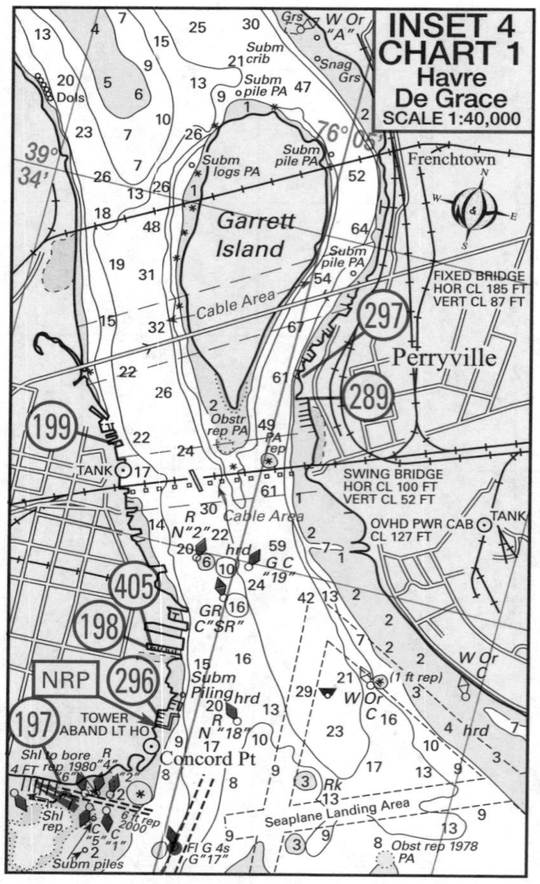

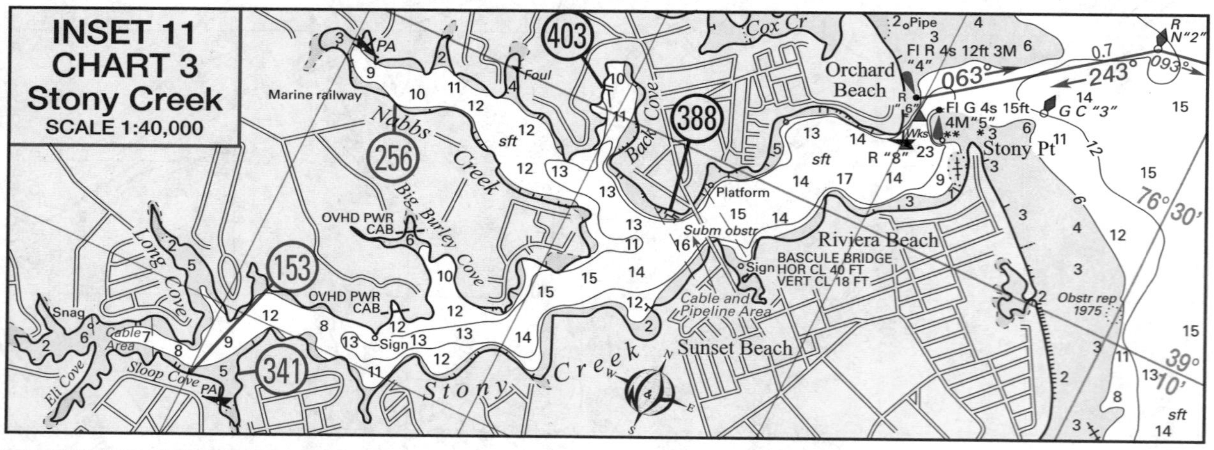

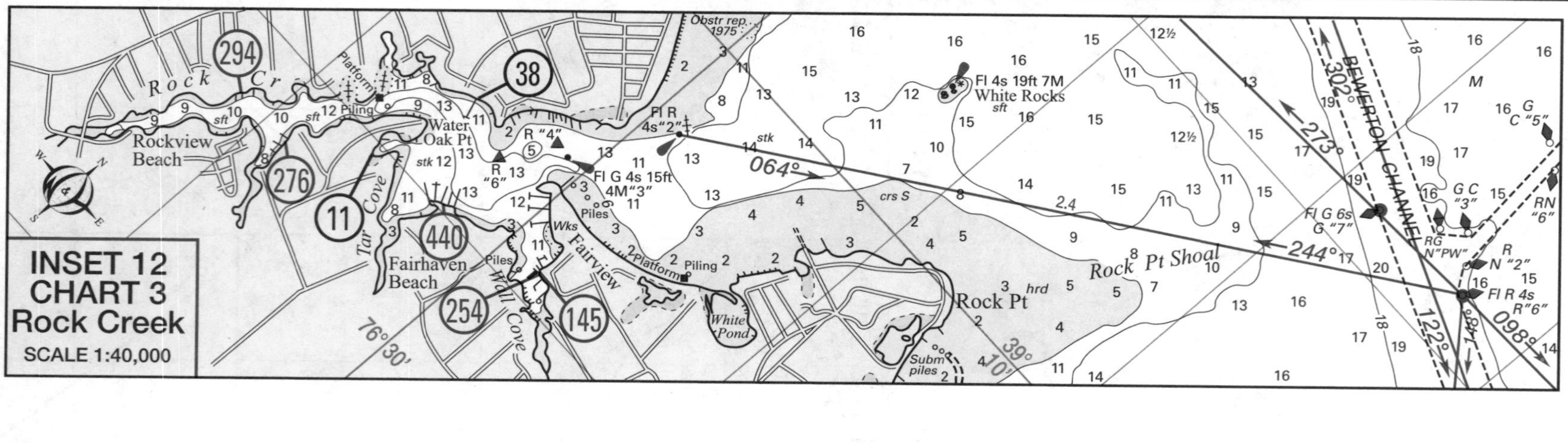

**INSET 1 - CHART 1**
**C&D Canal** SCALE 1:40,000

**INSET 10-CHART 3**
**Baltimore Harbor**
SCALE 1:40,000

**INSET 9**
**CHARTS 2 & 3**
**Middle River** SCALE 1:40,000

**INSET 4**
**CHART 1**
Havre De Grace
SCALE 1:40,000

**INSET 11**
**CHART 3**
**Stony Creek**
SCALE 1:40,000

**INSET 12**
**CHART 3**
**Rock Creek**
SCALE 1:40,000

# PAGE B OF INSETS

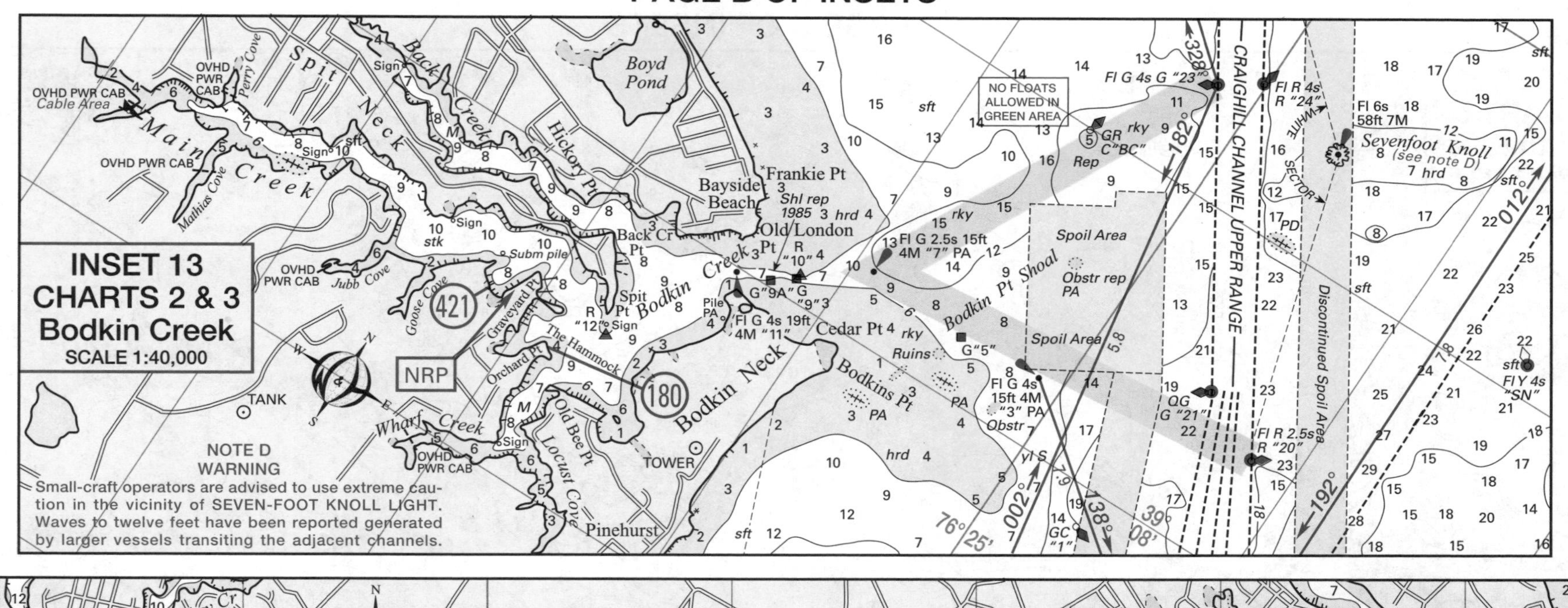

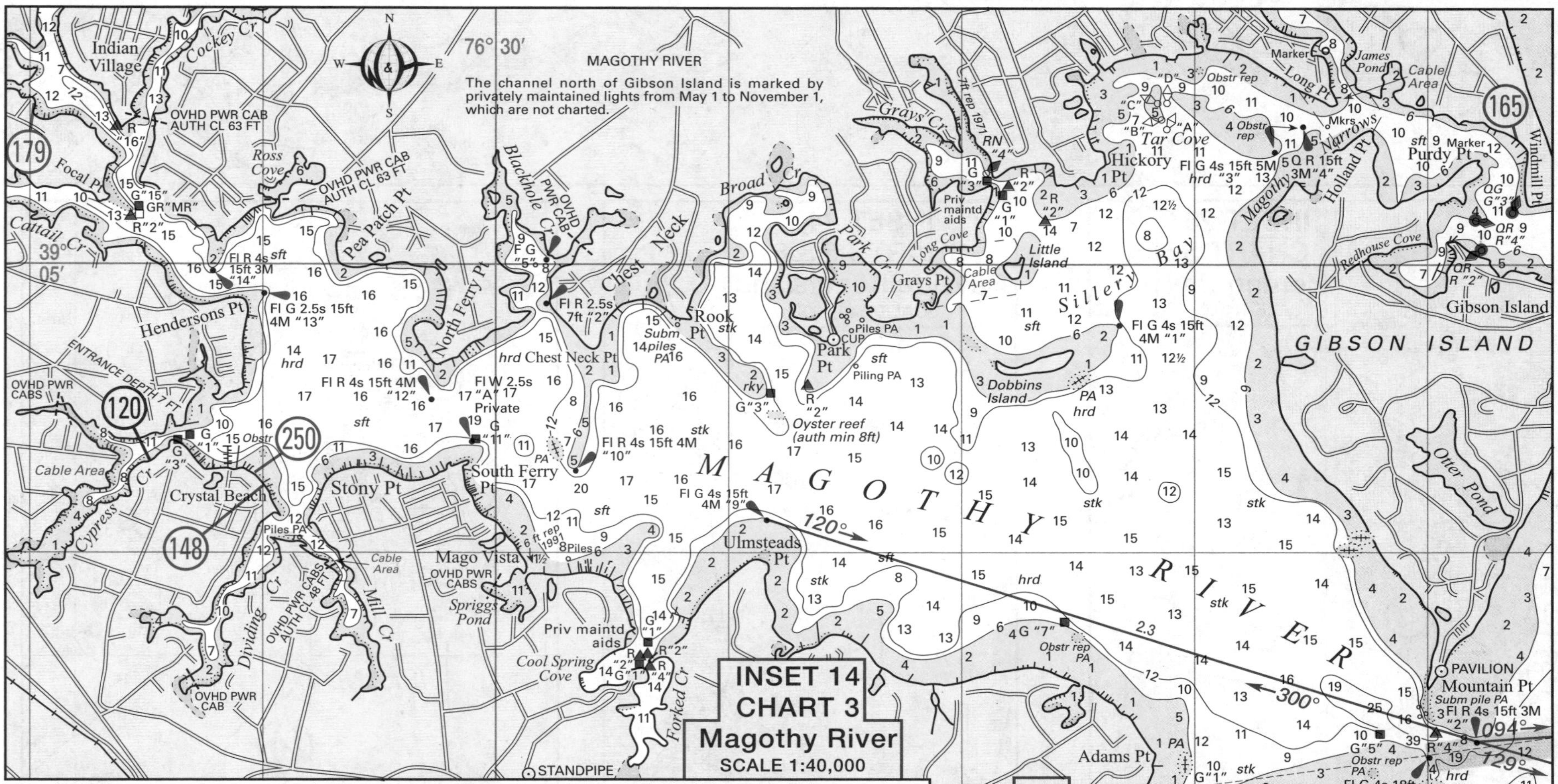

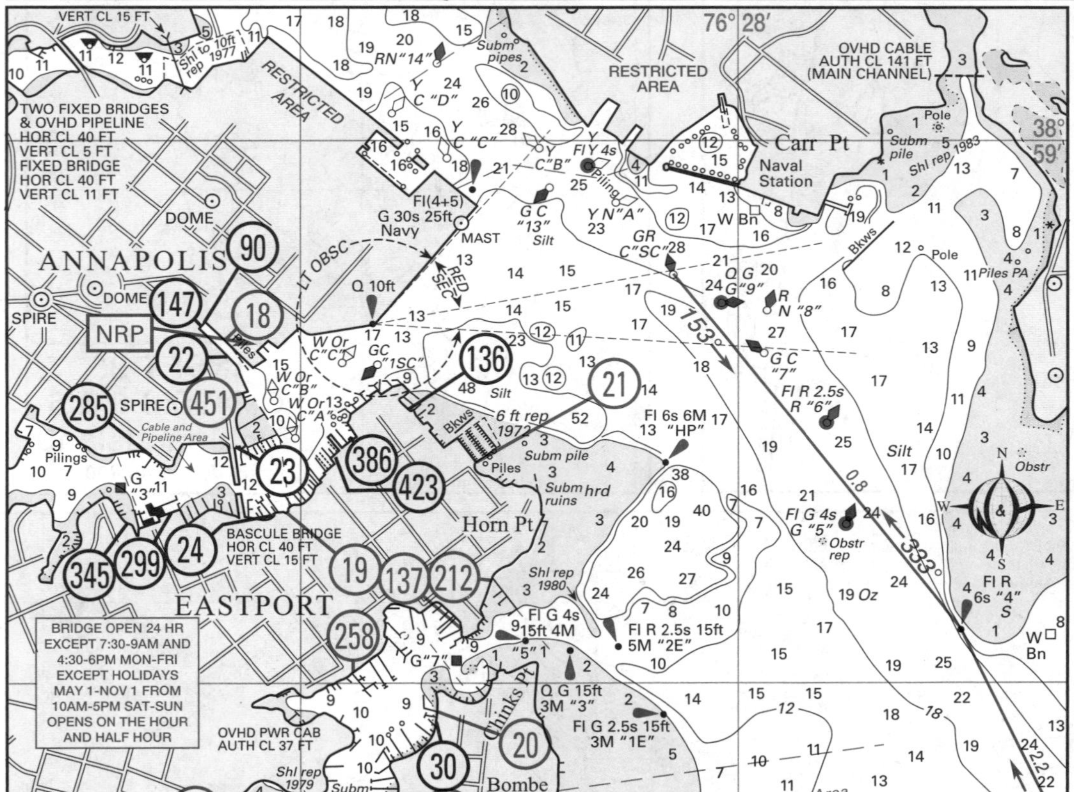

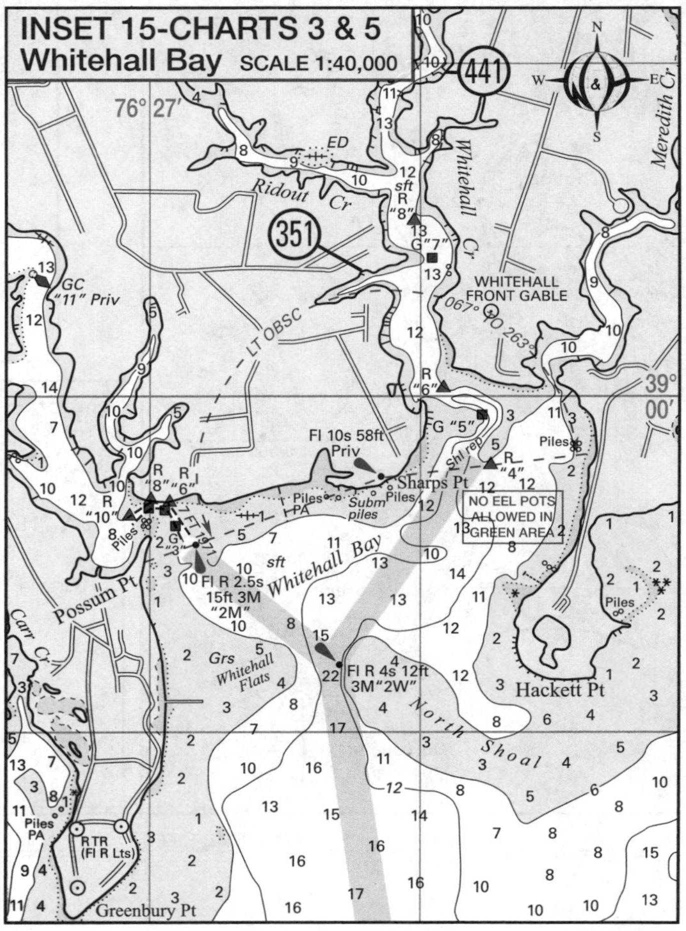

MAGOTHY RIVER

The channel north of Gibson Island is marked by privately maintained lights from May 1 to November 1, which are not charted.

NO CRAB POTS ALLOWED IN GREEN AREA

**INSET 14**
**CHART 3**
**Magothy River**
SCALE 1:40,000

TWO FIXED BRIDGES & OVHD PIPELINE HOR CL 40 FT VERT CL 5 FT FIXED BRIDGE HOR CL 40 FT VERT CL 11 FT

OVHD CABLE AUTH CL 141 FT (MAIN CHANNEL)

BASCULE BRIDGE HOR CL 40 FT VERT CL 15 FT

BRIDGE OPEN 24 HR EXCEPT 7:30-9AM AND 4:30-6PM MON-FRI EXCEPT HOLIDAYS MAY 1-NOV 1 FROM 10AM-5PM SAT-SUN OPENS ON THE HOUR AND HALF HOUR

7½ ft centerline rep Nov 2001

**INSET 20**
**CHARTS 3 & 5**
**Annapolis Harbor**
SCALE 1:25,000

**INSET 15-CHARTS 3 & 5**
**Whitehall Bay** SCALE 1:40,000

NO EEL POTS ALLOWED IN GREEN AREA

# PAGE C OF INSETS

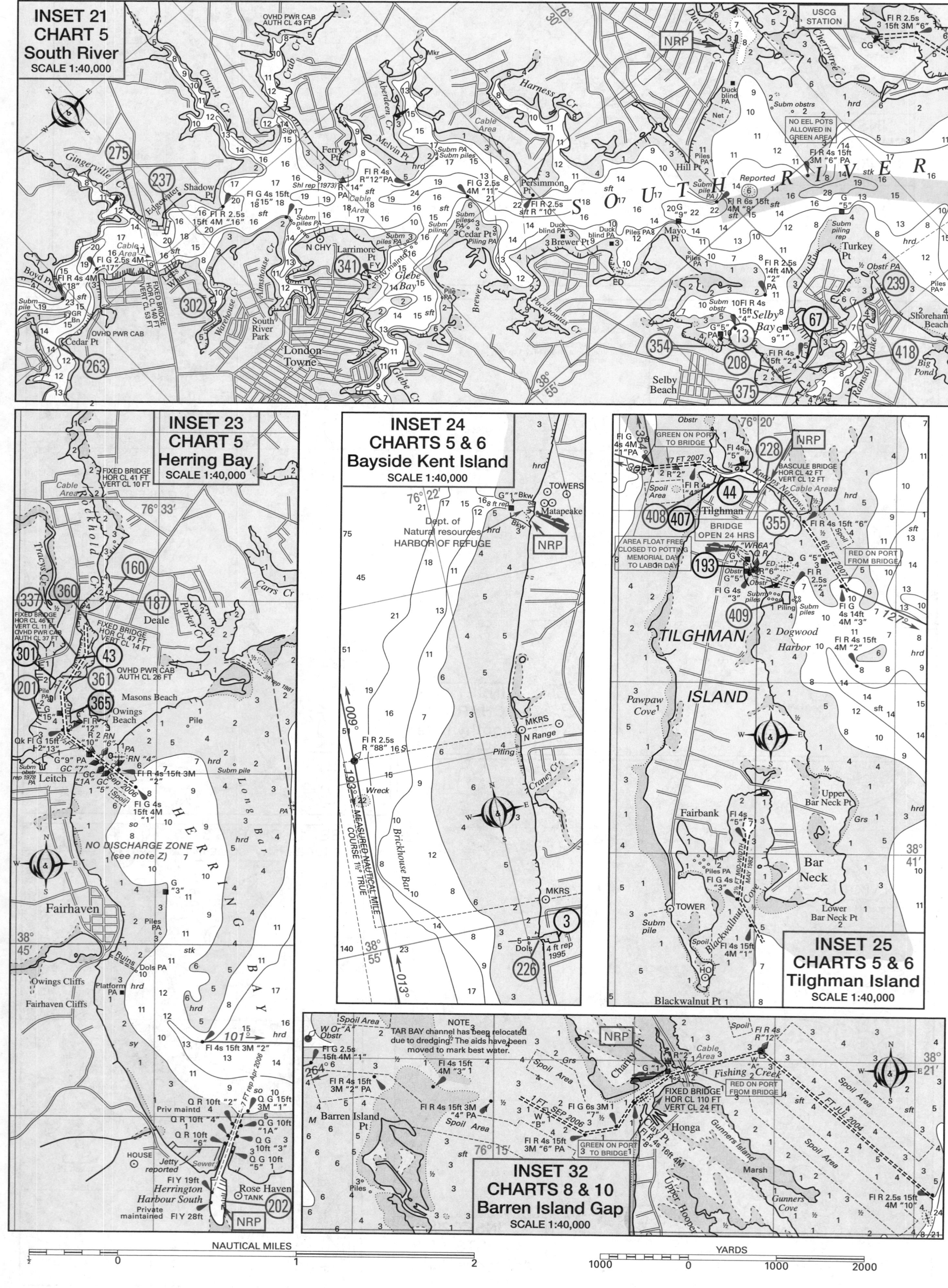

PAGE D OF INSETS

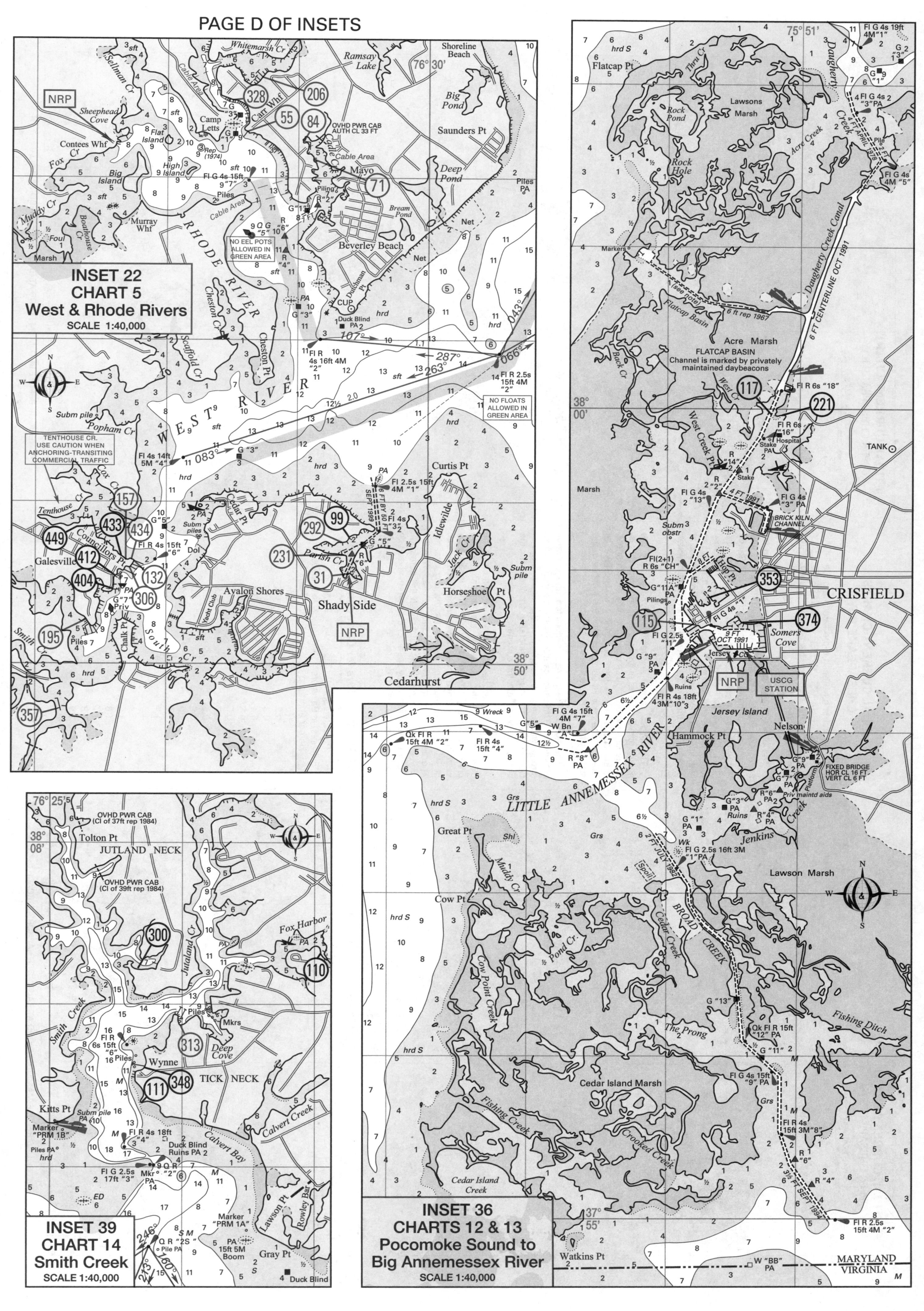

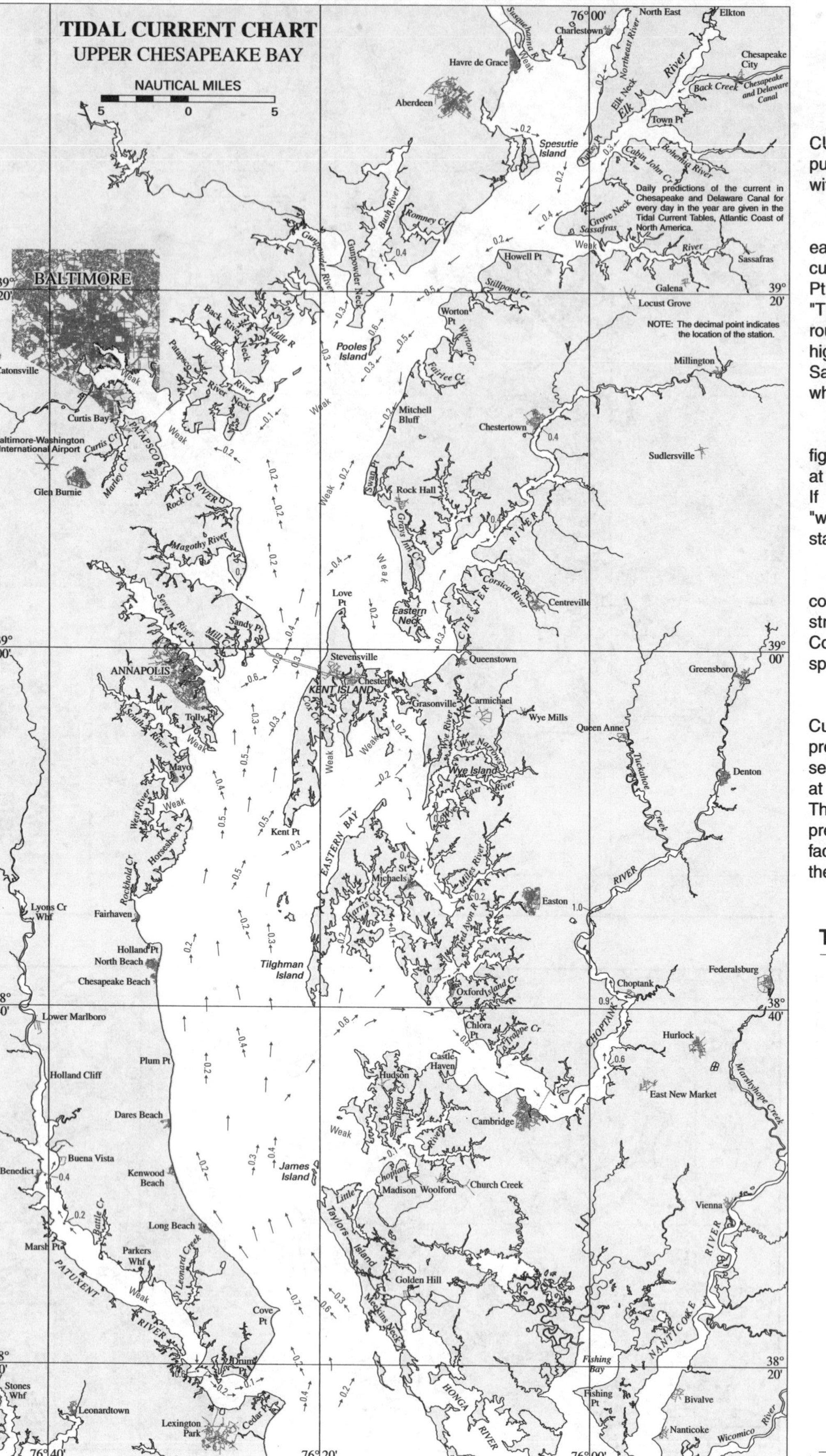


TWO HOURS BEFORE MAXIMUM FLOOD AT BALTIMORE HARBOR APPROACH (F–2)

## TIDAL CURRENT CHARTS CHESAPEAKE BAY

These charts have been reproduced from the TIDAL CURRENT CHARTS, UPPER CHESAPEAKE BAY published by the U.S. Coast & Geodetic Survey, ESSA with their permission.

The direction and speed of the current is given for each hour before and after "maximum flood and ebb current at Baltimore Harbor Approaches" (off Sandy Pt.). Although these charts should be used with the "Tidal Current Tables" of the USC&GS, a very, very rough estimate of Maximum Flood is one hour before high tide and Maximum Ebb, one hour before low tide at Sandy Pt. Current is the horizontal movement of water, whereas Tide is the vertical.

The arrows show the direction of the current; the figures give the speed at the time of spring tides, that is, at the time of new or full moon when they are strongest. If the speed is less than 0.1 knot it is described as "weak." The decimal point indicates the location of the station where the current was described.

The flow of the current is depicted under normal conditions. Therefore, caution should be exercised as strong winds or the opening of the flood gates of Conowingo Dam may considerably change both the speed and direction of the currents as shown.

These charts may be used for any year and, with the Current Tables, the speed of the current may be predicted for any time of any day. This is done by selecting the time and speed of Maximum Flood or Ebb at Baltimore Harbor Approaches for the day desired. The time will inform you which chart to use. With the predicted speed enter Table 1 to obtain the correction factor to be multiplied by speed of the current shown on the chart for the station desired.

### TABLE 1 Factors for Correcting Speeds

| Predicted Speed (knots) at Baltimore Harbor Approach (A) | Factor to apply to Speeds on charts (B) |
|---|---|
| 0.2 | 0.2 |
| 0.3 | 0.3 |
| 0.4 | 0.4 |
| 0.5 | 0.6 |
| 0.6 | 0.7 |
| 0.7 | 0.8 |
| 0.8 | 0.9 |
| 0.9 | 1.0 |
| 1.0 | 1.1 |
| 1.1 | 1.2 |
| 1.2 | 1.3 |
| 1.3 | 1.4 |
| 1.4 | 1.6 |
| 1.5 | 1.7 |
| 1.6 | 1.8 |
| 1.7 | 1.9 |
| 1.8 | 2.0 |
| 1.9 | 2.1 |
| 2.0 | 2.2 |

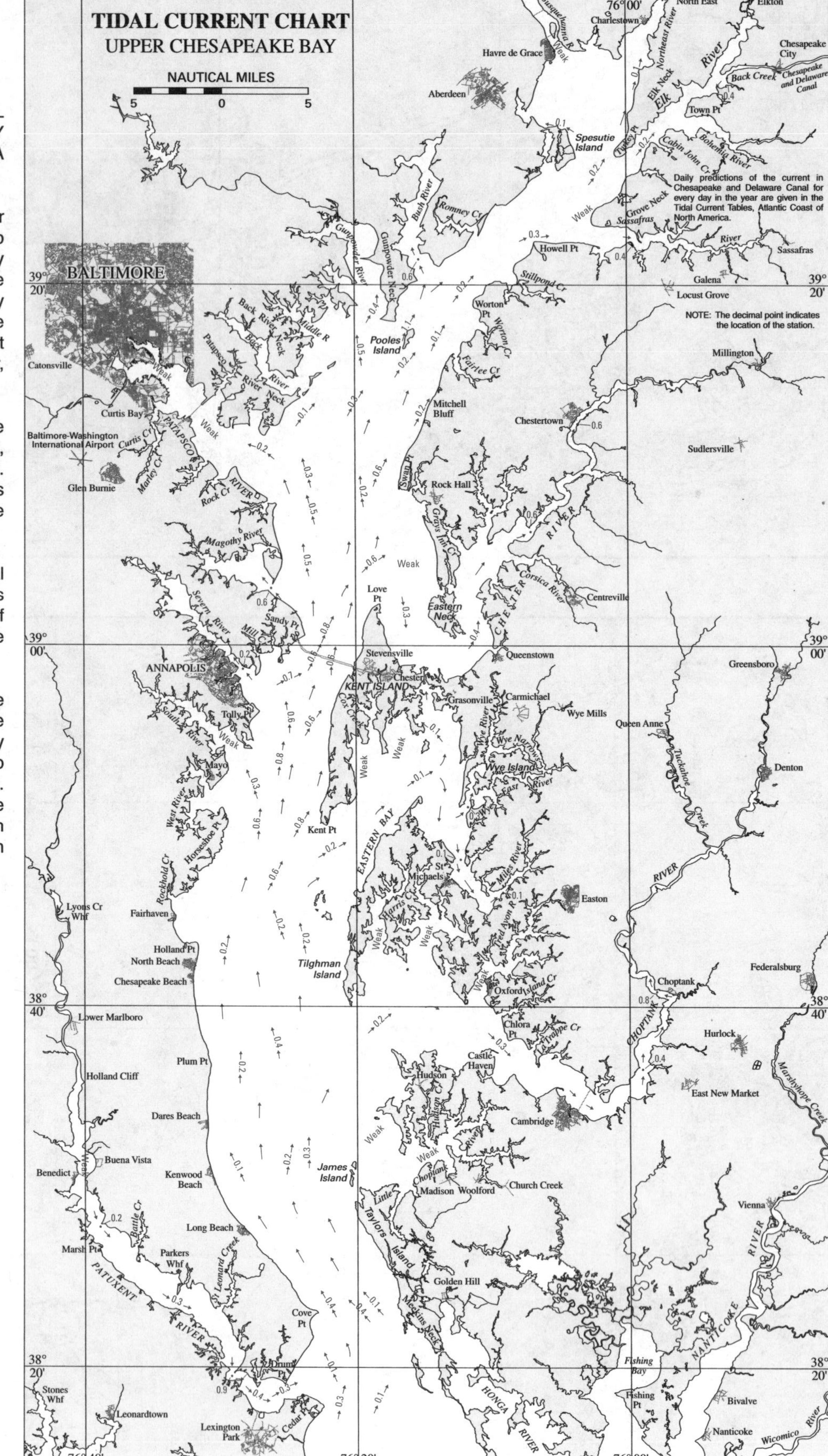


ONE HOUR BEFORE MAXIMUM FLOOD AT BALTIMORE HARBOR APPROACH (F–1)

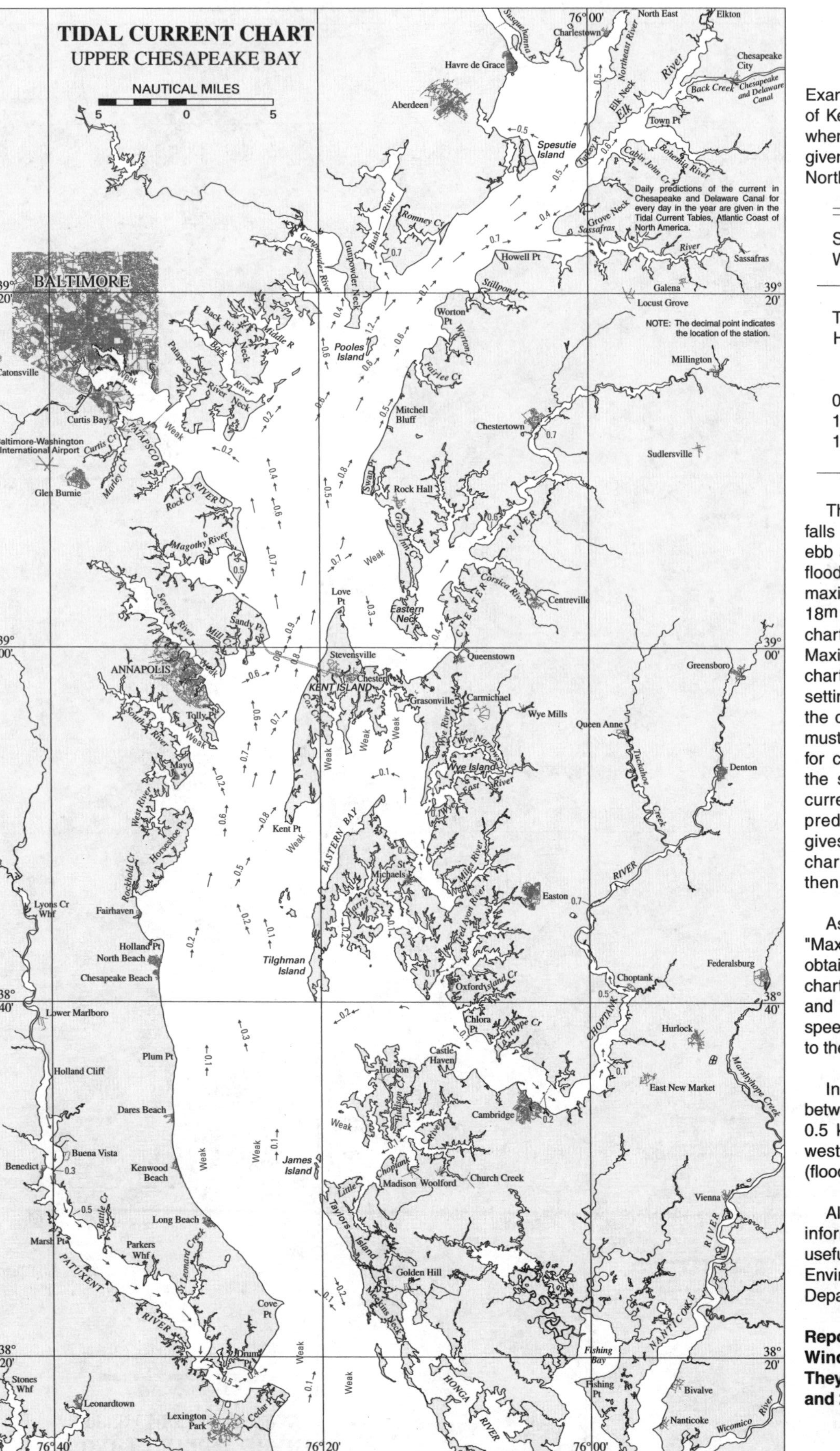


MAXIMUM FLOOD AT BALTIMORE HARBOR APPROACH (F)

Example — The speed and direction of the current west of Kent Pt. are desired for 1030 a.m. (E.S.T.) on a day when the predictions for Baltimore Harbor Approach as given in the "Tidal Current Tables, Atlantic Coast of North America" are as follows:

| Slack Water | Maximum Current | |
|---|---|---|
| Time H.M. | Time H.M. | Vel. Knots. |
| | 0242 | 0.8 E |
| 0536 | 0912 | 1.1 F |
| 1248 | 1554 | 0.9 E |
| 1930 | 2148 | 0.5 F |

The predictions show that the desired time of 1030 falls between maximum flood at 0912 and slack before ebb at 1248. Therefore, the current at the station was flooding at 1030, and one of the charts referring to maximum flood must be used. The desired time is 1h 18m after "Maximum Flood" at 0912. Therefore, the chart to be used is the one designated "One Hour After Maximum Flood at Baltimore Harbor Approach." This chart shows the current west of Kent Pt. is 0.6 knot setting northeast (flooding). To determine the speed of the current for this particular day and hour, this speed must be modified by a factor given in Table 1, "Factors for correcting speeds." From the tidal current tables the speed of the current at 0912 (time of maximum current used as reference) is 1.1 knots. For a predicted maximum speed of 1.1 knots the table gives a factor of 1.2 to be applied to the speed on the chart. The approximate speed west of Kent Pt. is then 1.2 x 0.6 = 0.7 knot.

As the actual time difference is 1h 18m after "Maximum Flood" a value for the specified time may be obtained by interpolating between values from the two charts designated "One Hour After Maximum Flood" and "Two Hors After Maximum Flood." The corrected speed derived from the latter chart by a process similar to the one just described is 1.2 x 0.4 = 0.5 knot.

Interpolating for 1h 18m after maximum flood between 0.7 knot at one hour after maximum flood and 0.5 knot at 2 hours after maximum flood, the current west of Kent Pt. is found to be setting northeast (flooding) with a speed of 0.6 knot.

All persons using these charts are invited to send information or suggestions for increasing their usefulness to the Director, Coast and Geodetic Survey, Environmental Science Services Administration, U.S. Department of Commerce, Rockville, Maryland 20852.

**Reports were generated by Tides and Currents for Windows from Nautical Software (503) 579-1414. They are for the 6 summer months of the years 2008 and 2009.**

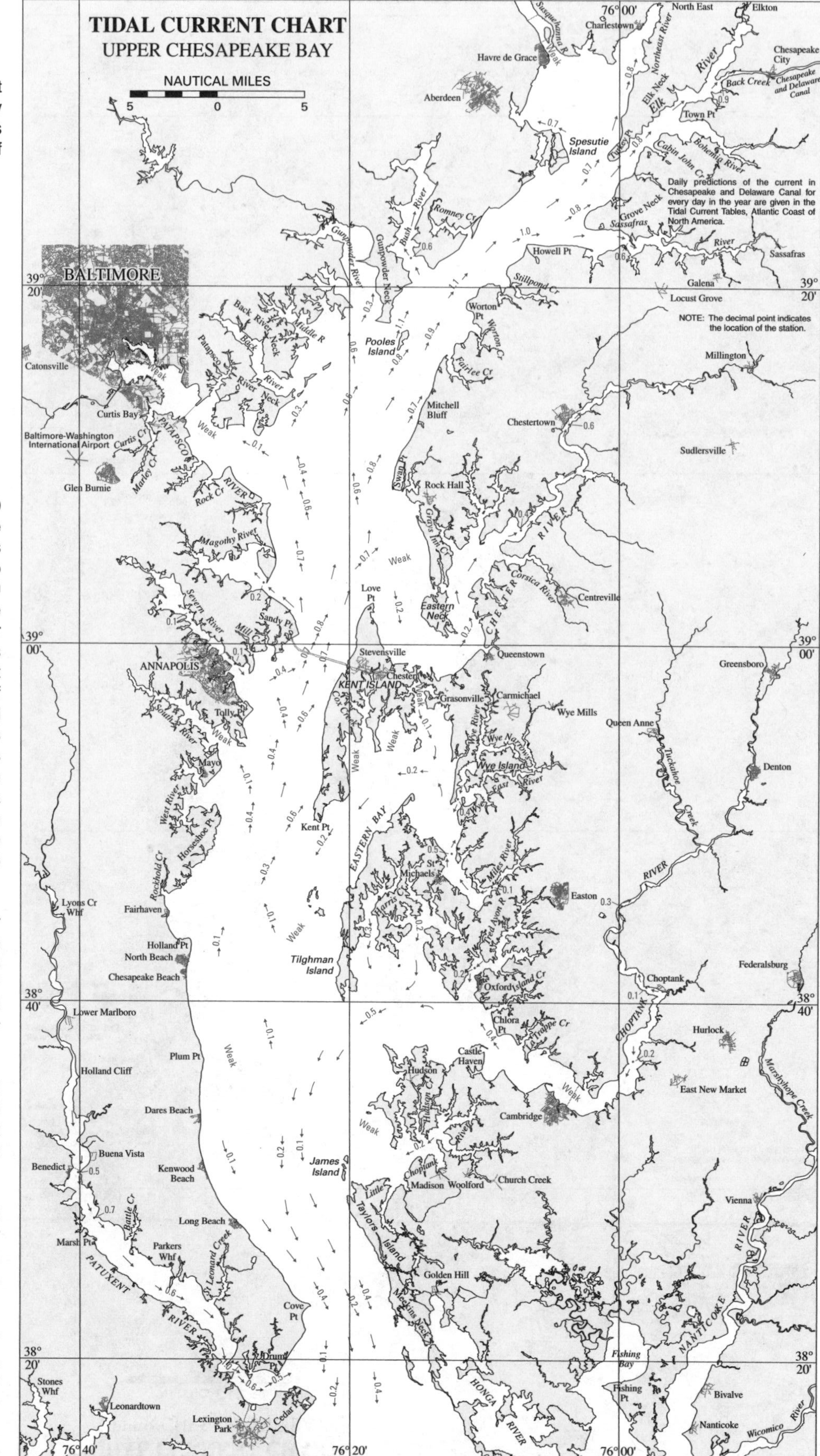


ONE HOUR AFTER MAXIMUM FLOOD AT BALTIMORE HARBOR APPROACH (F+1)

# TIDAL CURRENTS - 2008

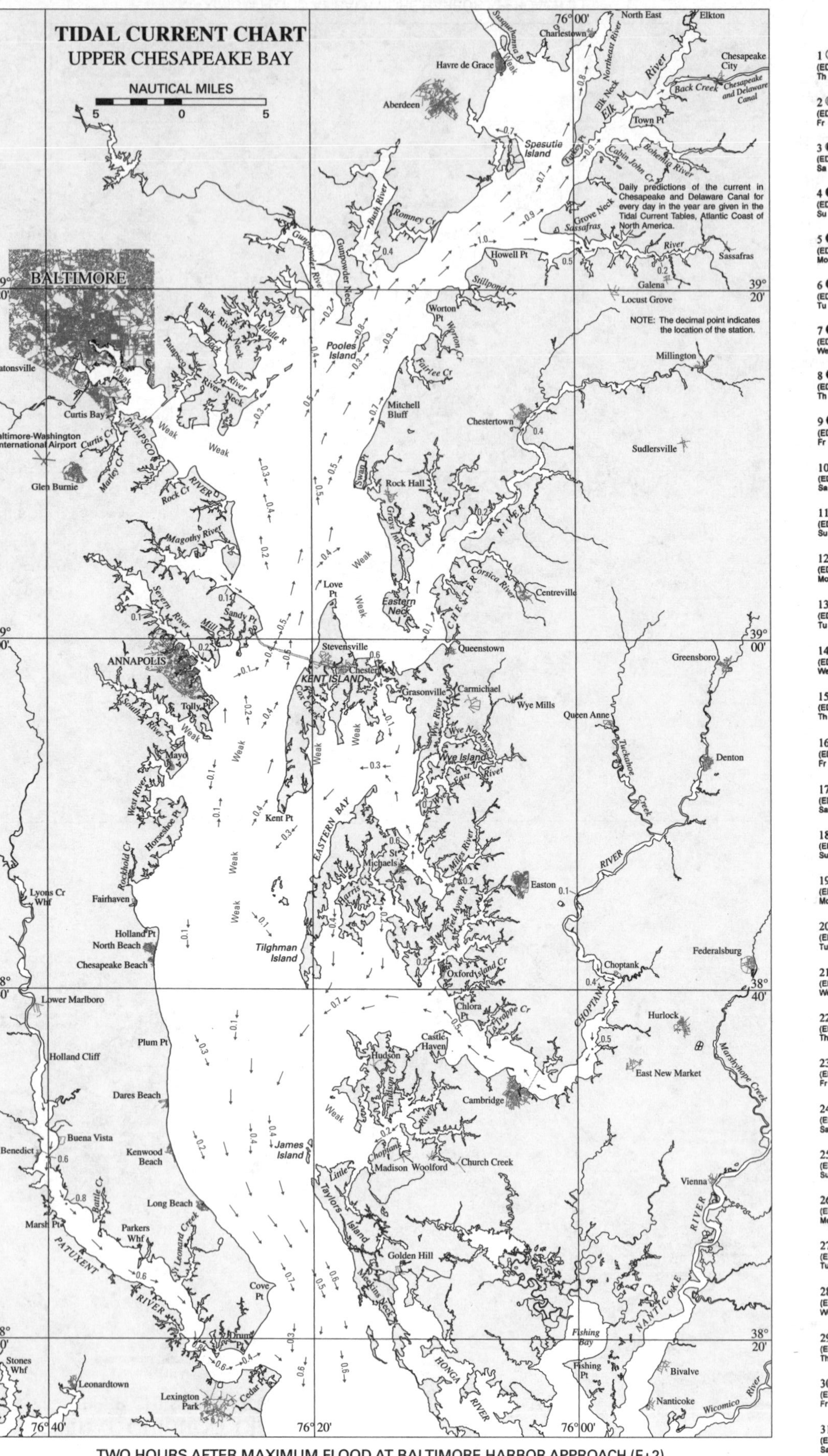


TWO HOURS AFTER MAXIMUM FLOOD AT BALTIMORE HARBOR APPROACH (F+2)

## May

| Day | Slack h m | Max h m | knots |
|---|---|---|---|
| 1 (EDT) Th | | 2:36a | 0.8F |
| | 5:54a | 8:55a | 0.7E |
| | 12:05p | 2:54p | 0.6F |
| | 5:42p | 8:53p | 0.7E |
| | 11:51p | | |
| 2 (EDT) Fr | | 3:18a | 0.9F |
| | 6:39a | 9:48a | 0.8E |
| | 1:09p | 3:47p | 0.5F |
| | 6:27p | 9:33p | 0.7E |
| 3 (EDT) Sa | 12:24a | 3:59a | 1.1F |
| | 7:25a | 10:37a | 1.0E |
| | 2:09p | 4:37p | 0.5F |
| | 7:10p | 10:14p | 0.7E |
| 4 (EDT) Su | 12:58a | 4:40a | 1.2F |
| | 8:10a | 11:25a | 1.1E |
| | 3:05p | 5:26p | 0.5F |
| | 7:54p | 10:56p | 0.7E |
| 5 (EDT) Mo | 1:36a | 5:23a | 1.3F |
| | 8:55a | 12:13p | 1.1E |
| | 3:58p | 6:15p | 0.5F |
| | 8:39p | 11:39p | 0.7E |
| 6 (EDT) Tu | 2:18a | 6:08a | 1.3F |
| | 9:42a | 1:00p | 1.2E |
| | 4:49p | 7:04p | 0.5F |
| | 9:28p | | |
| 7 (EDT) We | | 12:26a | 0.7E |
| | 3:03a | 6:55a | 1.3F |
| | 10:29a | 1:49p | 1.2E |
| | 5:39p | 7:55p | 0.5F |
| | 10:22p | | |
| 8 (EDT) Th | | 1:18a | 0.6E |
| | 3:54a | 7:44a | 1.3F |
| | 11:18a | 2:39p | 1.1E |
| | 6:28p | 8:50p | 0.5F |
| | 11:22p | | |
| 9 (EDT) Fr | | 2:14a | 0.6E |
| | 4:50a | 8:38a | 1.2F |
| | 12:08p | 3:31p | 1.1E |
| | 7:17p | 9:47p | 0.5F |
| 10 (EDT) Sa | 12:30a | 3:18a | 0.6E |
| | 5:53a | 9:35a | 1.0F |
| | 1:00p | 4:24p | 1.0E |
| | 8:04p | 10:46p | 0.6F |
| 11 (EDT) Su | 1:42a | 4:28a | 0.5E |
| | 7:06a | 10:38a | 0.9F |
| | 1:54p | 5:19p | 0.9E |
| | 8:51p | 11:46p | 0.7F |
| 12 (EDT) Mo | 2:55a | 5:42a | 0.5E |
| | 8:27a | 11:45a | 0.7F |
| | 2:50p | 6:14p | 0.9E |
| | 9:36p | | |
| 13 (EDT) Tu | | 12:45a | 0.8F |
| | 4:03a | 6:55a | 0.6E |
| | 9:51a | 12:52p | 0.6F |
| | 3:46p | 7:08p | 0.8E |
| | 10:20p | | |
| 14 (EDT) We | | 1:40a | 0.9F |
| | 5:04a | 8:03a | 0.7E |
| | 11:12a | 1:58p | 0.6F |
| | 4:42p | 7:59p | 0.8E |
| | 11:02p | | |
| 15 (EDT) Th | | 2:31a | 1.0F |
| | 5:59a | 9:03a | 0.8E |
| | 12:24p | 2:59p | 0.5F |
| | 5:35p | 8:48p | 0.7E |
| | 11:42p | | |
| 16 (EDT) Fr | | 3:18a | 1.0F |
| | 6:48a | 9:57a | 0.9E |
| | 1:28p | 3:55p | 0.5F |
| | 6:26p | 9:33p | 0.7E |
| 17 (EDT) Sa | 12:21a | 4:02a | 1.1F |
| | 7:33a | 10:46a | 0.9E |
| | 2:25p | 4:46p | 0.5F |
| | 7:15p | 10:17p | 0.6E |
| 18 (EDT) Su | 12:58a | 4:43a | 1.1F |
| | 8:15a | 11:32a | 1.0E |
| | 3:16p | 5:34p | 0.4F |
| | 8:02p | 10:58p | 0.6E |
| 19 (EDT) Mo | 1:34a | 5:23a | 1.1F |
| | 8:54a | 12:14p | 1.0E |
| | 4:04p | 6:20p | 0.4F |
| | 8:47p | 11:38p | 0.5E |
| 20 (EDT) Tu | 2:10a | 6:01a | 1.1F |
| | 9:33a | 12:56p | 1.0E |
| | 4:49p | 7:05p | 0.4F |
| | 9:33p | | |
| 21 (EDT) We | | 12:19a | 0.5E |
| | 2:45a | 6:40a | 1.1F |
| | 10:11a | 1:37p | 1.0E |
| | 5:33p | 7:49p | 0.4F |
| | 10:20p | | |
| 22 (EDT) Th | | 1:00a | 0.4E |
| | 3:23a | 7:19a | 1.0F |
| | 10:50a | 2:17p | 1.0E |
| | 6:16p | 8:34p | 0.4F |
| | 11:09p | | |
| 23 (EDT) Fr | | 1:44a | 0.4E |
| | 4:03a | 8:00a | 1.0F |
| | 11:29a | 2:59p | 1.0E |
| | 6:56p | 9:19p | 0.4F |
| 24 (EDT) Sa | 12:01a | 2:32a | 0.4E |
| | 4:49a | 8:44a | 0.9F |
| | 12:10p | 3:41p | 0.9E |
| | 7:35p | 10:05p | 0.4F |
| 25 (EDT) Su | 12:56a | 3:25a | 0.3E |
| | 5:43a | 9:32a | 0.8F |
| | 12:53p | 4:24p | 0.9E |
| | 8:10p | 10:52p | 0.5F |
| 26 (EDT) Mo | 1:53a | 4:24a | 0.3E |
| | 6:48a | 10:24a | 0.7F |
| | 1:37p | 5:07p | 0.8E |
| | 8:43p | 11:38p | 0.6F |
| 27 (EDT) Tu | 2:51a | 5:27a | 0.4E |
| | 8:02a | 11:21a | 0.6F |
| | 2:22p | 5:50p | 0.8E |
| | 9:14p | | |
| 28 (EDT) We | | 12:24a | 0.7F |
| | 3:46a | 6:32a | 0.5E |
| | 9:24a | 12:21p | 0.5F |
| | 3:08p | 6:33p | 0.7E |
| | 9:45p | | |
| 29 (EDT) Th | | 1:09a | 0.8F |
| | 4:38a | 7:34a | 0.6E |
| | 10:45a | 1:22p | 0.4F |
| | 3:55p | 7:17p | 0.7E |
| | 10:18p | | |
| 30 (EDT) Fr | | 1:54a | 0.9F |
| | 5:28a | 8:33a | 0.7E |
| | 12:01p | 2:22p | 0.4F |
| | 4:43p | 8:01p | 0.7E |
| | 10:53p | | |
| 31 (EDT) Sa | | 2:39a | 1.1F |
| | 6:16a | 9:28a | 0.9E |
| | 1:10p | 3:19p | 0.4F |
| | 5:32p | 8:47p | 0.7E |
| | 11:32p | | |

## June

| Day | Slack h m | Max h m | knots |
|---|---|---|---|
| 1 (EDT) Su | | 3:25a | 1.2F |
| | 7:03a | 10:19a | 1.0E |
| | 2:10p | 4:14p | 0.3F |
| | 6:24p | 9:34p | 0.7E |
| 2 (EDT) Mo | 12:15a | 4:11a | 1.3F |
| | 7:50a | 11:09a | 1.1E |
| | 3:04p | 5:07p | 0.4F |
| | 7:17p | 10:23p | 0.7E |
| 3 (EDT) Tu | 1:01a | 4:58a | 1.4F |
| | 8:37a | 11:57a | 1.2E |
| | 3:52p | 5:59p | 0.4F |
| | 8:13p | 11:15p | 0.7E |
| 4 (EDT) We | 1:50a | 5:47a | 1.4F |
| | 9:23a | 12:44p | 1.2E |
| | 4:38p | 6:50p | 0.5F |
| | 9:12p | | |
| 5 (EDT) Th | | 12:09a | 0.7E |
| | 2:43a | 6:36a | 1.3F |
| | 10:10a | 1:31p | 1.2E |
| | 5:21p | 7:42p | 0.5F |
| | 10:14p | | |
| 6 (EDT) Fr | | 1:06a | 0.6E |
| | 3:40a | 7:28a | 1.2F |
| | 10:57a | 2:19p | 1.2E |
| | 6:03p | 8:34p | 0.6F |
| | 11:19p | | |
| 7 (EDT) Sa | | 2:06a | 0.6E |
| | 4:41a | 8:21a | 1.1F |
| | 11:44a | 3:07p | 1.1E |
| | 6:44p | 9:28p | 0.7F |
| 8 (EDT) Su | 12:25a | 3:10a | 0.6E |
| | 5:48a | 9:17a | 0.9F |
| | 12:31p | 3:56p | 1.0E |
| | 7:26p | 10:22p | 0.8F |
| 9 (EDT) Mo | 1:33a | 4:17a | 0.6E |
| | 7:01a | 10:16a | 0.8F |
| | 1:19p | 4:45p | 1.0E |
| | 8:08p | 11:17p | 0.8F |
| 10 (EDT) Tu | 2:39a | 5:26a | 0.6E |
| | 8:19a | 11:19a | 0.6F |
| | 2:09p | 5:35p | 0.9E |
| | 8:51p | | |
| 11 (EDT) We | | 12:12a | 0.9F |
| | 3:43a | 6:35a | 0.6E |
| | 9:42a | 12:23p | 0.5F |
| | 3:00p | 6:26p | 0.8E |
| | 9:33p | | |
| 12 (EDT) Th | | 1:05a | 1.0F |
| | 4:41a | 7:41a | 0.7E |
| | 11:02a | 1:28p | 0.4F |
| | 3:54p | 7:16p | 0.7E |
| | 10:16p | | |
| 13 (EDT) Fr | | 1:56a | 1.0F |
| | 5:35a | 8:41a | 0.8E |
| | 12:16p | 2:31p | 0.4F |
| | 4:48p | 8:06p | 0.6E |
| | 10:57p | | |
| 14 (EDT) Sa | | 2:45a | 1.1F |
| | 6:24a | 9:36a | 0.9E |
| | 1:22p | 3:30p | 0.3F |
| | 5:44p | 8:55p | 0.6E |
| | 11:38p | | |
| 15 (EDT) Su | | 3:30a | 1.1F |
| | 7:08a | 10:26a | 0.9E |
| | 2:18p | 4:25p | 0.3F |
| | 6:38p | 9:42p | 0.5E |
| 16 (EDT) Mo | 12:18a | 4:14a | 1.1F |
| | 7:51a | 11:12a | 1.0E |
| | 3:08p | 5:15p | 0.3F |
| | 7:32p | 10:27p | 0.5E |
| 17 (EDT) Tu | 12:58a | 4:55a | 1.1F |
| | 8:30a | 11:54a | 1.0E |
| | 3:53p | 6:02p | 0.4F |
| | 8:23p | 11:11p | 0.5E |
| 18 (EDT) We | 1:37a | 5:36a | 1.1F |
| | 9:09a | 12:35p | 1.1E |
| | 4:34p | 6:46p | 0.4F |
| | 9:13p | 11:55p | 0.4E |
| 19 (EDT) Th | 2:18a | 6:16a | 1.1F |
| | 9:47a | 1:14p | 1.1E |
| | 5:12p | 7:29p | 0.4F |
| | 10:01p | | |
| 20 (EDT) Fr | | 12:39a | 0.4E |
| | 3:00a | 6:56a | 1.1F |
| | 10:25a | 1:52p | 1.0E |
| | 5:47p | 8:10p | 0.4F |
| | 10:50p | | |
| 21 (EDT) Sa | | 1:25a | 0.4E |
| | 3:46a | 7:37a | 1.0F |
| | 11:02a | 2:30p | 1.0E |
| | 6:19p | 8:50p | 0.5F |
| | 11:39p | | |
| 22 (EDT) Su | | 2:13a | 0.4E |
| | 4:36a | 8:20a | 0.9F |
| | 11:40a | 3:07p | 1.0E |
| | 6:49p | 9:31p | 0.5F |
| 23 (EDT) Mo | 12:30a | 3:05a | 0.4E |
| | 5:33a | 9:05a | 0.8F |
| | 12:18p | 3:44p | 0.9E |
| | 7:18p | 10:12p | 0.6F |
| 24 (EDT) Tu | 1:23a | 4:00a | 0.4E |
| | 6:38a | 9:54a | 0.6F |
| | 12:55p | 4:22p | 0.8E |
| | 7:46p | 10:54p | 0.7F |
| 25 (EDT) We | 2:17a | 5:00a | 0.5E |
| | 7:51a | 10:47a | 0.5F |
| | 1:34p | 5:01p | 0.8E |
| | 8:16p | 11:39p | 0.8F |
| 26 (EDT) Th | 3:12a | 6:03a | 0.6E |
| | 9:12a | 11:45a | 0.4F |
| | 2:14p | 5:42p | 0.7E |
| | 8:48p | | |
| 27 (EDT) Fr | | 12:26a | 0.9F |
| | 4:07a | 7:07a | 0.6E |
| | 10:37a | 12:47p | 0.3F |
| | 2:57p | 6:28p | 0.7E |
| | 9:25p | | |
| 28 (EDT) Sa | | 1:15a | 1.1F |
| | 5:01a | 8:09a | 0.8E |
| | 11:58a | 1:51p | 0.2F |
| | 3:47p | 7:17p | 0.6E |
| | 10:08p | | |
| 29 (EDT) Su | | 2:06a | 1.2F |
| | 5:53a | 9:07a | 0.9E |
| | 1:07p | 2:54p | 0.2F |
| | 4:45p | 8:10p | 0.6E |
| | 10:55p | | |
| 30 (EDT) Mo | | 2:57a | 1.3F |
| | 6:43a | 10:01a | 1.0E |
| | 2:04p | 3:54p | 0.3F |
| | 5:49p | 9:06p | 0.6E |
| | 11:47p | | |

## July

| Day | Slack h m | Max h m | knots |
|---|---|---|---|
| 1 (EDT) Tu | | 3:49a | 1.3F |
| | 7:32a | 10:52a | 1.1E |
| | 2:51p | 4:50p | 0.3F |
| | 6:55p | 10:04p | 0.6E |
| 2 (EDT) We | 12:42a | 4:41a | 1.3F |
| | 8:20a | 11:40a | 1.1E |
| | 3:33p | 5:43p | 0.4F |
| | 8:01p | 11:02p | 0.7E |
| 3 (EDT) Th | 1:39a | 5:32a | 1.3F |
| | 9:06a | 12:26p | 1.2E |
| | 4:12p | 6:33p | 0.5F |
| | 9:05p | | |
| 4 (EDT) Fr | | 12:00a | 0.7E |
| | 2:38a | 6:23a | 1.3F |
| | 9:51a | 1:11p | 1.2E |
| | 4:50p | 7:23p | 0.6F |
| | 10:07p | | |
| 5 (EDT) Sa | | 12:59a | 0.7E |
| | 3:38a | 7:14a | 1.2F |
| | 10:35a | 1:55p | 1.1E |
| | 5:28p | 8:12p | 0.7F |
| | 11:08p | | |
| 6 (EDT) Su | | 1:58a | 0.7E |
| | 4:40a | 8:06a | 1.0F |
| | 11:19a | 2:39p | 1.1E |
| | 6:06p | 9:02p | 0.8F |
| 7 (EDT) Mo | 12:10a | 2:58a | 0.7E |
| | 5:45a | 8:59a | 0.9F |
| | 12:02p | 3:24p | 1.0E |
| | 6:45p | 9:52p | 0.9F |
| 8 (EDT) Tu | 1:11a | 3:59a | 0.7E |
| | 6:53a | 9:53a | 0.7F |
| | 12:45p | 4:09p | 0.9E |
| | 7:25p | 10:43p | 0.9F |
| 9 (EDT) We | 2:11a | 5:02a | 0.6E |
| | 8:06a | 10:50a | 0.5F |
| | 1:30p | 4:55p | 0.8E |
| | 8:06p | 11:35p | 1.0F |
| 10 (EDT) Th | 3:11a | 6:07a | 0.7E |
| | 9:24a | 11:51a | 0.4F |
| | 2:17p | 5:44p | 0.7E |
| | 8:48p | | |
| 11 (EDT) Fr | | 12:27a | 1.0F |
| | 4:09a | 7:11a | 0.7E |
| | 10:43a | 12:55p | 0.3F |
| | 3:08p | 6:35p | 0.6E |
| | 9:31p | | |
| 12 (EDT) Sa | | 1:19a | 1.0F |
| | 5:03a | 8:12a | 0.7E |
| | 11:59a | 2:01p | 0.3F |
| | 4:06p | 7:27p | 0.6E |
| | 10:16p | | |
| 13 (EDT) Su | | 2:10a | 1.0F |
| | 5:53a | 9:09a | 0.8E |
| | 1:05p | 3:03p | 0.3F |
| | 5:07p | 8:20p | 0.5E |
| | 11:01p | | |
| 14 (EDT) Mo | | 2:59a | 1.1F |
| | 6:40a | 10:00a | 0.9E |
| | 1:59p | 4:00p | 0.3F |
| | 6:09p | 9:12p | 0.5E |
| | 11:46p | | |
| 15 (EDT) Tu | | 3:46a | 1.1F |
| | 7:24a | 10:46a | 0.9E |
| | 2:45p | 4:51p | 0.3F |
| | 7:08p | 10:02p | 0.5E |
| 16 (EDT) We | 12:31a | 4:30a | 1.1F |
| | 8:05a | 11:29a | 1.0E |
| | 3:25p | 5:37p | 0.4F |
| | 8:01p | 10:50p | 0.5E |
| 17 (EDT) Th | 1:17a | 5:13a | 1.1F |
| | 8:44a | 12:09p | 1.0E |
| | 4:01p | 6:19p | 0.4F |
| | 8:51p | 11:36p | 0.5E |
| 18 (EDT) Fr | 2:04a | 5:55a | 1.1F |
| | 9:22a | 12:46p | 1.0E |
| | 4:33p | 6:59p | 0.5F |
| | 9:38p | | |
| 19 (EDT) Sa | | 12:22a | 0.5E |
| | 2:51a | 6:36a | 1.0F |
| | 9:59a | 1:22p | 1.0E |
| | 5:02p | 7:36p | 0.5F |
| | 10:23p | | |
| 20 (EDT) Su | | 1:07a | 0.5E |
| | 3:41a | 7:17a | 1.0F |
| | 10:35a | 1:56p | 1.0E |
| | 5:29p | 8:13p | 0.6F |
| | 11:09p | | |
| 21 (EDT) Mo | | 1:54a | 0.6E |
| | 4:34a | 7:59a | 0.9F |
| | 11:10a | 2:30p | 0.9E |
| | 5:55p | 8:50p | 0.7F |
| | 11:56p | | |
| 22 (EDT) Tu | | 2:44a | 0.6E |
| | 5:30a | 8:42a | 0.7F |
| | 11:44a | 3:04p | 0.9E |
| | 6:21p | 9:29p | 0.8F |
| 23 (EDT) We | 12:47a | 3:37a | 0.6E |
| | 6:33a | 9:29a | 0.6F |
| | 12:18p | 3:39p | 0.8E |
| | 6:50p | 10:11p | 0.9F |
| 24 (EDT) Th | 1:40a | 4:34a | 0.6E |
| | 7:43a | 10:19a | 0.4F |
| | 12:52p | 4:17p | 0.7E |
| | 7:22p | 10:57p | 1.0F |
| 25 (EDT) Fr | 2:36a | 5:35a | 0.7E |
| | 9:02a | 11:16a | 0.3F |
| | 1:30p | 5:00p | 0.7E |
| | 8:00p | 11:47p | 1.0F |
| 26 (EDT) Sa | 3:34a | 6:40a | 0.7E |
| | 10:26a | 12:20p | 0.2F |
| | 2:15p | 5:49p | 0.6E |
| | 8:44p | | |
| 27 (EDT) Su | | 12:42a | 1.1F |
| | 4:32a | 7:44a | 0.8E |
| | 11:45a | 1:28p | 0.2F |
| | 3:12p | 6:46p | 0.6E |
| | 9:36p | | |
| 28 (EDT) Mo | | 1:39a | 1.2F |
| | 5:29a | 8:45a | 0.9E |
| | 12:50p | 2:35p | 0.2F |
| | 4:24p | 7:49p | 0.6E |
| | 10:34p | | |
| 29 (EDT) Tu | | 2:37a | 1.2F |
| | 6:23a | 9:41a | 0.9E |
| | 1:39p | 3:37p | 0.3F |
| | 5:40p | 8:54p | 0.6E |
| | 11:36p | | |
| 30 (EDT) We | | 3:34a | 1.2F |
| | 7:14a | 10:32a | 1.0E |
| | 2:21p | 4:33p | 0.4F |
| | 6:52p | 9:58p | 0.6E |
| 31 (EDT) Th | 12:39a | 4:29a | 1.2F |
| | 8:02a | 11:19a | 1.1E |
| | 2:58p | 5:24p | 0.5F |
| | 7:58p | 10:58p | 0.7E |

**Reports were generated by Tides and Currents for Windows from Nautical Software (503) 579-1414.**

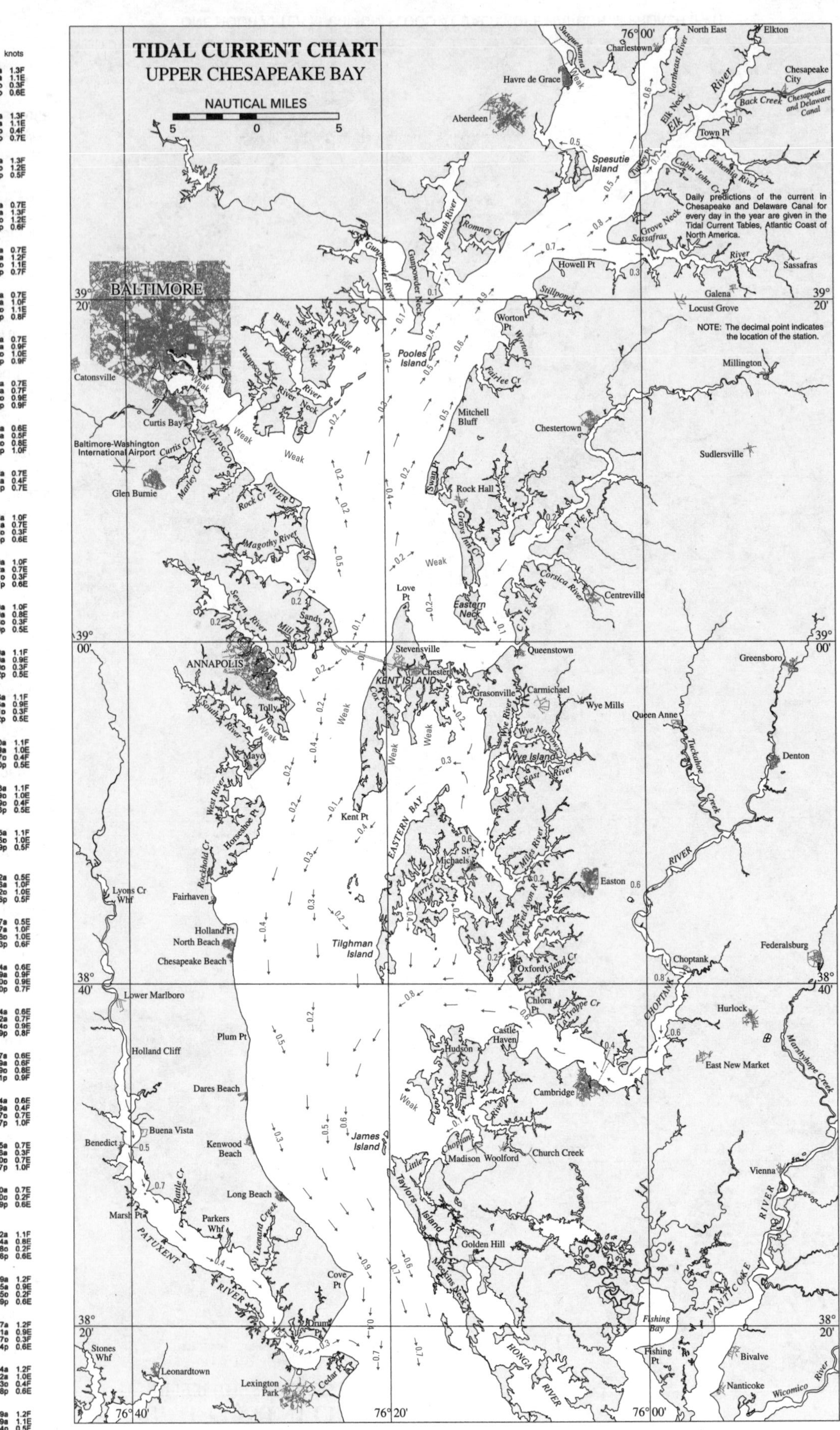


THREE HOURS AFTER MAXIMUM FLOOD AT BALTIMORE HARBOR APPROACH (F+3)

# TIDAL CURRENTS - 2008

TIDAL CURRENT CHART
UPPER CHESAPEAKE BAY

TWO HOURS BEFORE MAXIMUM EBB AT BALTIMORE HARBOR APPROACH (E–2)

## August

| Date | Slack h m | Max h m | knots |
|---|---|---|---|
| 1 (EDT) Fr | 1:42a<br>8:47a<br>3:34p<br>8:58p | 5:21a<br>12:03p<br>6:12p<br>11:56p | 1.2F<br>1.1E<br>0.7F<br>0.7E |
| 2 (EDT) Sa | 2:43a<br>9:31a<br>4:10p<br>9:55p | 6:12a<br>12:46p<br>6:59p | 1.1F<br>1.1E<br>0.8F |
| 3 (EDT) Su | 3:42a<br>10:13a<br>4:46p<br>10:51p | 12:52a<br>7:02a<br>1:27p<br>7:45p | 0.8E<br>1.0F<br>1.1E<br>0.9F |
| 4 (EDT) Mo | 4:41a<br>10:54a<br>5:23p<br>11:45p | 1:46a<br>7:50a<br>2:09p<br>8:30p | 0.8E<br>0.9F<br>1.0E<br>0.9F |
| 5 (EDT) Tu | 5:41a<br>11:34a<br>6:00p | 2:40a<br>8:39a<br>2:50p<br>9:17p | 0.8E<br>0.8F<br>0.9E<br>1.0F |
| 6 (EDT) We | 12:40a<br>6:43a<br>12:14p<br>6:39p | 3:36a<br>9:30a<br>3:32p<br>10:04p | 0.7E<br>0.6F<br>0.8E<br>1.0F |
| 7 (EDT) Th | 1:35a<br>7:49a<br>12:56p<br>7:19p | 4:33a<br>10:23a<br>4:16p<br>10:54p | 0.7E<br>0.5F<br>0.7E<br>1.0F |
| 8 (EDT) Fr | 2:31a<br>9:01a<br>1:42p<br>8:02p | 5:33a<br>11:21a<br>5:04p<br>11:46p | 0.7E<br>0.3F<br>0.6E<br>0.9F |
| 9 (EDT) Sa | 3:28a<br>10:17a<br>2:35p<br>8:48p | 6:35a<br>12:24p<br>5:56p | 0.7E<br>0.3F<br>0.5E |
| 10 (EDT) Su | 4:23a<br>11:30a<br>3:37p<br>9:37p | 12:39a<br>7:37a<br>1:31p<br>6:53p | 0.9F<br>0.7E<br>0.2F<br>0.5E |
| 11 (EDT) Mo | 5:16a<br>12:32p<br>4:45p<br>10:29p | 1:34a<br>8:35a<br>2:35p<br>7:51p | 0.9F<br>0.8E<br>0.3F<br>0.5E |
| 12 (EDT) Tu | 6:05a<br>1:23p<br>5:50p<br>11:22p | 2:27a<br>9:27a<br>3:32p<br>8:48p | 1.0F<br>0.8E<br>0.3F<br>0.5E |
| 13 (EDT) We | 6:52a<br>2:04p<br>6:49p | 3:18a<br>10:14a<br>4:21p<br>9:42p | 1.0F<br>0.9E<br>0.4F<br>0.5E |
| 14 (EDT) Th | 12:15a<br>7:35a<br>2:40p<br>7:40p | 4:05a<br>10:56a<br>5:05p<br>10:32p | 1.0F<br>0.9E<br>0.4F<br>0.5E |
| 15 (EDT) Fr | 1:07a<br>8:15a<br>3:11p<br>8:26p | 4:50a<br>11:34a<br>5:44p<br>11:19p | 1.0F<br>1.0E<br>0.5F<br>0.6E |
| 16 (EDT) Sa | 1:58a<br>8:54a<br>3:39p<br>9:10p | 5:33a<br>12:10p<br>6:20p | 1.0F<br>1.0E<br>0.6F |
| 17 (EDT) Su | 2:50a<br>9:31a<br>4:05p<br>9:53p | 12:04a<br>6:15a<br>12:44p<br>6:56p | 0.6E<br>1.0F<br>0.9E<br>0.7F |
| 18 (EDT) Mo | 3:41a<br>10:05a<br>4:31p<br>10:37p | 12:49a<br>6:57a<br>1:17p<br>7:31p | 0.7E<br>0.9F<br>0.9E<br>0.8F |
| 19 (EDT) Tu | 4:34a<br>10:39a<br>4:57p<br>11:23p | 1:35a<br>7:38a<br>1:49p<br>8:08p | 0.7E<br>0.8F<br>0.9E<br>0.9F |
| 20 (EDT) We | 5:31a<br>11:12a<br>5:25p | 2:23a<br>8:22a<br>2:23p<br>8:48p | 0.8E<br>0.7F<br>0.8E<br>1.0F |
| 21 (EDT) Th | 12:12a<br>6:31a<br>11:45a<br>5:57p | 3:14a<br>9:08a<br>2:59p<br>9:31p | 0.8E<br>0.5F<br>0.7E<br>1.0F |
| 22 (EDT) Fr | 1:05a<br>7:38a<br>12:21p<br>6:35p | 4:09a<br>9:58a<br>3:40p<br>10:20p | 0.8E<br>0.4F<br>0.7E<br>1.1F |
| 23 (EDT) Sa | 2:01a<br>8:51a<br>1:04p<br>7:21p | 5:09a<br>10:56a<br>4:28p<br>11:14p | 0.8E<br>0.3F<br>0.6E<br>1.1F |
| 24 (EDT) Su | 3:01a<br>10:07a<br>1:59p<br>8:15p | 6:13a<br>12:01p<br>5:25p | 0.8E<br>0.2F<br>0.6E |
| 25 (EDT) Mo | 4:02a<br>11:16a<br>3:11p<br>9:18p | 12:14a<br>7:17a<br>1:11p<br>6:32p | 1.1F<br>0.8E<br>0.2F<br>0.5E |
| 26 (EDT) Tu | 5:02a<br>12:11p<br>4:32p<br>10:28p | 1:18a<br>8:19a<br>2:19p<br>7:44p | 1.1F<br>0.8E<br>0.3F<br>0.6E |
| 27 (EDT) We | 5:58a<br>12:56p<br>5:48p<br>11:39p | 2:21a<br>9:15a<br>3:19p<br>8:54p | 1.1F<br>0.9E<br>0.4F<br>0.6E |
| 28 (EDT) Th | 6:51a<br>1:36p<br>6:55p | 3:22a<br>10:06a<br>4:13p<br>9:58p | 1.1F<br>0.9E<br>0.6F<br>0.7E |
| 29 (EDT) Fr | 12:47a<br>7:40a<br>2:13p<br>7:54p | 4:19a<br>10:52a<br>5:01p<br>10:57p | 1.0F<br>1.0E<br>0.7F<br>0.8E |
| 30 (EDT) Sa | 1:51a<br>8:25a<br>2:49p<br>8:48p | 5:11a<br>11:35a<br>5:47p<br>11:51p | 1.0F<br>1.0E<br>0.8F<br>0.9E |
| 31 (EDT) Su | 2:51a<br>9:08a<br>3:25p<br>9:39p | 6:01a<br>12:16p<br>6:31p | 0.9F<br>1.0E<br>0.9F |

## September

| Date | Slack h m | Max h m | knots |
|---|---|---|---|
| 1 (EDT) Mo | 3:47a<br>9:48a<br>4:00p<br>10:28p | 12:42a<br>6:48a<br>12:56p<br>7:14p | 0.9E<br>0.9F<br>0.9E<br>1.0F |
| 2 (EDT) Tu | 4:42a<br>10:28a<br>4:36p<br>11:17p | 1:32a<br>7:34a<br>1:36p<br>7:56p | 0.9E<br>0.8F<br>0.9E<br>1.0F |
| 3 (EDT) We | 5:37a<br>11:07a<br>5:13p | 2:21a<br>8:21a<br>2:15p<br>8:39p | 0.9E<br>0.6F<br>0.8E<br>1.0F |
| 4 (EDT) Th | 12:05a<br>6:34a<br>11:47a<br>5:51p | 3:11a<br>9:08a<br>2:56p<br>9:24p | 0.8E<br>0.5F<br>0.7E<br>1.0F |
| 5 (EDT) Fr | 12:55a<br>7:34a<br>12:30p<br>6:31p | 4:03a<br>9:59a<br>3:40p<br>10:12p | 0.8E<br>0.4F<br>0.6E<br>0.9F |
| 6 (EDT) Sa | 1:47a<br>8:38a<br>1:19p<br>7:15p | 4:58a<br>10:55a<br>4:28p<br>11:03p | 0.7E<br>0.3F<br>0.5E<br>0.9F |
| 7 (EDT) Su | 2:41a<br>9:46a<br>2:17p<br>8:05p | 5:56a<br>11:58a<br>5:23p<br>11:58p | 0.7E<br>0.3F<br>0.4E<br>0.8F |
| 8 (EDT) Mo | 3:36a<br>10:50a<br>3:25p<br>9:01p | 6:56a<br>1:03p<br>6:24p | 0.7E<br>0.3F<br>0.4E |
| 9 (EDT) Tu | 4:31a<br>11:45a<br>4:33p<br>10:02p | 12:56a<br>7:54a<br>2:04p<br>7:28p | 0.8F<br>0.7E<br>0.3F<br>0.4E |
| 10 (EDT) We | 5:23a<br>12:30p<br>5:36p<br>11:04p | 1:53a<br>8:46a<br>2:58p<br>8:28p | 0.8F<br>0.8E<br>0.4F<br>0.5E |
| 11 (EDT) Th | 6:12a<br>1:08p<br>6:29p | 2:48a<br>9:33a<br>3:44p<br>9:23p | 0.9F<br>0.8E<br>0.5F<br>0.5E |
| 12 (EDT) Fr | 12:05a<br>6:58a<br>1:40p<br>7:16p | 3:38a<br>10:14a<br>4:25p<br>10:14p | 0.9F<br>0.9E<br>0.6F<br>0.6E |
| 13 (EDT) Sa | 1:02a<br>7:40a<br>2:09p<br>8:00p | 4:26a<br>10:52a<br>5:03p<br>11:01p | 0.9F<br>0.9E<br>0.7F<br>0.7E |
| 14 (EDT) Su | 1:56a<br>8:19a<br>2:36p<br>8:42p | 5:10a<br>11:27a<br>5:38p<br>11:46p | 0.9F<br>0.9E<br>0.8F<br>0.8E |
| 15 (EDT) Mo | 2:50a<br>8:56a<br>3:03p<br>9:24p | 5:53a<br>12:01p<br>6:14p | 0.8F<br>0.8E<br>0.9F |
| 16 (EDT) Tu | 3:42a<br>9:31a<br>3:30p<br>10:07p | 12:31a<br>6:36a<br>12:34p<br>6:51p | 0.9E<br>0.7F<br>0.8E<br>1.0F |
| 17 (EDT) We | 4:36a<br>10:05a<br>4:00p<br>10:53p | 1:16a<br>7:19a<br>1:08p<br>7:29p | 0.9E<br>0.7F<br>0.8E<br>1.1F |
| 18 (EDT) Th | 5:31a<br>10:41a<br>4:34p<br>11:42p | 2:03a<br>8:03a<br>1:45p<br>8:11p | 0.9E<br>0.6F<br>0.7E<br>1.1F |
| 19 (EDT) Fr | 6:29a<br>11:19a<br>5:13p | 2:53a<br>8:51a<br>2:26p<br>8:57p | 0.9E<br>0.5F<br>0.7E<br>1.1F |
| 20 (EDT) Sa | 12:33a<br>7:31a<br>12:03p<br>5:59p | 3:46a<br>9:44a<br>3:13p<br>9:49p | 0.9E<br>0.4F<br>0.6E<br>1.1F |
| 21 (EDT) Su | 1:29a<br>8:35a<br>12:59p<br>6:53p | 4:44a<br>10:43a<br>4:09p<br>10:47p | 0.9E<br>0.3F<br>0.6E<br>1.0F |
| 22 (EDT) Mo | 2:28a<br>9:37a<br>2:09p<br>7:59p | 5:45a<br>11:49a<br>5:16p<br>11:51p | 0.8E<br>0.3F<br>0.5E<br>1.0F |
| 23 (EDT) Tu | 3:29a<br>10:33a<br>3:28p<br>9:14p | 6:48a<br>12:57p<br>6:31p | 0.8E<br>0.4F<br>0.5E |
| 24 (EDT) We | 4:30a<br>11:23a<br>4:45p<br>10:34p | 12:59a<br>7:48a<br>2:00p<br>7:46p | 0.9F<br>0.8E<br>0.5F<br>0.6E |
| 25 (EDT) Th | 5:28a<br>12:06p<br>5:53p<br>11:50p | 2:07a<br>8:43a<br>2:57p<br>8:55p | 0.9F<br>0.9E<br>0.6F<br>0.7E |
| 26 (EDT) Fr | 6:22a<br>12:47p<br>6:52p | 3:09a<br>9:33a<br>3:48p<br>9:56p | 0.9F<br>0.9E<br>0.8F<br>0.8E |
| 27 (EDT) Sa | 12:59a<br>7:11a<br>1:25p<br>7:45p | 4:07a<br>10:19a<br>4:35p<br>10:51p | 0.8F<br>0.9E<br>0.9F<br>0.9E |
| 28 (EDT) Su | 2:01a<br>7:57a<br>2:02p<br>8:33p | 4:59a<br>11:02a<br>5:19p<br>11:42p | 0.8F<br>0.9E<br>1.0F<br>1.0E |
| 29 (EDT) Mo | 2:58a<br>8:40a<br>2:38p<br>9:20p | 5:48a<br>11:43a<br>6:01p | 0.7F<br>0.8E<br>1.1F |
| 30 (EDT) Tu | 3:51a<br>9:21a<br>3:14p<br>10:04p | 12:29a<br>6:34a<br>12:23p<br>6:42p | 1.0E<br>0.7F<br>0.8E<br>1.1F |

## October

| Date | Slack h m | Max h m | knots |
|---|---|---|---|
| 1 (EDT) We | 4:43a<br>10:02a<br>3:49p<br>10:48p | 1:15a<br>7:19a<br>1:02p<br>7:22p | 1.0E<br>0.6F<br>0.7E<br>1.1F |
| 2 (EDT) Th | 5:34a<br>10:42a<br>4:26p<br>11:32p | 2:01a<br>8:04a<br>1:41p<br>8:03p | 1.0E<br>0.5F<br>0.6E<br>1.0F |
| 3 (EDT) Fr | 6:26a<br>11:25a<br>5:03p | 2:46a<br>8:51a<br>2:22p<br>8:46p | 0.9E<br>0.4F<br>0.6E<br>1.0F |
| 4 (EDT) Sa | 12:17a<br>7:19a<br>12:13p<br>5:44p | 3:34a<br>9:41a<br>3:07p<br>9:31p | 0.9E<br>0.4F<br>0.5E<br>0.9F |
| 5 (EDT) Su | 1:04a<br>8:15a<br>1:08p<br>6:30p | 4:25a<br>10:35a<br>3:58p<br>10:21p | 0.8E<br>0.3F<br>0.4E<br>0.8F |
| 6 (EDT) Mo | 1:53a<br>9:11a<br>2:11p<br>7:24p | 5:18a<br>11:34a<br>4:56p<br>11:17p | 0.8E<br>0.3F<br>0.4E<br>0.8F |
| 7 (EDT) Tu | 2:46a<br>10:04a<br>3:18p<br>8:29p | 6:13a<br>12:33p<br>6:00p | 0.8E<br>0.4F<br>0.3E |
| 8 (EDT) We | 3:40a<br>10:50a<br>4:21p<br>9:39p | 12:16a<br>7:07a<br>1:29p<br>7:05p | 0.7F<br>0.8E<br>0.4F<br>0.4E |
| 9 (EDT) Th | 4:34a<br>11:29a<br>5:17p<br>10:50p | 1:16a<br>7:57a<br>2:18p<br>8:07p | 0.7F<br>0.8E<br>0.5F<br>0.5E |
| 10 (EDT) Fr | 5:24a<br>12:04p<br>6:06p<br>11:56p | 2:14a<br>8:43a<br>3:02p<br>9:02p | 0.7F<br>0.8E<br>0.6F<br>0.6E |
| 11 (EDT) Sa | 6:12a<br>12:35p<br>6:50p | 3:08a<br>9:25a<br>3:42p<br>9:53p | 0.7F<br>0.8E<br>0.8F<br>0.7E |
| 12 (EDT) Su | 12:58a<br>6:56a<br>1:04p<br>7:33p | 3:58a<br>10:03a<br>4:20p<br>10:41p | 0.7F<br>0.8E<br>0.9F<br>0.8E |
| 13 (EDT) Mo | 1:55a<br>7:36a<br>1:32p<br>8:15p | 4:45a<br>10:39a<br>4:57p<br>11:27p | 0.7F<br>0.7E<br>1.0F<br>0.9E |
| 14 (EDT) Tu | 2:50a<br>8:15a<br>2:02p<br>8:58p | 5:30a<br>11:15a<br>5:35p | 0.6F<br>0.7E<br>1.1F |
| 15 (EDT) We | 3:44a<br>8:53a<br>2:35p<br>9:42p | 12:12a<br>6:15a<br>11:52a<br>6:15p | 1.0E<br>0.6F<br>0.7E<br>1.2F |
| 16 (EDT) Th | 4:37a<br>9:32a<br>3:12p<br>10:28p | 12:58a<br>7:00a<br>12:31p<br>6:56p | 1.1E<br>0.5F<br>0.7E<br>1.2F |
| 17 (EDT) Fr | 5:30a<br>10:14a<br>3:53p<br>11:16p | 1:45a<br>7:47a<br>1:13p<br>7:41p | 1.1E<br>0.5F<br>0.7E<br>1.2F |
| 18 (EDT) Sa | 6:23a<br>11:02a<br>4:40p | 2:34a<br>8:38a<br>2:01p<br>8:30p | 1.1E<br>0.4F<br>0.6E<br>1.2F |
| 19 (EDT) Su | 12:06a<br>7:16a<br>11:59a<br>5:34p | 3:26a<br>9:33a<br>2:57p<br>9:25p | 1.0E<br>0.4F<br>0.6E<br>1.1F |
| 20 (EDT) Mo | 12:59a<br>8:09a<br>1:07p<br>6:38p | 4:20a<br>10:32a<br>4:01p<br>10:25p | 1.0E<br>0.4F<br>0.5E<br>1.0F |
| 21 (EDT) Tu | 1:55a<br>9:00a<br>2:22p<br>7:53p | 5:17a<br>11:35a<br>5:14p<br>11:31p | 0.9E<br>0.5F<br>0.5E<br>0.9F |
| 22 (EDT) We | 2:53a<br>9:48a<br>3:37p<br>9:17p | 6:15a<br>12:37p<br>6:30p | 0.9E<br>0.6F<br>0.5E |
| 23 (EDT) Th | 3:52a<br>10:33a<br>4:46p<br>10:41p | 12:41a<br>7:12a<br>1:36p<br>7:44p | 0.8F<br>0.8E<br>0.7F<br>0.6E |
| 24 (EDT) Fr | 4:50a<br>11:17a<br>5:47p<br>11:58p | 1:49a<br>8:06a<br>2:31p<br>8:50p | 0.7F<br>0.8E<br>0.8F<br>0.7E |
| 25 (EDT) Sa | 5:45a<br>11:58a<br>6:41p | 2:52a<br>8:56a<br>3:21p<br>9:48p | 0.7F<br>0.8E<br>1.0F<br>0.9E |
| 26 (EST) Su | 12:06a<br>5:36a<br>11:37a<br>6:30p | 2:50a<br>8:43a<br>3:07p<br>9:41p | 0.6F<br>0.8E<br>1.1F<br>0.9E |
| 27 (EST) Mo | 1:07a<br>6:24a<br>12:16p<br>7:16p | 3:43a<br>9:27a<br>3:50p<br>10:29p | 0.6F<br>0.7E<br>1.1F<br>1.0E |
| 28 (EST) Tu | 2:02a<br>7:10a<br>12:53p<br>7:59p | 4:33a<br>10:09a<br>4:32p<br>11:15p | 0.6F<br>0.7E<br>1.2F<br>1.0E |
| 29 (EST) We | 2:53a<br>7:54a<br>1:29p<br>8:41p | 5:19a<br>10:50a<br>5:12p<br>11:59p | 0.5F<br>0.6E<br>1.1F<br>1.0E |
| 30 (EST) Th | 3:42a<br>8:38a<br>2:05p<br>9:21p | 6:05a<br>11:30a<br>5:51p | 0.5F<br>0.6E<br>1.1F |
| 31 (EST) Fr | 4:29a<br>9:23a<br>2:42p<br>10:01p | 12:41a<br>6:50a<br>12:11p<br>6:31p | 1.0E<br>0.4F<br>0.5E<br>1.1F |

Reports were generated by Tides and Currents for Windows from Nautical Software (503) 579-1414.

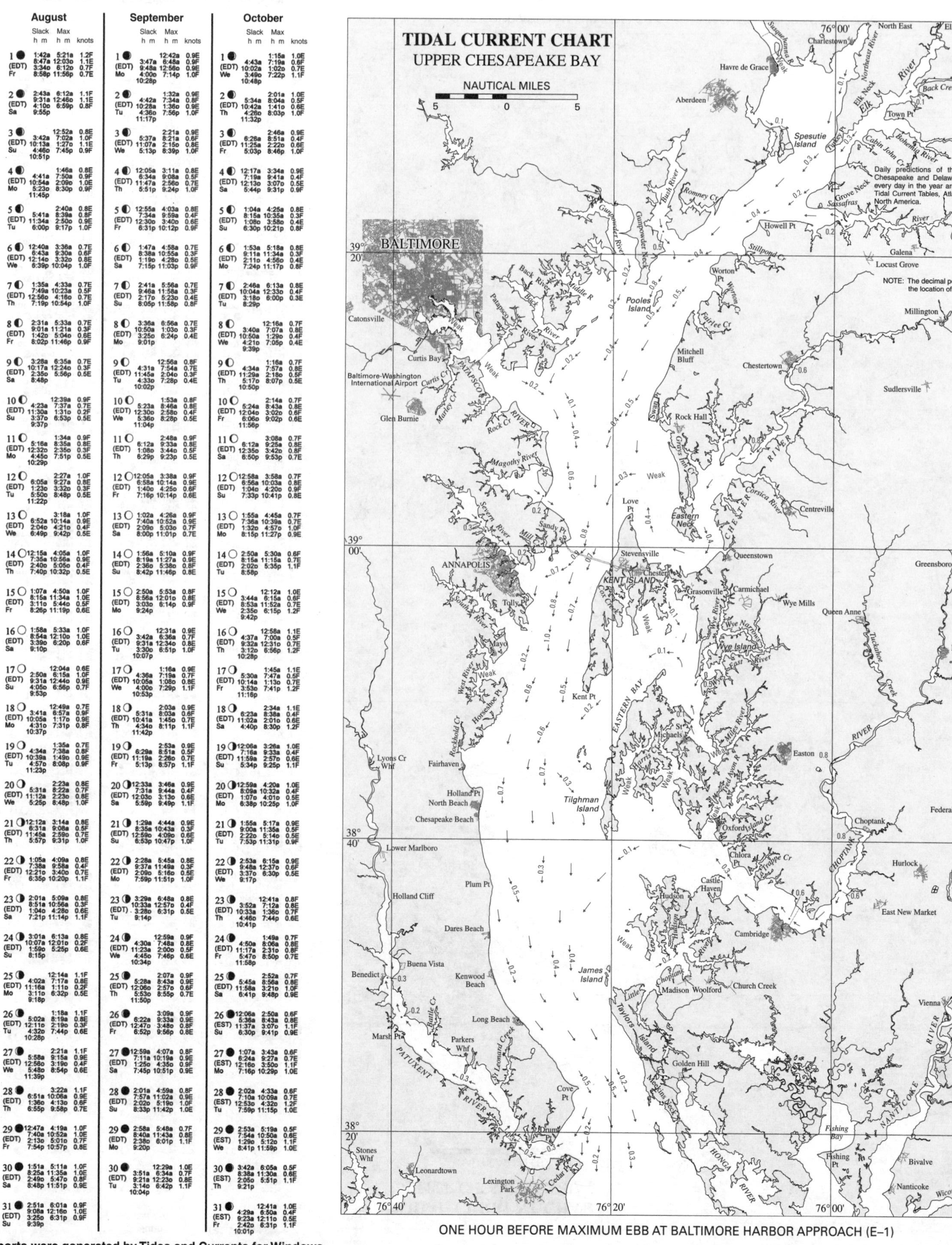


ONE HOUR BEFORE MAXIMUM EBB AT BALTIMORE HARBOR APPROACH (E–1)

# TIDAL CURRENTS - 2009

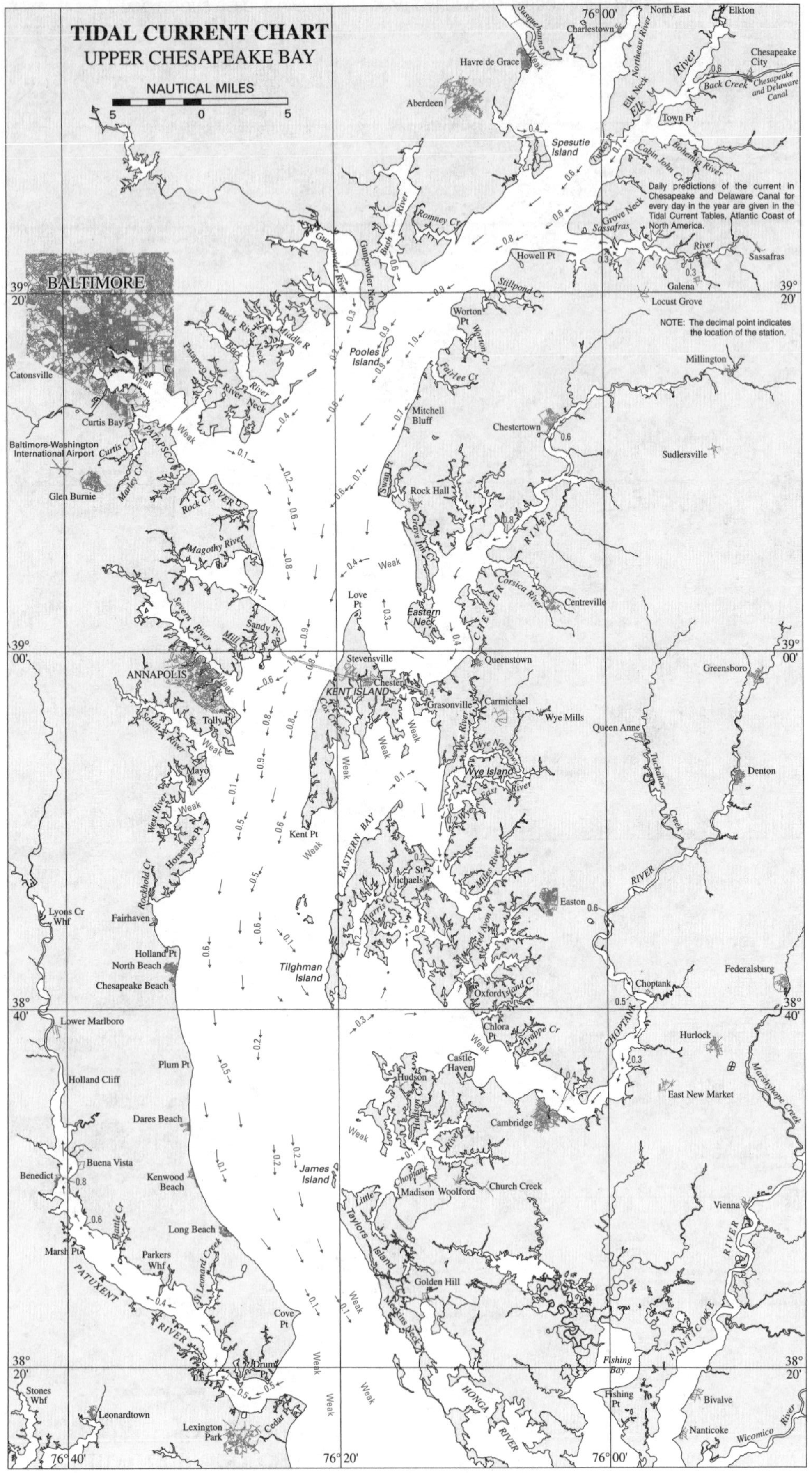

## TIDAL CURRENT CHART
### UPPER CHESAPEAKE BAY

NAUTICAL MILES
5 0 5

Daily predictions of the current in Chesapeake and Delaware Canal for every day in the year are given in the Tidal Current Tables, Atlantic Coast of North America.

NOTE: The decimal point indicates the location of the station.

MAXIMUM EBB AT BALTIMORE HARBOR APPROACH (E)

### May

| Day | Slack h m | Max h m | knots |
|---|---|---|---|
| 1 (EDT) Fr | 1:54a | 4:43a | 0.5E |
| | 7:22a | 10:58a | 0.9F |
| | 2:17p | 5:40p | 0.9E |
| | 9:12p | | |
| 2 (EDT) Sa | | 12:04a | 0.6F |
| | 3:07a | 5:58a | 0.5E |
| | 8:45a | 12:05p | 0.8F |
| | 3:14p | 6:35p | 0.8E |
| | 9:56p | | |
| 3 (EDT) Su | | 1:02a | 0.7F |
| | 4:16a | 7:12a | 0.6E |
| | 10:10a | 1:14p | 0.7F |
| | 4:12p | 7:29p | 0.8E |
| | 10:39p | | |
| 4 (EDT) Mo | | 1:57a | 0.9F |
| | 5:18a | 8:20a | 0.7E |
| | 11:30a | 2:20p | 0.6F |
| | 5:08p | 8:21p | 0.8E |
| | 11:22p | | |
| 5 (EDT) Tu | | 2:49a | 1.0F |
| | 6:13a | 9:21a | 0.9E |
| | 12:42p | 3:21p | 0.6F |
| | 6:02p | 9:11p | 0.8E |
| 6 (EDT) We | 12:04a | 3:38a | 1.1F |
| | 7:05a | 10:16a | 1.0E |
| | 1:46p | 4:17p | 0.6F |
| | 6:53p | 9:58p | 0.7E |
| 7 (EDT) Th | 12:45a | 4:24a | 1.2F |
| | 7:52a | 11:07a | 1.0E |
| | 2:43p | 5:09p | 0.5F |
| | 7:43p | 10:43p | 0.7E |
| 8 (EDT) Fr | 1:25a | 5:08a | 1.2F |
| | 8:37a | 11:54a | 1.1E |
| | 3:36p | 5:59p | 0.5F |
| | 8:30p | 11:27p | 0.7E |
| 9 (EDT) Sa | 2:05a | 5:50a | 1.2F |
| | 9:20a | 12:39p | 1.1E |
| | 4:24p | 6:46p | 0.5F |
| | 9:18p | | |
| 10 (EDT) Su | | 12:10a | 0.6E |
| | 2:45a | 6:32a | 1.2F |
| | 10:02a | 1:23p | 1.1E |
| | 5:11p | 7:32p | 0.5F |
| | 10:06p | | |
| 11 (EDT) Mo | | 12:54a | 0.5E |
| | 3:25a | 7:13a | 1.1F |
| | 10:43a | 2:06p | 1.0E |
| | 5:56p | 8:19p | 0.5F |
| | 10:56p | | |
| 12 (EDT) Tu | | 1:39a | 0.5E |
| | 4:06a | 7:55a | 1.0F |
| | 11:23a | 2:49p | 1.0E |
| | 6:39p | 9:06p | 0.4F |
| | 11:49p | | |
| 13 (EDT) We | | 2:26a | 0.4E |
| | 4:51a | 8:39a | 0.9F |
| | 12:04p | 3:32p | 0.9E |
| | 7:22p | 9:54p | 0.5F |
| 14 (EDT) Th | 12:46a | 3:18a | 0.4E |
| | 5:41a | 9:26a | 0.8F |
| | 12:47p | 4:17p | 0.9E |
| | 8:04p | 10:44p | 0.5F |
| 15 (EDT) Fr | 1:45a | 4:15a | 0.4E |
| | 6:39a | 10:17a | 0.7F |
| | 1:32p | 5:03p | 0.8E |
| | 8:43p | 11:34p | 0.5F |
| 16 (EDT) Sa | 2:45a | 5:17a | 0.4E |
| | 7:46a | 11:13a | 0.6F |
| | 2:19p | 5:50p | 0.8E |
| | 9:21p | | |
| 17 (EDT) Su | | 12:23a | 0.6F |
| | 3:42a | 6:21a | 0.4E |
| | 9:01a | 12:12p | 0.5F |
| | 3:08p | 6:36p | 0.7E |
| | 9:57p | | |
| 18 (EDT) Mo | | 1:10a | 0.7F |
| | 4:34a | 7:22a | 0.5E |
| | 10:19a | 1:12p | 0.5F |
| | 3:57p | 7:21p | 0.7E |
| | 10:30p | | |
| 19 (EDT) Tu | | 1:54a | 0.8F |
| | 5:22a | 8:20a | 0.6E |
| | 11:33a | 2:11p | 0.4F |
| | 4:46p | 8:04p | 0.7E |
| | 11:03p | | |
| 20 (EDT) We | | 2:37a | 0.9F |
| | 6:07a | 9:14a | 0.7E |
| | 12:41p | 3:06p | 0.4F |
| | 5:34p | 8:46p | 0.6E |
| | 11:36p | | |
| 21 (EDT) Th | | 3:18a | 1.0F |
| | 6:51a | 10:03a | 0.9E |
| | 1:42p | 3:59p | 0.4F |
| | 6:20p | 9:28p | 0.6E |
| 22 (EDT) Fr | 12:11a | 4:00a | 1.1F |
| | 7:34a | 10:51a | 1.0E |
| | 2:39p | 4:49p | 0.4F |
| | 7:06p | 10:10p | 0.6E |
| 23 (EDT) Sa | 12:48a | 4:41a | 1.2F |
| | 8:17a | 11:37a | 1.1E |
| | 3:30p | 5:37p | 0.4F |
| | 7:52p | 10:53p | 0.6E |
| 24 (EDT) Su | 1:28a | 5:24a | 1.3F |
| | 9:01a | 12:22p | 1.1E |
| | 4:17p | 6:25p | 0.4F |
| | 8:41p | 11:39p | 0.6E |
| 25 (EDT) Mo | 2:13a | 6:09a | 1.3F |
| | 9:45a | 1:07p | 1.2E |
| | 5:01p | 7:12p | 0.4F |
| | 9:34p | | |
| 26 (EDT) Tu | | 12:29a | 0.6E |
| | 3:02a | 6:56a | 1.3F |
| | 10:30a | 1:52p | 1.2E |
| | 5:43p | 8:02p | 0.5F |
| | 10:31p | | |
| 27 (EDT) We | | 1:23a | 0.6E |
| | 3:56a | 7:46a | 1.2F |
| | 11:16a | 2:38p | 1.1E |
| | 6:24p | 8:53p | 0.5F |
| | 11:34p | | |
| 28 (EDT) Th | | 2:22a | 0.6E |
| | 4:57a | 8:39a | 1.1F |
| | 12:03p | 3:26p | 1.1E |
| | 7:05p | 9:46p | 0.6F |
| 29 (EDT) Fr | 12:41a | 3:27a | 0.6E |
| | 6:05a | 9:36a | 0.9F |
| | 12:52p | 4:15p | 1.0E |
| | 7:46p | 10:41p | 0.7F |
| 30 (EDT) Sa | 1:50a | 4:36a | 0.6E |
| | 7:21a | 10:38a | 0.8F |
| | 1:42p | 5:06p | 0.9E |
| | 8:28p | 11:38p | 0.8F |
| 31 (EDT) Su | 2:58a | 5:48a | 0.6E |
| | 8:44a | 11:43a | 0.6F |
| | 2:35p | 5:58p | 0.9E |
| | 9:12p | | |

### June

| Day | Slack h m | Max h m | knots |
|---|---|---|---|
| 1 (EDT) Mo | | 12:34a | 0.9F |
| | 4:02a | 6:59a | 0.7E |
| | 10:09a | 12:51p | 0.5F |
| | 3:30p | 6:51p | 0.8E |
| | 9:55p | | |
| 2 (EDT) Tu | | 1:28a | 1.0F |
| | 5:02a | 8:06a | 0.8E |
| | 11:30a | 1:58p | 0.5F |
| | 4:26p | 7:44p | 0.7E |
| | 10:40p | | |
| 3 (EDT) We | | 2:21a | 1.1F |
| | 5:57a | 9:06a | 0.9E |
| | 12:43p | 3:01p | 0.4F |
| | 5:23p | 8:36p | 0.7E |
| | 11:24p | | |
| 4 (EDT) Th | | 3:11a | 1.2F |
| | 6:47a | 10:02a | 1.0E |
| | 1:46p | 4:00p | 0.4F |
| | 6:19p | 9:26p | 0.6E |
| 5 (EDT) Fr | 12:08a | 3:58a | 1.2F |
| | 7:34a | 10:52a | 1.0E |
| | 2:42p | 4:54p | 0.4F |
| | 7:14p | 10:14p | 0.6E |
| 6 (EDT) Sa | 12:51a | 4:44a | 1.2F |
| | 8:18a | 11:39a | 1.1E |
| | 3:31p | 5:44p | 0.4F |
| | 8:07p | 11:01p | 0.6E |
| 7 (EDT) Su | 1:33a | 5:27a | 1.2F |
| | 9:00a | 12:22p | 1.1E |
| | 4:15p | 6:31p | 0.4F |
| | 8:59p | 11:47p | 0.5E |
| 8 (EDT) Mo | 2:15a | 6:08a | 1.1F |
| | 9:39a | 1:03p | 1.1E |
| | 4:56p | 7:16p | 0.4F |
| | 9:50p | | |
| 9 (EDT) Tu | | 12:32a | 0.5E |
| | 2:58a | 6:49a | 1.1F |
| | 10:17a | 1:43p | 1.1E |
| | 5:35p | 8:00p | 0.5F |
| | 10:41p | | |
| 10 (EDT) We | | 1:18a | 0.4E |
| | 3:41a | 7:30a | 1.0F |
| | 10:55a | 2:23p | 1.0E |
| | 6:11p | 8:43p | 0.5F |
| | 11:33p | | |
| 11 (EDT) Th | | 2:06a | 0.4E |
| | 4:28a | 8:13a | 0.9F |
| | 11:33a | 3:01p | 1.0E |
| | 6:47p | 9:26p | 0.5F |
| 12 (EDT) Fr | 12:25a | 2:56a | 0.4E |
| | 5:19a | 8:57a | 0.8F |
| | 12:11p | 3:41p | 0.9E |
| | 7:21p | 10:10p | 0.6F |
| 13 (EDT) Sa | 1:19a | 3:50a | 0.4E |
| | 6:18a | 9:44a | 0.7F |
| | 12:51p | 4:21p | 0.9E |
| | 7:53p | 10:54p | 0.6F |
| 14 (EDT) Su | 2:13a | 4:47a | 0.4E |
| | 7:24a | 10:36a | 0.6F |
| | 1:31p | 5:01p | 0.8E |
| | 8:25p | 11:38p | 0.7F |
| 15 (EDT) Mo | 3:06a | 5:48a | 0.5E |
| | 8:40a | 11:31a | 0.5F |
| | 2:13p | 5:43p | 0.7E |
| | 8:57p | | |
| 16 (EDT) Tu | | 12:23a | 0.8F |
| | 3:58a | 6:50a | 0.5E |
| | 10:01a | 12:31p | 0.4F |
| | 2:57p | 6:26p | 0.7E |
| | 9:30p | | |
| 17 (EDT) We | | 1:09a | 0.9F |
| | 4:49a | 7:50a | 0.6E |
| | 11:21a | 1:33p | 0.3F |
| | 3:44p | 7:10p | 0.6E |
| | 10:05p | | |
| 18 (EDT) Th | | 1:55a | 1.0F |
| | 5:37a | 8:47a | 0.8E |
| | 12:35p | 2:33p | 0.3F |
| | 4:34p | 7:57p | 0.6E |
| | 10:44p | | |
| 19 (EDT) Fr | | 2:41a | 1.1F |
| | 6:24a | 9:40a | 0.9E |
| | 1:39p | 3:31p | 0.2F |
| | 5:27p | 8:45p | 0.6E |
| | 11:26p | | |
| 20 (EDT) Sa | | 3:27a | 1.2F |
| | 7:11a | 10:30a | 1.0E |
| | 2:32p | 4:25p | 0.3F |
| | 6:23p | 9:35p | 0.6E |
| 21 (EDT) Su | 12:12a | 4:14a | 1.3F |
| | 7:56a | 11:16a | 1.1E |
| | 3:17p | 5:16p | 0.3F |
| | 7:22p | 10:27p | 0.6E |
| 22 (EDT) Mo | 1:02a | 5:02a | 1.3F |
| | 8:41a | 12:01p | 1.1E |
| | 3:57p | 6:05p | 0.4F |
| | 8:21p | 11:21p | 0.6E |
| 23 (EDT) Tu | 1:55a | 5:50a | 1.3F |
| | 9:25a | 12:45p | 1.2E |
| | 4:34p | 6:53p | 0.5F |
| | 9:21p | | |
| 24 (EDT) We | | 12:16a | 0.6E |
| | 2:52a | 6:40a | 1.3F |
| | 10:09a | 1:29p | 1.2E |
| | 5:11p | 7:41p | 0.6F |
| | 10:23p | | |
| 25 (EDT) Th | | 1:14a | 0.7E |
| | 3:52a | 7:31a | 1.2F |
| | 10:53a | 2:13p | 1.1E |
| | 5:47p | 8:30p | 0.7F |
| | 11:25p | | |
| 26 (EDT) Fr | | 2:14a | 0.7E |
| | 4:56a | 8:23a | 1.0F |
| | 11:38a | 2:58p | 1.1E |
| | 6:25p | 9:21p | 0.8F |
| 27 (EDT) Sa | 12:28a | 3:17a | 0.7E |
| | 6:04a | 9:19a | 0.9F |
| | 12:23p | 3:44p | 1.0E |
| | 7:05p | 10:13p | 0.9F |
| 28 (EDT) Su | 1:32a | 4:22a | 0.7E |
| | 7:18a | 10:17a | 0.7F |
| | 1:09p | 4:32p | 0.9E |
| | 7:47p | 11:07p | 1.0F |
| 29 (EDT) Mo | 2:36a | 5:30a | 0.7E |
| | 8:38a | 11:20a | 0.5F |
| | 1:58p | 5:22p | 0.8E |
| | 8:30p | | |
| 30 (EDT) Tu | | 12:02a | 1.0F |
| | 3:39a | 6:38a | 0.7E |
| | 10:00a | 12:25p | 0.4F |
| | 2:50p | 6:15p | 0.8E |
| | 9:16p | | |

### July

| Day | Slack h m | Max h m | knots |
|---|---|---|---|
| 1 (EDT) We | | 12:57a | 1.1F |
| | 4:38a | 7:44a | 0.8E |
| | 11:21a | 1:33p | 0.3F |
| | 3:47p | 7:09p | 0.7E |
| | 10:03p | | |
| 2 (EDT) Th | | 1:52a | 1.1F |
| | 5:34a | 8:46a | 0.9E |
| | 12:34p | 2:39p | 0.3F |
| | 4:48p | 8:04p | 0.6E |
| | 10:50p | | |
| 3 (EDT) Fr | | 2:44a | 1.1F |
| | 6:25a | 9:42a | 0.9E |
| | 1:35p | 3:40p | 0.3F |
| | 5:51p | 8:59p | 0.6E |
| | 11:38p | | |
| 4 (EDT) Sa | | 3:34a | 1.2F |
| | 7:13a | 10:33a | 1.0E |
| | 2:28p | 4:35p | 0.3F |
| | 6:52p | 9:51p | 0.5E |
| 5 (EDT) Su | 12:26a | 4:21a | 1.1F |
| | 7:57a | 11:18a | 1.0E |
| | 3:12p | 5:25p | 0.4F |
| | 7:49p | 10:41p | 0.5E |
| 6 (EDT) Mo | 1:12a | 5:06a | 1.1F |
| | 8:37a | 12:00p | 1.0E |
| | 3:52p | 6:11p | 0.4F |
| | 8:42p | 11:29p | 0.5E |
| 7 (EDT) Tu | 1:57a | 5:48a | 1.1F |
| | 9:16a | 12:40p | 1.1E |
| | 4:27p | 6:53p | 0.5F |
| | 9:32p | | |
| 8 (EDT) We | | 12:15a | 0.5E |
| | 2:43a | 6:29a | 1.0F |
| | 9:53a | 1:17p | 1.0E |
| | 5:01p | 7:33p | 0.5F |
| | 10:20p | | |
| 9 (EDT) Th | | 1:00a | 0.5E |
| | 3:29a | 7:09a | 1.0F |
| | 10:29a | 1:53p | 1.0E |
| | 5:32p | 8:12p | 0.6F |
| | 11:07p | | |
| 10 (EDT) Fr | | 1:46a | 0.5E |
| | 4:17a | 7:50a | 0.9F |
| | 11:04a | 2:28p | 1.0E |
| | 6:02p | 8:50p | 0.6F |
| | 11:54p | | |
| 11 (EDT) Sa | | 2:33a | 0.5E |
| | 5:09a | 8:32a | 0.8F |
| | 11:39a | 3:03p | 0.9E |
| | 6:31p | 9:29p | 0.7F |
| 12 (EDT) Su | 12:42a | 3:23a | 0.5E |
| | 6:05a | 9:16a | 0.6F |
| | 12:14p | 3:39p | 0.8E |
| | 7:00p | 10:09p | 0.7F |
| 13 (EDT) Mo | 1:32a | 4:17a | 0.5E |
| | 7:10a | 10:04a | 0.5F |
| | 12:49p | 4:15p | 0.8E |
| | 7:29p | 10:52p | 0.8F |
| 14 (EDT) Tu | 2:25a | 5:15a | 0.5E |
| | 8:23a | 10:56a | 0.4F |
| | 1:25p | 4:54p | 0.7E |
| | 8:01p | 11:37p | 0.9F |
| 15 (EDT) We | 3:19a | 6:17a | 0.6E |
| | 9:44a | 11:54a | 0.3F |
| | 2:04p | 5:36p | 0.6E |
| | 8:36p | | |
| 16 (EDT) Th | | 12:25a | 1.0F |
| | 4:13a | 7:19a | 0.7E |
| | 11:08a | 12:58p | 0.2F |
| | 2:48p | 6:24p | 0.6E |
| | 9:17p | | |
| 17 (EDT) Fr | | 1:16a | 1.0F |
| | 5:06a | 8:19a | 0.8E |
| | 12:24p | 2:03p | 0.2F |
| | 3:44p | 7:17p | 0.6E |
| | 10:04p | | |
| 18 (EDT) Sa | | 2:08a | 1.1F |
| | 5:58a | 9:15a | 0.9E |
| | 1:23p | 3:04p | 0.2F |
| | 4:50p | 8:14p | 0.6E |
| | 10:56p | | |
| 19 (EDT) Su | | 3:01a | 1.2F |
| | 6:47a | 10:06a | 0.9E |
| | 2:08p | 4:01p | 0.3F |
| | 6:00p | 9:14p | 0.6E |
| | 11:53p | | |
| 20 (EDT) Mo | | 3:53a | 1.2F |
| | 7:34a | 10:53a | 1.0E |
| | 2:45p | 4:53p | 0.4F |
| | 7:07p | 10:13p | 0.6E |
| 21 (EDT) Tu | 12:53a | 4:45a | 1.3F |
| | 8:20a | 11:37a | 1.1E |
| | 3:20p | 5:42p | 0.5F |
| | 8:11p | 11:12p | 0.7E |
| 22 (EDT) We | 1:53a | 5:36a | 1.2F |
| | 9:04a | 12:20p | 1.1E |
| | 3:54p | 6:29p | 0.6F |
| | 9:11p | | |
| 23 (EDT) Th | | 12:09a | 0.7E |
| | 2:54a | 6:27a | 1.2F |
| | 9:47a | 1:03p | 1.1E |
| | 4:29p | 7:16p | 0.8F |
| | 10:10p | | |
| 24 (EDT) Fr | | 1:06a | 0.8E |
| | 3:55a | 7:17a | 1.1F |
| | 10:30a | 1:45p | 1.1E |
| | 5:05p | 8:03p | 0.9F |
| | 11:08p | | |
| 25 (EDT) Sa | | 2:04a | 0.8E |
| | 4:58a | 8:08a | 0.9F |
| | 11:12a | 2:28p | 1.0E |
| | 5:43p | 8:51p | 1.0F |
| 26 (EDT) Su | 12:07a | 3:02a | 0.8E |
| | 6:03a | 9:01a | 0.8F |
| | 11:55a | 3:13p | 1.0E |
| | 6:23p | 9:41p | 1.0F |
| 27 (EDT) Mo | 1:06a | 4:03a | 0.8E |
| | 7:12a | 9:57a | 0.6F |
| | 12:40p | 3:59p | 0.9E |
| | 7:05p | 10:34p | 1.1F |
| 28 (EDT) Tu | 2:07a | 5:06a | 0.8E |
| | 8:25a | 10:56a | 0.5F |
| | 1:27p | 4:48p | 0.8E |
| | 7:51p | 11:28p | 1.1F |
| 29 (EDT) We | 3:07a | 6:11a | 0.8E |
| | 9:43a | 12:00p | 0.4F |
| | 2:19p | 5:42p | 0.7E |
| | 8:39p | | |
| 30 (EDT) Th | | 12:24a | 1.1F |
| | 4:07a | 7:16a | 0.8E |
| | 11:00a | 1:08p | 0.3F |
| | 3:19p | 6:39p | 0.6E |
| | 9:29p | | |
| 31 (EDT) Fr | | 1:21a | 1.1F |
| | 5:04a | 8:19a | 0.8E |
| | 12:10p | 2:15p | 0.3F |
| | 4:25p | 7:38p | 0.5E |
| | 10:22p | | |

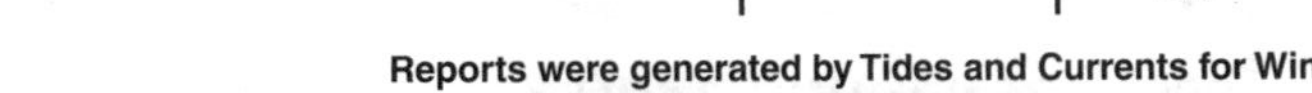

Reports were generated by Tides and Currents for Windows from Nautical Software (503) 579-1414.

## TIDAL CURRENT CHART
### UPPER CHESAPEAKE BAY

NAUTICAL MILES
5 0 5

Daily predictions of the current in Chesapeake and Delaware Canal for every day in the year are given in the Tidal Current Tables, Atlantic Coast of North America.

NOTE: The decimal point indicates the location of the station.

ONE HOUR AFTER MAXIMUM EBB AT BALTIMORE HARBOR APPROACH (E+1)

# TIDAL CURRENTS - 2009

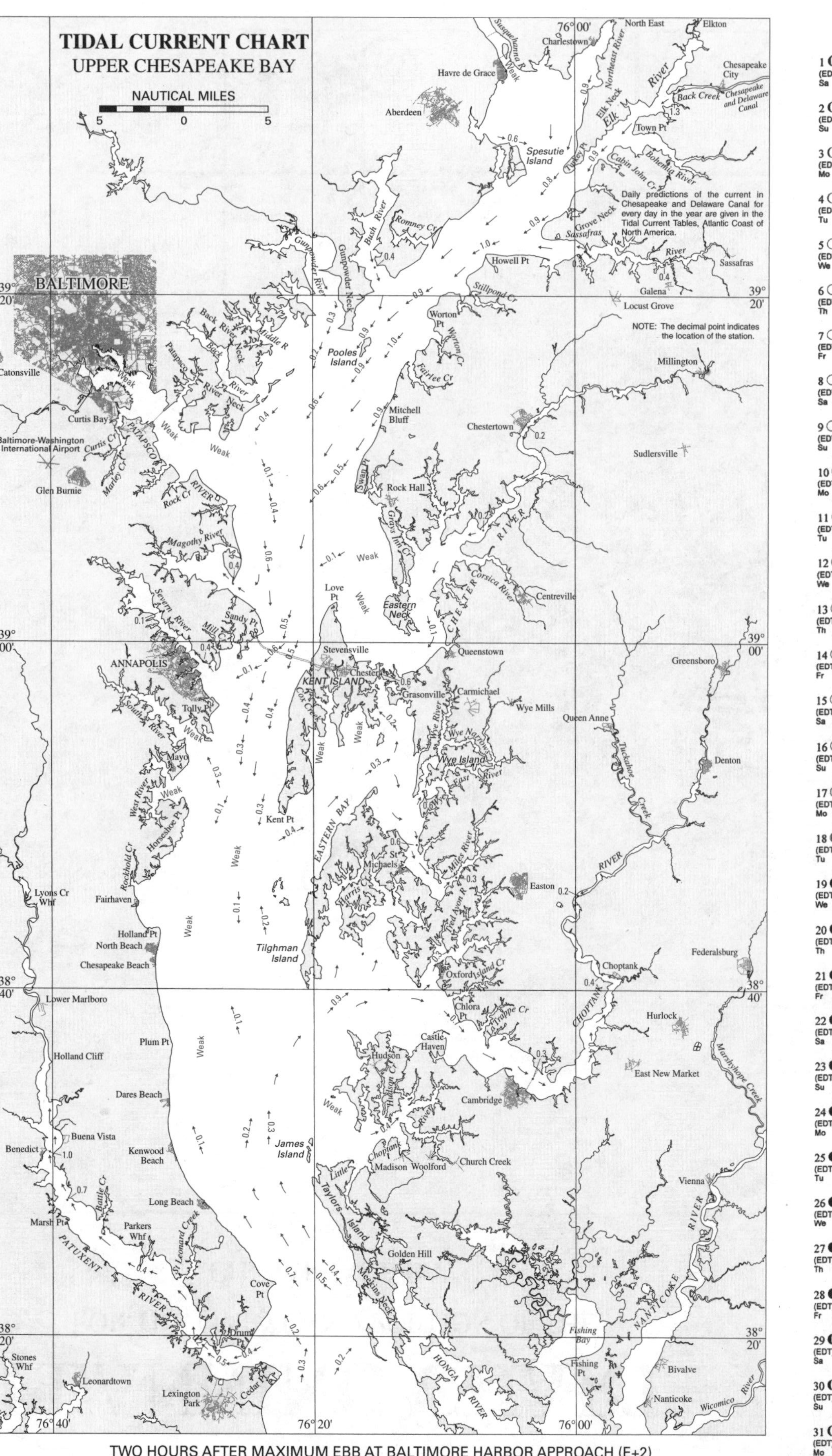


TWO HOURS AFTER MAXIMUM EBB AT BALTIMORE HARBOR APPROACH (E+2)

**August**

| Day | Slack h m | Max h m | knots |
|---|---|---|---|
| 1 (EDT) Sa | 5:57a<br>1:08p<br>5:33p<br>11:16p | 2:17a<br>9:15a<br>3:17p<br>8:37p | 1.0F<br>0.9E<br>0.3F<br>0.5E |
| 2 (EDT) Su | 6:46a<br>1:55p<br>6:37p | 3:10a<br>10:06a<br>4:11p<br>9:33p | 1.0F<br>0.9E<br>0.4F<br>0.5E |
| 3 (EDT) Mo | 12:09a<br>7:30a<br>2:36p<br>7:33p | 3:59a<br>10:51a<br>4:59p<br>10:25p | 1.0F<br>1.0E<br>0.4F<br>0.5E |
| 4 (EDT) Tu | 12:59a<br>8:11a<br>3:11p<br>8:23p | 4:45a<br>11:31a<br>5:42p<br>11:13p | 1.0F<br>1.0E<br>0.5F<br>0.6E |
| 5 (EDT) We | 1:48a<br>8:49a<br>3:44p<br>9:09p | 5:27a<br>12:09p<br>6:21p<br>11:58p | 1.0F<br>1.0E<br>0.6F<br>0.6E |
| 6 (EDT) Th | 2:36a<br>9:26a<br>4:14p<br>9:52p | 6:08a<br>12:44p<br>6:58p | 1.0F<br>1.0E<br>0.6F |
| 7 (EDT) Fr | 3:24a<br>10:01a<br>4:42p<br>10:35p | 12:42a<br>6:49a<br>1:18p<br>7:33p | 0.6E<br>0.9F<br>0.9E<br>0.7F |
| 8 (EDT) Sa | 4:13a<br>10:35a<br>5:09p<br>11:18p | 1:25a<br>7:29a<br>1:51p<br>8:09p | 0.6E<br>0.8F<br>0.9E<br>0.8F |
| 9 (EDT) Su | 5:04a<br>11:08a<br>5:36p | 2:10a<br>8:09a<br>2:24p<br>8:46p | 0.6E<br>0.7F<br>0.8E<br>0.8F |
| 10 (EDT) Mo | 12:03a<br>6:00a<br>11:41a<br>6:03p | 2:57a<br>8:52a<br>2:57p<br>9:25p | 0.6E<br>0.6F<br>0.8E<br>0.9F |
| 11 (EDT) Tu | 12:51a<br>7:01a<br>12:13p<br>6:33p | 3:48a<br>9:38a<br>3:32p<br>10:07p | 0.6E<br>0.5F<br>0.7E<br>0.9F |
| 12 (EDT) We | 1:43a<br>8:11a<br>12:47p<br>7:08p | 4:44a<br>10:28a<br>4:11p<br>10:54p | 0.7E<br>0.3F<br>0.6E<br>0.9F |
| 13 (EDT) Th | 2:38a<br>9:29a<br>1:26p<br>7:50p | 5:44a<br>11:26a<br>4:56p<br>11:46p | 0.7E<br>0.2F<br>0.6E<br>1.0F |
| 14 (EDT) Fr | 3:35a<br>10:47a<br>2:17p<br>8:40p | 6:47a<br>12:31p<br>5:50p | 0.7E<br>0.2F<br>0.5E |
| 15 (EDT) Sa | 4:33a<br>11:53a<br>3:26p<br>9:39p | 12:42a<br>7:48a<br>1:38p<br>6:53p | 1.0F<br>0.8E<br>0.2F<br>0.5E |
| 16 (EDT) Su | 5:28a<br>12:43p<br>4:43p<br>10:43p | 1:41a<br>8:45a<br>2:41p<br>8:00p | 1.1F<br>0.8E<br>0.3F<br>0.5E |
| 17 (EDT) Mo | 6:20a<br>1:22p<br>5:57p<br>11:50p | 2:40a<br>9:37a<br>3:37p<br>9:06p | 1.1F<br>0.9E<br>0.4F<br>0.6E |
| 18 (EDT) Tu | 7:10a<br>1:58p<br>7:03p | 3:37a<br>10:24a<br>4:28p<br>10:08p | 1.1F<br>1.0E<br>0.5F<br>0.7E |
| 19 (EDT) We | 12:56a<br>7:56a<br>2:32p<br>8:04p | 4:32a<br>11:08a<br>5:16p<br>11:07p | 1.1F<br>1.0E<br>0.7F<br>0.8E |
| 20 (EDT) Th | 2:00a<br>8:40a<br>3:07p<br>9:00p | 5:24a<br>11:51a<br>6:02p | 1.1F<br>1.0E<br>0.8F |
| 21 (EDT) Fr | 3:01a<br>9:23a<br>3:43p<br>9:54p | 12:03a<br>6:14a<br>12:33p<br>6:47p | 0.9E<br>1.0F<br>1.0E<br>1.0F |
| 22 (EDT) Sa | 4:00a<br>10:05a<br>4:21p<br>10:47p | 12:57a<br>7:04a<br>1:15p<br>7:33p | 0.9E<br>0.9F<br>1.0E<br>1.1F |
| 23 (EDT) Su | 5:00a<br>10:47a<br>5:00p<br>11:41p | 1:50a<br>7:53a<br>1:57p<br>8:20p | 0.9E<br>0.8F<br>0.9E<br>1.1F |
| 24 (EDT) Mo | 6:00a<br>11:30a<br>5:41p | 2:44a<br>8:44a<br>2:41p<br>9:08p | 0.9E<br>0.7F<br>0.9E<br>1.1F |
| 25 (EDT) Tu | 12:36a<br>7:03a<br>12:15p<br>6:24p | 3:40a<br>9:37a<br>3:27p<br>9:59p | 0.9E<br>0.6F<br>0.8E<br>1.1F |
| 26 (EDT) We | 1:32a<br>8:09a<br>1:04p<br>7:11p | 4:38a<br>10:34a<br>4:17p<br>10:52p | 0.8E<br>0.4F<br>0.7E<br>1.0F |
| 27 (EDT) Th | 2:30a<br>9:19a<br>2:00p<br>8:02p | 5:40a<br>11:37a<br>5:12p<br>11:49p | 0.8E<br>0.4F<br>0.6E<br>1.0F |
| 28 (EDT) Fr | 3:28a<br>10:28a<br>3:05p<br>8:58p | 6:42a<br>12:43p<br>6:13p | 0.8E<br>0.3F<br>0.5E |
| 29 (EDT) Sa | 4:25a<br>11:30a<br>4:15p<br>9:58p | 12:48a<br>7:43a<br>1:49p<br>7:17p | 0.9F<br>0.8E<br>0.3F<br>0.5E |
| 30 (EDT) Su | 5:20a<br>12:23p<br>5:23p<br>10:58p | 1:47a<br>8:39a<br>2:48p<br>8:19p | 0.9F<br>0.8E<br>0.4F<br>0.5E |
| 31 (EDT) Mo | 6:10a<br>1:07p<br>6:22p<br>11:57p | 2:43a<br>9:29a<br>3:40p<br>9:17p | 0.9F<br>0.8E<br>0.5F<br>0.5E |

**September**

| Day | Slack h m | Max h m | knots |
|---|---|---|---|
| 1 (EDT) Tu | 6:56a<br>1:45p<br>7:14p | 3:34a<br>10:14a<br>4:25p<br>10:08p | 0.9F<br>0.9E<br>0.5F<br>0.6E |
| 2 (EDT) We | 12:51a<br>7:38a<br>2:18p<br>7:59p | 4:21a<br>10:54a<br>5:05p<br>10:55p | 0.9F<br>0.9E<br>0.6F<br>0.6E |
| 3 (EDT) Th | 1:43a<br>8:18a<br>2:49p<br>8:41p | 5:05a<br>11:31a<br>5:42p<br>11:39p | 0.9F<br>0.9E<br>0.7F<br>0.7E |
| 4 (EDT) Fr | 2:33a<br>8:55a<br>3:17p<br>9:22p | 5:47a<br>12:05p<br>6:18p | 0.9F<br>0.9E<br>0.8F |
| 5 (EDT) Sa | 3:22a<br>9:31a<br>3:44p<br>10:02p | 12:22a<br>6:28a<br>12:38p<br>6:52p | 0.8E<br>0.8F<br>0.8E<br>0.9F |
| 6 (EDT) Su | 4:12a<br>10:05a<br>4:11p<br>10:44p | 1:05a<br>7:08a<br>1:11p<br>7:27p | 0.8E<br>0.7F<br>0.8E<br>0.9F |
| 7 (EDT) Mo | 5:03a<br>10:37a<br>4:38p<br>11:27p | 1:48a<br>7:49a<br>1:43p<br>8:04p | 0.8E<br>0.6F<br>0.7E<br>1.0F |
| 8 (EDT) Tu | 5:58a<br>11:10a<br>5:08p | 2:34a<br>8:32a<br>2:17p<br>8:43p | 0.8E<br>0.5F<br>0.7E<br>1.0F |
| 9 (EDT) We | 12:14a<br>6:57a<br>11:43a<br>5:43p | 3:23a<br>9:18a<br>2:54p<br>9:27p | 0.8E<br>0.4F<br>0.6E<br>1.0F |
| 10 (EDT) Th | 1:05a<br>8:01a<br>12:23p<br>6:24p | 4:16a<br>10:09a<br>3:37p<br>10:16p | 0.8E<br>0.3F<br>0.6E<br>1.0F |
| 11 (EDT) Fr | 1:59a<br>9:08a<br>1:13p<br>7:15p | 5:13a<br>11:07a<br>4:29p<br>11:12p | 0.8E<br>0.2F<br>0.5E<br>1.0F |
| 12 (EDT) Sa | 2:57a<br>10:11a<br>2:18p<br>8:17p | 6:14a<br>12:12p<br>5:33p | 0.8E<br>0.2F<br>0.5E |
| 13 (EDT) Su | 3:56a<br>11:04a<br>3:36p<br>9:29p | 12:14a<br>7:14a<br>1:17p<br>6:45p | 0.9F<br>0.8E<br>0.3F<br>0.5E |
| 14 (EDT) Mo | 4:54a<br>11:49a<br>4:52p<br>10:45p | 1:19a<br>8:11a<br>2:17p<br>7:57p | 0.9F<br>0.8E<br>0.4F<br>0.6E |
| 15 (EDT) Tu | 5:49a<br>12:28p<br>5:59p<br>11:58p | 2:23a<br>9:03a<br>3:12p<br>9:04p | 0.9F<br>0.8E<br>0.6F<br>0.7E |
| 16 (EDT) We | 6:40a<br>1:05p<br>6:59p | 3:23a<br>9:50a<br>4:02p<br>10:05p | 0.9F<br>0.9E<br>0.7F<br>0.8E |
| 17 (EDT) Th | 1:06a<br>7:28a<br>1:42p<br>7:54p | 4:19a<br>10:35a<br>4:49p<br>11:01p | 0.9F<br>0.9E<br>0.9F<br>0.9E |
| 18 (EDT) Fr | 2:09a<br>8:13a<br>2:20p<br>8:46p | 5:11a<br>11:19a<br>5:34p<br>11:54p | 0.9F<br>0.9E<br>1.0F<br>1.0E |
| 19 (EDT) Sa | 3:08a<br>8:57a<br>2:58p<br>9:36p | 6:01a<br>12:01p<br>6:19p | 0.8F<br>0.9E<br>1.1F |
| 20 (EDT) Su | 4:05a<br>9:40a<br>3:37p<br>10:25p | 12:45a<br>6:50a<br>12:43p<br>7:03p | 1.0E<br>0.8F<br>0.9E<br>1.2F |
| 21 (EDT) Mo | 5:00a<br>10:23a<br>4:17p<br>11:14p | 1:35a<br>7:39a<br>1:26p<br>7:49p | 1.1E<br>0.7F<br>0.8E<br>1.2F |
| 22 (EDT) Tu | 5:56a<br>11:08a<br>4:59p | 2:25a<br>8:28a<br>2:11p<br>8:35p | 1.0E<br>0.6F<br>0.7E<br>1.1F |
| 23 (EDT) We | 12:04a<br>6:52a<br>11:56a<br>5:44p | 3:17a<br>9:20a<br>2:58p<br>9:24p | 1.0E<br>0.5F<br>0.6E<br>1.0F |
| 24 (EDT) Th | 12:55a<br>7:51a<br>12:50p<br>6:33p | 4:10a<br>10:16a<br>3:50p<br>10:16p | 0.9E<br>0.4F<br>0.6E<br>1.0F |
| 25 (EDT) Fr | 1:48a<br>8:51a<br>1:51p<br>7:27p | 5:06a<br>11:16a<br>4:47p<br>11:12p | 0.8E<br>0.4F<br>0.5E<br>0.9F |
| 26 (EDT) Sa | 2:43a<br>9:49a<br>2:59p<br>8:28p | 6:04a<br>12:18p<br>5:51p | 0.8E<br>0.4F<br>0.4E |
| 27 (EDT) Su | 3:38a<br>10:42a<br>4:08p<br>9:35p | 12:12a<br>7:01a<br>1:19p<br>6:57p | 0.8F<br>0.8E<br>0.4F<br>0.4E |
| 28 (EDT) Mo | 4:32a<br>11:29a<br>5:10p<br>10:42p | 1:12a<br>7:55a<br>2:14p<br>8:00p | 0.8F<br>0.8E<br>0.5F<br>0.5E |
| 29 (EDT) Tu | 5:24a<br>12:09p<br>6:03p<br>11:45p | 2:10a<br>8:44a<br>3:02p<br>8:57p | 0.7F<br>0.8E<br>0.6F<br>0.5E |
| 30 (EDT) We | 6:12a<br>12:45p<br>6:50p | 3:04a<br>9:28a<br>3:45p<br>9:48p | 0.7F<br>0.8E<br>0.7F<br>0.6E |

**October**

| Day | Slack h m | Max h m | knots |
|---|---|---|---|
| 1 (EDT) Th | 12:44a<br>6:57a<br>1:18p<br>7:32p | 3:53a<br>10:09a<br>4:24p<br>10:34p | 0.7F<br>0.8E<br>0.8F<br>0.7E |
| 2 (EDT) Fr | 1:38a<br>7:39a<br>1:48p<br>8:13p | 4:39a<br>10:46a<br>5:01p<br>11:19p | 0.7F<br>0.8E<br>0.9F<br>0.8E |
| 3 (EDT) Sa | 2:30a<br>8:18a<br>2:17p<br>8:52p | 5:23a<br>11:21a<br>5:37p | 0.7F<br>0.8E<br>0.9F |
| 4 (EDT) Su | 3:21a<br>8:55a<br>2:45p<br>9:32p | 12:02a<br>6:06a<br>11:55a<br>6:12p | 0.9E<br>0.6F<br>0.7E<br>1.0F |
| 5 (EDT) Mo | 4:12a<br>9:30a<br>3:14p<br>10:14p | 12:45a<br>6:48a<br>12:29p<br>6:49p | 0.9E<br>0.6F<br>0.7E<br>1.1F |
| 6 (EDT) Tu | 5:04a<br>10:05a<br>3:45p<br>10:57p | 1:28a<br>7:31a<br>1:04p<br>7:27p | 1.0E<br>0.5F<br>0.6E<br>1.1F |
| 7 (EDT) We | 5:56a<br>10:42a<br>4:21p<br>11:43p | 2:13a<br>8:15a<br>1:42p<br>8:09p | 1.0E<br>0.4F<br>0.6E<br>1.1F |
| 8 (EDT) Th | 6:50a<br>11:24a<br>5:03p | 3:01a<br>9:03a<br>2:25p<br>8:55p | 0.9E<br>0.4F<br>0.5E<br>1.1F |
| 9 (EDT) Fr | 12:32a<br>7:45a<br>12:15p<br>5:53p | 3:51a<br>9:55a<br>3:16p<br>9:47p | 0.9E<br>0.3F<br>0.5E<br>1.0F |
| 10 (EDT) Sa | 1:24a<br>8:37a<br>1:19p<br>6:55p | 4:45a<br>10:53a<br>4:17p<br>10:46p | 0.9E<br>0.3F<br>0.5E<br>0.9F |
| 11 (EDT) Su | 2:20a<br>9:27a<br>2:32p<br>8:08p | 5:41a<br>11:54a<br>5:28p<br>11:51p | 0.8E<br>0.4F<br>0.5E<br>0.8F |
| 12 (EDT) Mo | 3:18a<br>10:12a<br>3:47p<br>9:30p | 6:38a<br>12:55p<br>6:43p | 0.8E<br>0.5F<br>0.5E |
| 13 (EDT) Tu | 4:15a<br>10:54a<br>4:55p<br>10:52p | 12:59a<br>7:33a<br>1:52p<br>7:55p | 0.8F<br>0.8E<br>0.7F<br>0.6E |
| 14 (EDT) We | 5:12a<br>11:35a<br>5:56p | 2:05a<br>8:25a<br>2:45p<br>9:01p | 0.7F<br>0.8E<br>0.8F<br>0.8E |
| 15 (EDT) Th | 12:08a<br>6:05a<br>12:15p<br>6:51p | 3:07a<br>9:14a<br>3:35p<br>10:00p | 0.7F<br>0.8E<br>1.0F<br>0.9E |
| 16 (EDT) Fr | 1:16a<br>6:55a<br>12:55p<br>7:42p | 4:05a<br>10:01a<br>4:22p<br>10:53p | 0.7F<br>0.8E<br>1.1F<br>1.0E |
| 17 (EDT) Sa | 2:17a<br>7:43a<br>1:35p<br>8:31p | 4:58a<br>10:46a<br>5:07p<br>11:44p | 0.7F<br>0.8E<br>1.2F<br>1.1E |
| 18 (EDT) Su | 3:14a<br>8:30a<br>2:15p<br>9:18p | 5:49a<br>11:30a<br>5:52p | 0.6F<br>0.8E<br>1.2F |
| 19 (EDT) Mo | 4:08a<br>9:16a<br>2:56p<br>10:04p | 12:33a<br>6:38a<br>12:14p<br>6:36p | 1.1E<br>0.6F<br>0.7E<br>1.2F |
| 20 (EDT) Tu | 4:59a<br>10:02a<br>3:38p<br>10:49p | 1:20a<br>7:26a<br>12:58p<br>7:20p | 1.1E<br>0.6F<br>0.7E<br>1.2F |
| 21 (EDT) We | 5:50a<br>10:51a<br>4:21p<br>11:34p | 2:07a<br>8:15a<br>1:44p<br>8:05p | 1.1E<br>0.5F<br>0.6E<br>1.1F |
| 22 (EDT) Th | 6:40a<br>11:44a<br>5:07p | 2:54a<br>9:05a<br>2:32p<br>8:52p | 1.0E<br>0.5F<br>0.5E<br>1.0F |
| 23 (EDT) Fr | 12:20a<br>7:29a<br>12:42p<br>5:57p | 3:42a<br>9:58a<br>3:25p<br>9:41p | 0.9E<br>0.5F<br>0.4E<br>0.9F |
| 24 (EDT) Sa | 1:07a<br>8:18a<br>1:45p<br>6:53p | 4:32a<br>10:53a<br>4:24p<br>10:35p | 0.9E<br>0.5F<br>0.4E<br>0.8F |
| 25 (EST) Su | 12:55a<br>8:06a<br>1:50p<br>6:58p | 4:23a<br>10:49a<br>4:28p<br>10:32p | 0.8E<br>0.5F<br>0.4E<br>0.7F |
| 26 (EST) Mo | 1:46a<br>8:50a<br>2:53p<br>8:10p | 5:15a<br>11:43a<br>5:33p<br>11:32p | 0.8E<br>0.5F<br>0.4E<br>0.6F |
| 27 (EST) Tu | 2:38a<br>9:31a<br>3:48p<br>9:22p | 6:05a<br>12:34p<br>6:35p | 0.8E<br>0.6F<br>0.5E |
| 28 (EST) We | 3:30a<br>10:09a<br>4:37p<br>10:31p | 12:32a<br>6:52a<br>1:20p<br>7:32p | 0.6F<br>0.7E<br>0.7F<br>0.6E |
| 29 (EST) Th | 4:20a<br>10:43a<br>5:22p<br>11:35p | 1:28a<br>7:37a<br>2:02p<br>8:24p | 0.6F<br>0.7E<br>0.8F<br>0.7E |
| 30 (EST) Fr | 5:07a<br>11:16a<br>6:04p | 2:21a<br>8:18a<br>2:42p<br>9:12p | 0.6F<br>0.7E<br>0.9F<br>0.8E |
| 31 (EST) Sa | 12:33a<br>5:52a<br>11:47a<br>6:45p | 3:11a<br>8:57a<br>3:20p<br>9:57p | 0.5F<br>0.7E<br>1.0F<br>0.9E |

**Reports were generated by Tides and Currents for Windows from Nautical Software (503) 579-1414.**

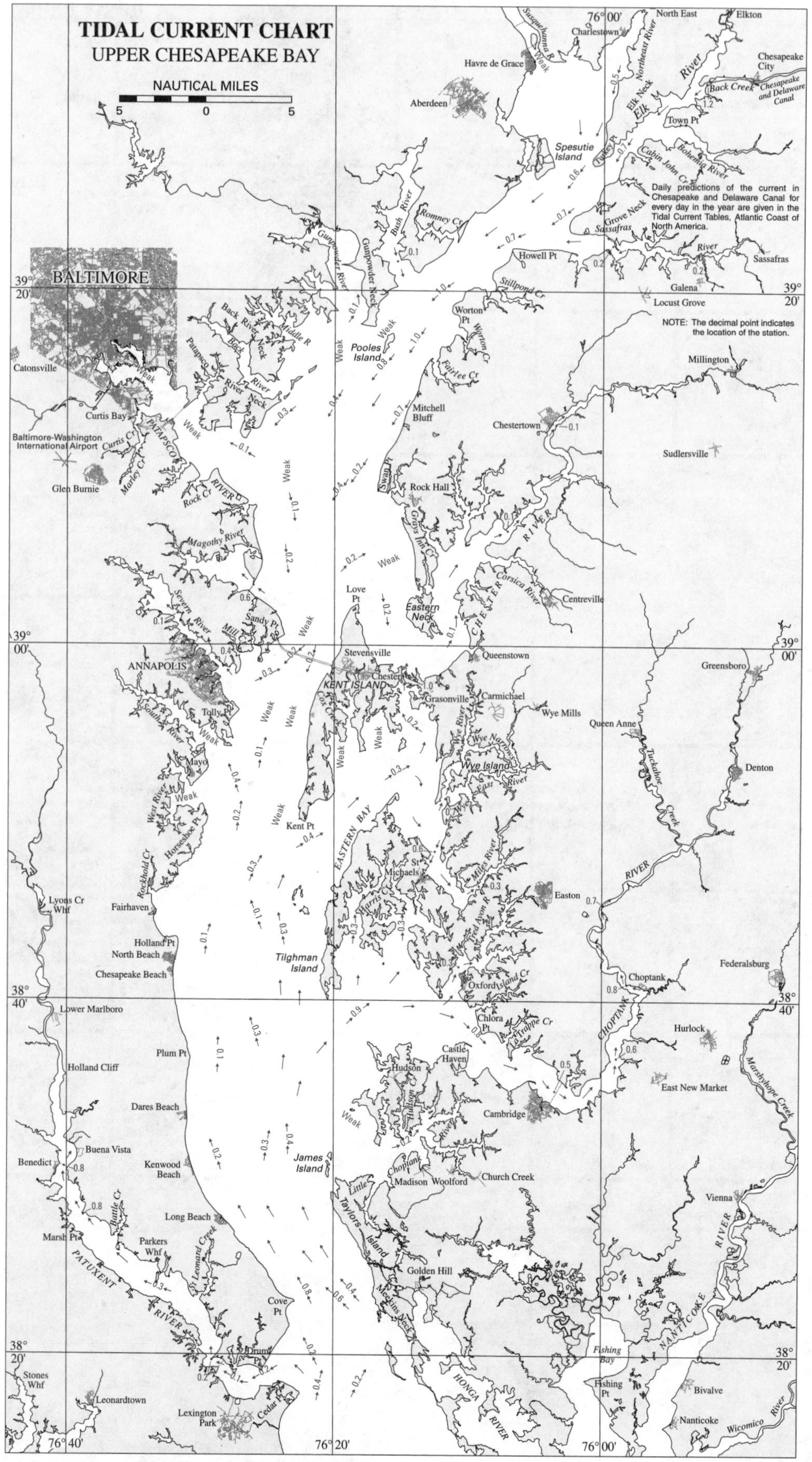

TIDAL CURRENT CHART
UPPER CHESAPEAKE BAY

NAUTICAL MILES

NOTE: The decimal point indicates the location of the station.

Daily predictions of the current in Chesapeake and Delaware Canal for every day in the year are given in the Tidal Current Tables, Atlantic Coast of North America.

THREE HOURS AFTER MAXIMUM EBB AT BALTIMORE HARBOR APPROACH (E+3)

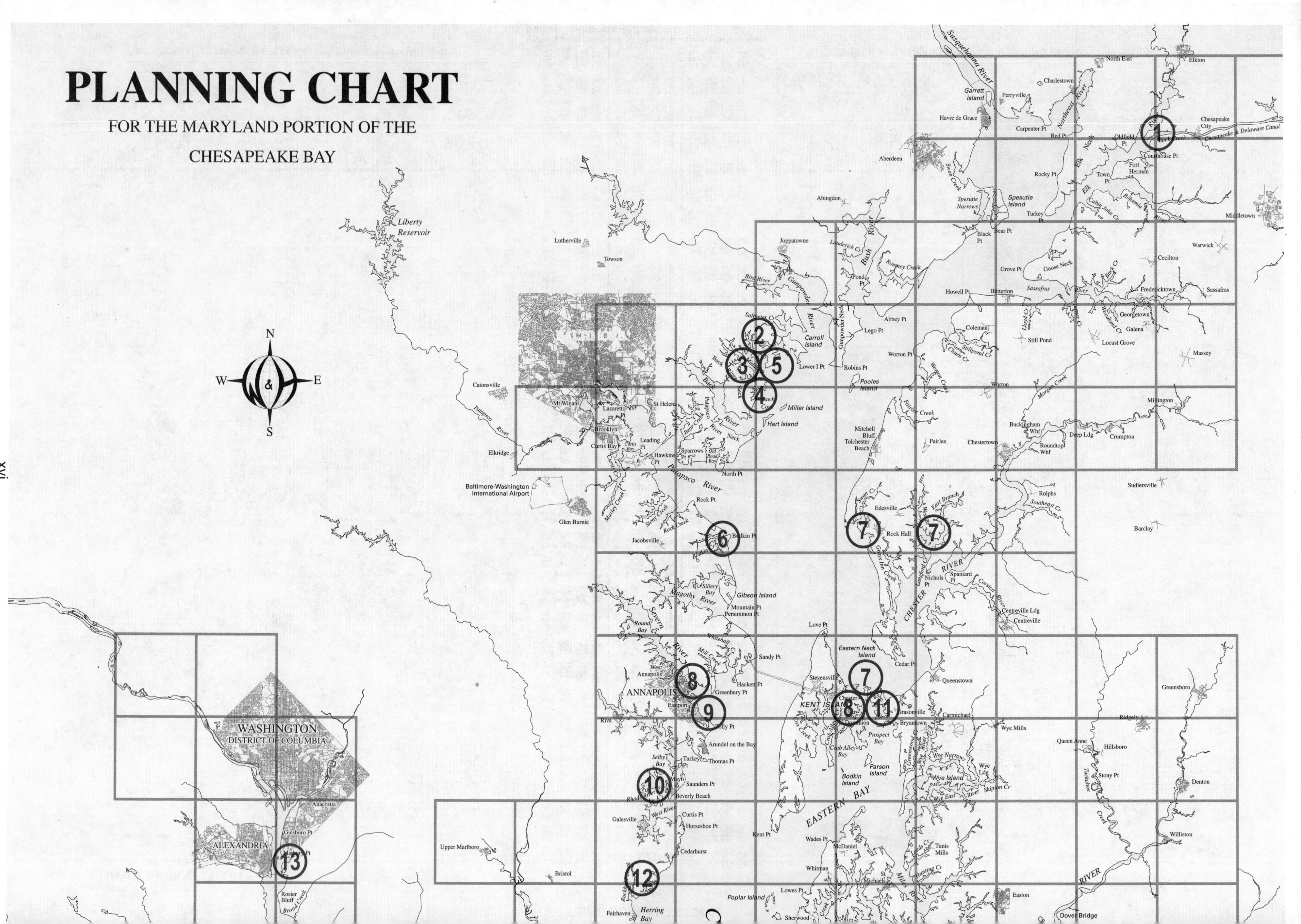
PLANNING CHART
FOR THE MARYLAND PORTION OF THE
CHESAPEAKE BAY
N
E
S
W
Liberty Reservoir
Lutherville
Towson
Catonsville
Elkridge
Baltimore-Washington International Airport
Glen Burnie
Jacobsville
Susquehanna River
Garrett Island
Havre de Grace
Perryville
Charlestown
North East
Elkton
Chesapeake City
Chesapeake & Delaware Canal
Aberdeen
Abingdon
Joppatowne
Bush River
Gunpowder River
Carroll Island
Miller Island
Hart Island
Patapsco River
Rock Pt
Bodkin Pt
Magothy River
Gibson Island
Severn River
ANNAPOLIS
West Annapolis
Eastport
Greenbury Pt
Sandy Pt
Galesville
Herring Bay
Fairhaven
Upper Marlboro
Bristol
WASHINGTON
DISTRICT OF COLUMBIA
ALEXANDRIA
Anacostia
Rosier Bluff
Broad Creek
Chestertown
Rock Hall
Edesville
Chester River
Centreville
Eastern Neck Island
Kent Island
Stevensville
Queenstown
Wye Mills
Wye Island
Eastern Bay
Poplar Island
St Michaels
Easton
Greensboro
Denton
Williston
Dover Bridge
Sassafras River
Massey
Sudlersville
Barclay
1
2
3
4
5
6
7
7
7
8
8
9
10
11
12
13

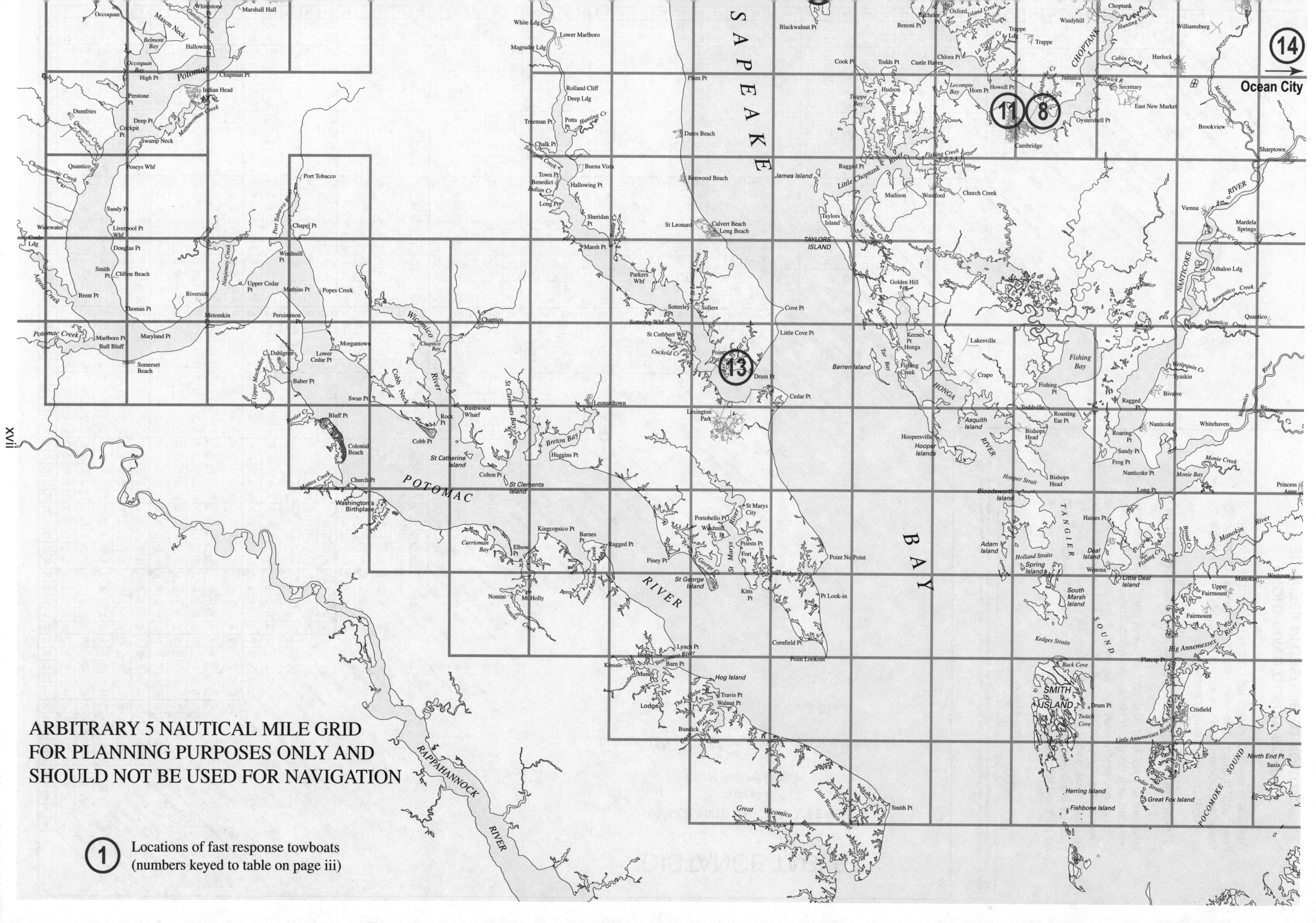

ARBITRARY 5 NAUTICAL MILE GRID
FOR PLANNING PURPOSES ONLY AND
SHOULD NOT BE USED FOR NAVIGATION
1 Locations of fast response towboats
(numbers keyed to table on page iii)
14
Ocean City
11
8
13
SAPEAKE
BAY
TANGIER
SOUND
POCOMOKE
SOUND
POTOMAC
RIVER
RAPPAHANNOCK
RIVER
CHOPTANK
NANTICOKE
RIVER
HONGA
RIVER
TAYLORS
ISLAND
SMITH
ISLAND
Occoquan
Mason Neck
Marshall Hall
Indian Head
Dumfries
Quantico
Cambridge
Oxford
Trappe
Hurlock
Secretary
East New Market
Williamsburg
Sharptown
Vienna
Mardela Springs
Crisfield
Princess Anne
Westover
Lexington Park
Leonardtown
Colonial Beach
Washington's Birthplace
Point Lookout
Point No Point
St Marys City
St George Island
Kinsale
Lodge
Smith Pt
Hog Island
Barren Island
Hooper Islands
Bloodsworth Island
South Marsh Island
Deal Island
Fishing Bay
Chaptico
Port Tobacco
Morgantown
Dahlgren
Calvert Beach
Long Beach
St Leonard
Cove Pt
Drum Pt
Cedar Pt
Kenwood Beach
Dares Beach
Plum Pt
Blackwalnut Pt
James Island
Benedict
Hallowing Pt
Lower Marlboro
Great Fox Island
Herring Island
Fishbone Island
Saxis
North End Pt

## CAUTION TO BE USED IN RELIANCE UPON AIDS TO NAVIGATION

The aids to navigation depicted on charts comprise a system of fixed and floating aids with varying degrees of reliability. Therefore, prudent mariners will not rely solely on any single aid to navigation, particularly a floating aid.

### Removal or Replacement of Aids to Navigation

Mariners are advised that lighted buoys may be removed or replaced with unlighted buoys in anticipation of ice conditions. Lighting equipment may be removed from aid structures in areas of little night use where ice may form and destroy the aids. The structures with daymarkers intact will remain in place. As soon as the threat of ice has passed, all aids to navigation will be restored to normal operation.

LOGARITHMIC SPEED SCALE

1 2 3 4 5 6 7 8 9 10 15 20 25 30 40 50 60

To find SPEED, place one point of dividers on distance run (in any unit) and the other on minutes run. Without changing divider spread, place right point on 60 and left point will then indicate speed in units per hour. Example: with 4.0 nautical miles run in 15 minutes, the speed is 16.0 knots

# DISTANCE TABLE

*APPROXIMATE NAUTICAL MILEAGE*
*between*
*Major Boating Centers*

*1 Nautical Mile = 1.15 Statute Miles (6,076 feet approx.)*

◥ Via Kent Narrows ◣ Via Knapps Narrows

1 — Annapolis (Severn River)
2 — Back River Bridge
3 — Baltimore - Ft. McHenry (Patapsco River)
4 — Big Annamessex & Manokin R. Ent. (Fl R 2.5sec "2")
5 — Bloody Point Light
6 — Bodkin Cr. (Fl G 2.5sec "7") (Patapsco R.)
7 — Bohemia River Bridge
8 — Bush River Bridge
9 — Cambridge
10 — Charlestown (Northeast River)
11 — Chesapeake Bay Bridge
12 — Chesapeake City (C & D Canal)
13 — Chestertown
14 — Colonial Beach, Virginia
15 — Corsica River Entrance (N "RG")
16 — Cove Point Light
17 — Craighill Channel Light (Fl 3sec 39ft 9M)
18 — Crisfield
19 — Deal, Deal Island
20 — Denton (Choptank River)
21 — Ft. Carroll (Patapsco River)
22 — Georgetown (Sassafras River)
23 — Gunpowder River Bridge
24 — Havre de Grace (Bridge)
25 — Herring Bay (Fl 4sec "2")
26 — Hooper Island Light
27 — Hooper Strait Light (Ent. to Honga R.)
28 — Howell Point Light
29 — Kent Narrows Bridge
30 — Love Point Light (Chester River Ent.)
31 — Leonardtown
32 — Little Choptank River (Fl G 2.5sec "1")
33 — Magothy River Entrance (Fl 4sec "3")
34 — Manokin & Annamessex R. Ent. (Fl R 2.5sec "2")
35 — Middle River (R "4" QR)
36 — Nanticoke
37 — Ocean City via C&D Canal
38 — Ocean City via Cape Charles
39 — Oxford
40 — Pocomoke City
41 — Poole's Island Light
42 — Potomac R. Ent. (RW "A" Mo (A) GONG)
43 — Queenstown
44 — Rhode & West River Ent. (Fl R 2.5sec)
45 — Rock Cr. (Fl G 4sec "3") (Patapsco R.)
46 — Rock Hall
47 — St. Mary's City
48 — St. Michaels via Bloody Point
49 — St. Michaels via Kent Narrows
50 — Salisbury
51 — Sandy Point Light
52 — 7' Knoll (Fl R 6sec 42ft 7M)
53 — Sharps Island Light (Choptank R. Ent.)
54 — Shark Fin Shoal Light (Fishing Bay Ent.)
55 — Smith Island (Big Thoroughfare Channel)
56 — Smith Point Light, Va.
57 — Solomons Island
58 — South River Entrance (Fl R "4")
59 — Tilghmans Island (Knapps Narrows)
60 — Washington, D. C.
61 — West & Rhode R. Ent. (Fl R 2.5sec)
62 — Worton Cr. (Gp Fl R 2.5sec R "2")

| | 1 | 2 | 3 | 4 | 5 | 6 | 7 | 8 | 9 | 10 | 11 | 12 | 13 | 14 | 15 | 16 | 17 | 18 | 19 | 20 | 21 | 22 | 23 | 24 | 25 | 26 | 27 | 28 | 29 | 30 | 31 | 32 | 33 | 34 | 35 | 36 | 37 | 38 | 39 | 40 | 41 | 42 | 43 | 44 | 45 | 46 | 47 | 48 | 49 | 50 | 51 | 52 | 53 | 54 | 55 | 56 | 57 | 58 | 59 | 60 | 61 | 62 |
|---|---|---|---|---|---|---|---|---|---|---|---|---|---|---|---|---|---|---|---|---|---|---|---|---|---|---|---|---|---|---|---|---|---|---|---|---|---|---|---|---|---|---|---|---|---|---|---|---|---|---|---|---|---|---|---|---|---|---|---|---|---|---|
| 1 | |
| 2 | 33 |
| 3 | 26 | 26 |
| 4 | 70 | 95 | 89 |
| 5 | 10 | 36 | 30 | 59 |
| 6 | 17 | 19 | 11 | 80 | 21 |
| 7 | 47 | 38 | 43 | 108 | 49 | 36 |
| 8 | 34 | 25 | 30 | 95 | 36 | 23 | 27 |
| 9 | 34 | 60 | 54 | 61 | 24 | 45 | 73 | 60 |
| 10 | 47 | 37 | 42 | 108 | 49 | 35 | 18 | 27 | 73 |
| 11 | 6 | 27 | 20 | 70 | 10 | 11 | 41 | 28 | 34 | 41 |
| 12 | 50 | 41 | 45 | 111 | 52 | 38 | 11 | 30 | 72 | 21 | 44 |
| 13 | 36 | 47 | 42 | 90 | 35 | 32 | 60 | 47 | 55 | 60 | 30 | 63 |
| 14 | 98 | 124 | 118 | 57 | 88 | 109 | 137 | 124 | 88 | 137 | 98 | 140 | 118 |
| 15 | 24 | 35 | 30 | 79 | 24 | 21 | 49 | 36 | 44 | 48 | 19 | 51 | 12 | 107 |
| 16 | 38 | 67 | 60 | 33 | 29 | 51 | 81 | 68 | 28 | 81 | 40 | 84 | 58 | 60 | 47 |
| 17 | 17 | 16 | 11 | 81 | 22 | 4 | 32 | 19 | 46 | 32 | 12 | 35 | 33 | 110 | 21 | 52 |
| 18 | 77 | 102 | 96 | 9 | 66 | 87 | 115 | 102 | 68 | 115 | 77 | 118 | 97 | 61 | 86 | 40 | 88 |
| 19 | 65 | 90 | 84 | 10 | 54 | 75 | 103 | 90 | 56 | 103 | 64 | 106 | 85 | 61 | 74 | 28 | 76 | 17 |
| 20 | 64 | 90 | 84 | 91 | 54 | 75 | 103 | 90 | 31 | 103 | 64 | 102 | 85 | 118 | 74 | 58 | 76 | 98 | 86 |
| 21 | 21 | 22 | 4 | 84 | 25 | 6 | 38 | 26 | 49 | 38 | 15 | 41 | 38 | 113 | 26 | 55 | 6 | 91 | 79 | 79 |
| 22 | 42 | 34 | 39 | 103 | 44 | 32 | 20 | 24 | 68 | 21 | 38 | | 56 | 132 | 45 | 78 | 29 | 110 | 98 | 98 | 35 |
| 23 | 31 | 18 | 24 | 93 | 34 | 17 | 36 | 23 | 57 | 35 | 25 | 39 | 45 | 122 | 33 | 65 | 14 | 100 | 88 | 87 | 20 | 32 |
| 24 | 47 | 38 | 43 | 108 | 49 | 36 | 17 | 27 | 73 | 16 | 41 | 20 | 60 | 137 | 49 | 81 | 32 | 115 | 103 | 103 | 39 | 21 | 36 |
| 25 | 17 | 45 | 37 | 55 | 9 | 29 | 59 | 46 | 26 | 59 | 18 | 62 | 44 | 82 | 33 | 22 | 30 | 62 | 50 | 56 | 33 | 56 | 43 | 59 |
| 26 | 47 | 72 | 66 | 23 | 36 | 57 | 85 | 72 | 38 | 85 | 46 | 88 | 67 | 52 | 56 | 10 | 58 | 30 | 18 | 68 | 61 | 80 | 70 | 85 | 32 |
| 27 | 56 | 81 | 75 | 18 | 45 | 66 | 94 | 81 | 47 | 94 | 55 | 97 | 76 | 54 | 65 | 19 | 67 | 25 | 9 | 77 | 70 | 89 | 79 | 94 | 41 | 9 |
| 28 | 32 | 23 | 28 | 93 | 34 | 21 | 15 | 13 | 58 | 24 | 26 | 18 | 46 | 122 | 34 | 66 | 17 | 100 | 88 | 88 | 24 | 12 | 21 | 15 | 44 | 70 | 79 |
| 29 | 19 | 31 | 25 | 69 | 14 | 16 | 44 | 31 | 34 | 44 | 14 | 47 | 21 | 97 | 10 | 37 | 16 | 76 | 64 | 64 | 21 | 41 | 29 | 44 | 23 | 46 | 55 | 29 |
| 30 | 12 | 24 | 18 | 75 | 16 | 9 | 37 | 24 | 40 | 37 | 7 | 40 | 23 | 104 | 12 | 45 | 10 | 82 | 70 | 70 | 14 | 34 | 22 | 37 | 24 | 52 | 61 | 22 | 7 |
| 31 | 89 | 115 | 109 | 48 | 79 | 100 | 128 | 115 | 79 | 128 | 89 | 131 | 109 | 21 | 98 | 51 | 101 | 52 | 52 | 109 | 104 | 123 | 113 | 128 | 73 | 43 | 45 | 113 | 88 | 95 |
| 32 | 29 | 54 | 48 | 45 | 18 | 39 | 67 | 54 | 18 | 67 | 28 | 70 | 49 | 72 | 38 | 12 | 40 | 52 | 40 | 48 | 43 | 62 | 52 | 67 | 17 | 22 | 31 | 52 | 28 | 34 | 63 |
| 33 | 10 | 25 | 18 | 74 | 15 | 9 | 40 | 27 | 39 | 40 | 4 | 43 | 30 | 103 | 19 | 44 | 10 | 81 | 69 | 69 | 13 | 37 | 23 | 40 | 22 | 51 | 60 | 25 | 14 | 7 | 94 | 33 |
| 34 | 70 | 95 | 89 | – | 59 | 80 | 108 | 95 | 61 | 108 | 70 | 111 | 90 | 57 | 79 | 33 | 81 | 9 | 10 | 91 | 84 | 103 | 93 | 108 | 55 | 23 | 18 | 93 | 69 | 75 | 48 | 45 | 74 |
| 35 | 26 | 13 | 19 | 88 | 29 | 12 | 30 | 18 | 53 | 30 | 20 | 33 | 40 | 117 | 28 | 60 | 8 | 95 | 83 | 83 | 15 | 27 | 9 | 31 | 38 | 65 | 74 | 16 | 24 | 17 | 108 | 47 | 18 | 88 |
| 36 | 68 | 93 | 87 | 16 | 57 | 78 | 106 | 93 | 59 | 106 | 67 | 109 | 88 | 66 | 77 | 31 | 79 | 23 | 8 | 89 | 82 | 101 | 91 | 106 | 53 | 21 | 12 | 91 | 67 | 73 | 57 | 43 | 73 | 16 | 86 |
| 37 | 142 | 133 | 137 | 203 | 144 | 130 | 103 | 122 | 168 | 113 | 136 | 92 | 155 | 232 | 143 | 176 | 127 | 210 | 198 | 198 | 133 | 122 | 131 | 112 | 154 | 180 | 189 | 110 | 139 | 132 | 223 | 162 | 135 | 203 | 125 | 201 |
| 38 | 211 | 236 | 230 | 151 | 200 | 221 | 249 | 236 | 202 | 249 | 211 | 252 | 231 | 193 | 220 | 174 | 222 | 146 | 161 | 232 | 225 | 244 | 234 | 249 | 196 | 164 | 161 | 234 | 210 | 216 | 184 | 186 | 215 | 151 | 229 | 167 | 344 |
| 39 | 28 | 54 | 48 | 55 | 18 | 39 | 67 | 54 | 10 | 67 | 28 | 70 | 49 | 83 | 38 | 23 | 40 | 62 | 50 | 40 | 43 | 62 | 51 | 67 | 20 | 32 | 41 | 52 | 28 | 34 | 74 | 13 | 33 | 55 | 47 | 53 | 162 | 196 |
| 40 | 111 | 136 | 130 | 39 | 100 | 121 | 149 | 136 | 102 | 149 | 111 | 152 | 131 | 95 | 120 | 74 | 123 | 35 | 49 | 132 | 125 | 144 | 134 | 149 | 96 | 64 | 59 | 134 | 110 | 116 | 86 | 86 | 115 | 39 | 129 | 57 | 244 | 175 | 96 |
| 41 | 24 | 13 | 18 | 88 | 29 | 11 | 25 | 12 | 53 | 25 | 19 | 28 | 36 | 117 | 24 | 59 | 7 | 95 | 83 | 83 | 13 | 22 | 11 | 25 | 37 | 65 | 74 | 10 | 20 | 13 | 108 | 47 | 17 | 88 | 5 | 86 | 120 | 229 | 47 | 129 |
| 42 | 62 | 88 | 82 | 21 | 52 | 73 | 101 | 88 | 52 | 101 | 62 | 104 | 82 | 36 | 71 | 24 | 74 | 25 | 25 | 82 | 77 | 96 | 86 | 101 | 46 | 16 | 18 | 86 | 61 | 68 | 27 | 36 | 67 | 21 | 81 | 30 | 196 | 157 | 47 | 59 | 81 |
| 43 | 20 | 32 | 26 | 74 | 19 | 17 | 45 | 32 | 39 | 45 | 15 | 48 | 19 | 102 | 7 | 42 | 18 | 81 | 69 | 69 | 22 | 42 | 30 | 45 | 25 | 51 | 60 | 30 | 5 | 8 | 93 | 33 | 15 | 74 | 25 | 73 | 140 | 215 | 33 | 115 | 21 | 66 |
| 44 | 12 | 40 | 32 | 63 | 6 | 24 | 54 | 41 | 30 | 54 | 15 | 57 | 41 | 92 | 30 | 32 | 25 | 70 | 59 | 60 | 28 | 51 | 38 | 54 | 11 | 40 | 49 | 39 | 20 | 19 | 83 | 22 | 17 | 63 | 33 | 61 | 149 | 204 | 24 | 104 | 32 | 56 | 25 |
| 45 | 20 | 22 | 8 | 83 | 24 | 6 | 38 | 25 | 48 | 37 | 14 | 41 | 37 | 112 | 25 | 54 | 6 | 90 | 78 | 78 | 4 | 35 | 20 | 38 | 32 | 60 | 69 | 23 | 20 | 13 | 103 | 42 | 12 | 83 | 14 | 81 | 133 | 224 | 42 | 124 | 13 | 76 | 21 | 27 |
| 46 | 16 | 21 | 18 | 80 | 21 | 9 | 35 | 22 | 45 | 34 | 10 | 37 | 28 | 109 | 17 | 50 | 8 | 87 | 75 | 75 | 14 | 31 | 19 | 35 | 28 | 57 | 66 | 20 | 12 | 5 | 100 | 39 | 11 | 80 | 14 | 78 | 129 | 221 | 39 | 121 | 10 | 73 | 13 | 23 | 13 |
| 47 | 74 | 100 | 94 | 33 | 64 | 85 | 113 | 100 | 64 | 113 | 74 | 116 | 94 | 36 | 83 | 36 | 85 | 37 | 37 | 94 | 89 | 108 | 98 | 113 | 58 | 28 | 30 | 98 | 73 | 80 | 26 | 48 | 79 | 33 | 93 | 42 | 208 | 169 | 59 | 71 | 93 | 12 | 78 | 68 | 88 | 85 |
| 48 | 24 | 50 | 44 | 69 | 14 | 35 | 63 | 50 | 36 | 63 | 26 | 66 | 49 | 97 | 38 | 37 | 36 | 76 | 63 | 66 | 39 | 58 | 48 | 63 | 23 | 46 | 54 | 48 | – | 30 | 88 | 28 | 29 | 69 | 43 | 66 | 158 | 210 | 28 | 110 | 43 | 61 | 34 | 20 | 38 | 35 | 73 |
| 49 | 31 | 42 | 37 | – | – | 27 | 55 | 43 | – | 55 | 25 | 58 | 35 | – | 21 | – | 28 | – | – | – | 33 | 52 | 40 | 56 | – | – | – | 41 | 11 | 18 | – | – | 26 | – | 35 | – | 150 | – | – | – | 31 | – | 16 | – | 32 | 23 | – | – |
| 50 | 87 | 112 | 106 | 35 | 76 | 97 | 125 | 112 | 78 | 125 | 86 | 128 | 117 | 85 | 97 | 50 | 98 | 42 | 26 | 108 | 101 | 120 | 110 | 125 | 72 | 40 | 31 | 110 | 86 | 92 | 76 | 62 | 91 | 35 | 105 | 31 | 220 | 186 | 72 | 76 | 105 | 49 | 91 | 80 | 100 | 97 | 61 | 85 | – |
| 51 | 7 | 26 | 19 | 69 | 11 | 10 | 40 | 27 | 35 | 40 | 1 | 43 | 29 | 99 | 17 | 41 | 11 | 76 | 65 | 65 | 14 | 37 | 24 | 40 | 19 | 47 | 56 | 25 | 12 | 5 | 90 | 29 | 3 | 69 | 19 | 68 | 135 | 211 | 29 | 110 | 18 | 63 | 13 | 14 | 13 | 9 | 75 | 25 | 24 | 87 |
| 52 | 15 | 18 | 10 | 78 | 19 | 2 | 34 | 21 | 43 | 34 | 9 | 37 | 31 | 107 | 20 | 49 | 2 | 85 | 73 | 73 | 6 | 31 | 16 | 34 | 27 | 55 | 64 | 19 | 15 | 8 | 98 | 37 | 7 | 78 | 10 | 76 | 129 | 219 | 37 | 119 | 9 | 71 | 16 | 22 | 5 | 8 | 83 | 33 | 26 | 95 | 8 |
| 53 | 22 | 48 | 42 | 49 | 12 | 33 | 61 | 48 | 17 | 61 | 23 | 64 | 43 | 75 | 32 | 15 | 34 | 54 | 42 | 47 | 37 | 56 | 46 | 61 | 11 | 24 | 33 | 46 | 22 | 28 | 66 | 6 | 27 | 49 | 41 | 45 | 156 | 188 | 11 | 88 | 41 | 39 | 27 | 16 | 36 | 33 | 51 | 22 | – | 64 | 23 | 31 |
| 54 | 62 | 87 | 81 | 12 | 51 | 72 | 100 | 87 | 53 | 100 | 61 | 103 | 82 | 60 | 71 | 25 | 73 | 19 | 3 | 83 | 76 | 95 | 85 | 100 | 47 | 15 | 6 | 85 | 61 | 67 | 51 | 37 | 66 | 12 | 80 | 6 | 195 | 163 | 47 | 53 | 80 | 24 | 66 | 55 | 75 | 72 | 36 | 60 | – | 25 | 62 | 70 | 39 |
| 55 | 65 | 90 | 84 | 5 | 54 | 75 | 103 | 90 | 56 | 103 | 65 | 106 | 85 | 49 | 74 | 28 | 76 | 6 | 15 | 86 | 79 | 98 | 88 | 103 | 50 | 18 | 15 | 88 | 64 | 70 | 40 | 40 | 69 | 5 | 83 | 21 | 198 | 146 | 50 | 42 | 83 | 13 | 69 | 58 | 78 | 75 | 25 | 64 | – | 40 | 65 | 73 | 42 | 17 |
| 56 | 70 | 95 | 89 | 19 | 59 | 80 | 108 | 95 | 61 | 108 | 69 | 111 | 90 | 47 | 79 | 33 | 81 | 20 | 23 | 91 | 84 | 103 | 93 | 108 | 55 | 23 | 18 | 93 | 69 | 75 | 38 | 45 | 73 | 19 | 88 | 30 | 203 | 146 | 55 | 49 | 88 | 11 | 74 | 63 | 83 | 80 | 23 | 69 | – | 48 | 70 | 78 | 47 | 25 | 9 |
| 57 | 46 | 75 | 68 | 34 | 37 | 59 | 89 | 76 | 36 | 89 | 48 | 92 | 66 | 60 | 55 | 8 | 60 | 41 | 29 | 66 | 63 | 86 | 73 | 89 | 30 | 11 | 20 | 74 | 45 | 53 | 51 | 20 | 52 | 34 | 68 | 32 | 184 | 175 | 31 | 75 | 67 | 24 | 50 | 40 | 62 | 58 | 36 | 45 | – | 51 | 49 | 57 | 23 | 26 | 29 | 34 |
| 58 | 8 | 36 | 29 | 64 | 7 | 20 | 50 | 37 | 30 | 50 | 11 | 53 | 38 | 92 | 27 | 32 | 21 | 71 | 59 | 60 | 24 | 47 | 34 | 50 | 11 | 41 | 50 | 35 | 20 | 15 | 83 | 23 | 13 | 64 | 29 | 62 | 145 | 205 | 24 | 105 | 28 | 56 | 23 | 4 | 23 | 19 | 68 | 21 | – | 81 | 10 | 18 | 17 | 56 | 59 | 64 | 40 |
| 59 | 14 | 40 | 34 | 55 | 4 | 25 | 53 | 40 | 16 | 53 | 14 | 56 | 35 | 81 | 24 | 21 | 26 | 60 | 48 | 46 | 29 | 48 | 37 | 53 | 6 | 30 | 39 | 38 | 14 | 20 | 72 | 12 | 19 | 55 | 33 | 51 | 148 | 194 | 14 | 94 | 33 | 45 | 19 | 10 | 28 | 25 | 57 | 18 | – | 70 | 15 | 23 | 6 | 45 | 48 | 53 | 29 | 10 |
| 60 | 154 | 180 | 174 | 113 | 144 | 165 | 193 | 180 | 144 | 193 | 154 | 196 | 175 | 63 | 163 | 116 | 166 | 117 | 117 | 174 | 169 | 188 | 178 | 193 | 138 | 108 | 110 | 178 | 153 | 160 | 77 | 128 | 159 | 113 | 173 | 122 | 288 | 249 | 139 | 151 | 173 | 92 | 158 | 148 | 168 | 165 | 92 | 153 | – | 141 | 155 | 163 | 131 | 116 | 105 | 103 | 116 | 149 | 137 |
| 61 | 12 | 40 | 32 | 63 | 6 | 24 | 54 | 41 | 30 | 54 | 15 | 57 | 41 | 92 | 30 | 32 | 25 | 70 | 59 | 60 | 28 | 51 | 38 | 54 | 11 | 40 | 49 | 39 | 20 | 19 | 83 | 22 | 17 | 63 | 33 | 61 | 149 | 204 | 24 | 104 | 32 | 56 | 25 | – | 27 | 23 | 68 | 20 | – | 80 | 14 | 22 | 16 | 55 | 58 | 63 | 40 | 4 | 10 | 148 |
| 62 | 28 | 18 | 23 | 89 | 30 | 16 | 23 | 12 | 54 | 23 | 22 | 26 | 41 | 118 | 29 | 62 | 13 | 96 | 84 | 84 | 19 | 20 | 16 | 23 | 40 | 66 | 75 | 8 | 25 | 18 | 109 | 48 | 21 | 89 | 11 | 87 | 118 | 230 | 48 | 130 | 6 | 82 | 26 | 35 | 19 | 15 | 94 | 44 | 36 | 106 | 21 | 15 | 42 | 81 | 84 | 89 | 70 | 31 | 34 | 174 | 35 |

## CRUISING / SAILING LOG

| Date | Occasion | Departure Time | Return Time | Fuel/Gal |
|---|---|---|---|---|
| | | | | |

| Guests | Date | Destination | Departure | ETA | Temp | Barometer | Waves | Wind | Direction |
|---|---|---|---|---|---|---|---|---|---|
| | | | | | | | | | |
| | | | | | | | | | |
| | | | | | | | | | |
| | | | | | | | | | |
| | | | | | | | | | |

## CRUISING / SAILING LOG

| Date | Occasion | Departure Time | Return Time | Fuel/Gal |
|---|---|---|---|---|
| | | | | |

| Guests | Date | Destination | Departure | ETA | Temp | Barometer | Waves | Wind | Direction |
|---|---|---|---|---|---|---|---|---|---|
| | | | | | | | | | |
| | | | | | | | | | |
| | | | | | | | | | |
| | | | | | | | | | |
| | | | | | | | | | |

## FISHING LOG

| Date | Destination | Fuel/Gal | Departure Time | Return Time | Temperature Air | Water | Barometer | Waves | Wind |
|---|---|---|---|---|---|---|---|---|---|
| | | | | | | | | | |

| Anglers | Catch | Coordinate Numbers | | Comments |
|---|---|---|---|---|
| | | | | |
| | | | | |
| | | | | |
| | | | | |
| | | | | |

## FISHING LOG

| Date | Destination | Fuel/Gal | Departure Time | Return Time | Temperature Air | Water | Barometer | Waves | Wind |
|---|---|---|---|---|---|---|---|---|---|
| | | | | | | | | | |

| Anglers | Catch | Coordinate Numbers | | Comments |
|---|---|---|---|---|
| | | | | |
| | | | | |
| | | | | |
| | | | | |
| | | | | |

# INDEX

This index gives the chart number and inset number locating over 300 places, rivers, and creeks. Space prevents the listing of every creek and cove, so only the ones most frequently cruised are included.

When a place is included on more than one chart, all chart numbers are given with the first listed being preferred.

When a place is also shown on an inset, the inset number is given in red, within brackets after the chart number.